Peachpit Learning Series
Mac OS X 10.4 Tiger

Robin Williams

 **Peachpit Press**

Mac OS X 10.4 Tiger: Peachpit Learning Series
Robin Williams
Copyright ©2005 Robin Williams

Published by Peachpit Press. For information on Peachpit Press books, contact:

Peachpit Press
1249 Eighth Street
Berkeley, CA 94710
510.524.2178 voice
510.524.2221 fax
www.peachpit.com
To report errors, please send a note to errata@peachpit.com
Peachpit Press is a division of Pearson Education

Editor: Nancy Davis
Interior layout design: Frances Baca and Robin Williams
Interior divider page and chapter opener design: John Tollett
Section divider images: John Tollett
Chapter opener images: iStockPhoto.com
Compositor: Robin Williams
Indexer: Robin Williams

ISBN 0-321-33022-6
9 8 7 6 5 4 3
Printed and bound in the United States of America

Getting Started

Tiger is the latest operating system for our Macs, and once again Apple surprises us with new ways of working and enjoying ourselves. As large as this book is, it contains just enough to get you started!

The first section, "Upgrade to Tiger," helps you get Tiger installed on your Mac, if it isn't already. Check out the great "migrating" feature for getting your files from your old Mac to your new one.

For new Mac OS X users, "Mac OS X Basics for New Users" gets you up and running, covering all the basics of working in this operating system. Experienced users might be surprised at what they learn here!

Then new and experienced users both move on to the third section, "Make Tiger Work For You," where you will learn how to customize your Mac to suit your needs and discover the new Tiger features in so many of the Apple applications that came with your computer.

And the fourth section, "A New Way of Working," explains the big new features of Tiger, the ones that change the way you use your Mac.

It's so great to be a Mac user.   ;-)

Robin

p.s. There is so much to Tiger that it just can't be contained in this one book. If you want to know lots more, see *The Robin Williams Mac OS X Book, Tiger Edition,* and *Cool Mac Apps, second edition,* both by John Tollett and me!

Contents at a Glance

Contents in Detail

Mac OS X Basics for New Users

Make Tiger Work For You

A New Way of Working on Your Mac

1

Goals

Know what to have on hand before you install or upgrade.

Walk through the easy and non-intimidating installation process.

Upgrade Your Mac to Tiger

You may have just gotten a brand-new Mac with Tiger already installed—in which case you can skip this chapter altogether (except page 14). You might want to read Lesson 2, however, about transferring your files from an old machine to your new one.

If you just got a new DVD with the Tiger installation, Mac OS X version 10.4, then you have a few choices to make before you upgrade. This chapter explains the choices you will need to make along the way and walks you through the process.

Remember, before you do anything serious like upgrade your operating system, first backup your important files. The easiest thing to do is drag your entire hard disk onto a FireWire hard disk. Always create at least two backups and store them in a different places—it won't do any good if all your important backups are in the same office that gets burglarized or burned down! Of course, we *know* we're suppposed to backup but we don't do it until we have our own personal catastrophes. Be forewarned.

Know Your System Requirements

Not all older Macs can run Mac OS X. If you have a Mac that has been running some version of OS X just fine, then there should be no problem installing Tiger on it.

But if you are planning to put OS X on a Mac for the first time, make sure the computer fulfills these requirements:

▼ **PowerPC G3, G4, or G5 processor.** If you're not sure, go to the Apple menu and choose "About This Mac." This will display the window shown below, which tells you which processor your Mac is using.

▼ **Apple DVD drive.** It's possible you can install it from a third-party external DVD drive, but Apple does not support it (meaning they won't give you any tech support for it.)

▼ **Built-in FireWire port.** Look for a port with this symbol:

▼ **At least 256 megabytes of RAM (memory).** More is always better. Lots more. The window shown above also tells you how much memory your Mac has.

▼ **At least 3 gigabytes of empty disk space** on your main hard disk. You'll need 4 gigabytes if you plan to install the developer tools. If you need just a little more room than what you have, see page 10 for one option during the installation process.

▼ **Built-in monitor or an Apple monitor.** If you bought a different monitor, it must be connected to an Apple video card supported by your Mac.

Do you need to update the firmware?

If you're planning to install Tiger on an *older* one-piece iMac (not the bubble-bottom kind or the new all-in-the-monitor kind, but the ones that are all one piece and colored blue or orange or red, etc.) or any other older Macintosh, you may need to update the firmware. Sometimes the installer software will warn you if you need to do this, but sometimes it doesn't. If you have an old machine, it's best to go check Apple's web site and see if there is a firmware update for your particular Mac. Go to www.apple.com/support/downloads.

Upgrading from Mac OS 9?

If you are upgrading your Mac **from** OS 9 **to** OS X version 10.4 Tiger, first make sure your Mac fulfills the system requirements as explained on the opposite page. And make sure you have all the documents, applications, and other files you need backed up onto another hard disk, CD, or DVD *before* you install the new operating system. If you don't, there is no guarantee you will ever see your files again.

If you're upgrading from a previous version of OS X, you don't need to worry about your files or even your Internet settings and Mail settings, etc., because they will be preserved and handed over to the new OS (depending, of course, on which option you choose; see pages 8–9).

If you decide it's time to **completely erase your existing hard disk** before you install a clean version of Tiger (called a "clean install"), then of course you *must* back up all files before you begin.

Know your Connection Specifications

In the installation process, you will be asked for your Internet and email specifications. If you don't know them, call your ISP and ask. Or write down as much information from your existing Internet dialog boxes as you can.

The Installation Process

Of course you need the DVD installation disk from Apple to start the process. Put the DVD in. This is what you'll see:

I suggest you read the file called "Welcome to Tiger." It gives you a good overview of the new features.

The file called "Read Before You Install" is essentially the same as this chapter, but in less detail. It is probably, however, more up-to-date, plus it has some technical details that I haven't included here.

It's always a good idea to read the "Read Me" files before you do something like install a brand-new operating system that can potentially destroy everything on your Mac. So I suggest you read it. In fact, I suggest you **print it** before you start to install so you can have it to refer to.

To start the installation process, double-click the file "Install Mac OS X." This will restart your Mac and make it boot up with the install disc. If you are upgrading a Mac running some version of OS X, you will be asked for the Administrator name and password.

Or you could do this: Insert the DVD into your Mac. Then **restart and hold down the C key,** which will force the Mac to boot from the DVD.

During the process

The first thing you will be asked to do is choose the language in which you want to see all the menus and dialog boxes. Choose it and then click the button to continue.

Welcome to the Installer

Become familiar with this first Installer screen because you may need to come back here again someday. Check out the Utilities menu and all the options available there. This is a wonderfully useful troubleshooting stop—when things go really wrong with your Mac, restart from the Installer DVD and use one of these utilities. They are explained in a little more detail on page 14.

If you need to quit

If you decide you need to quit the installation process at this point—*after* you restart with the disc but *before* you actually click the "Install" button—you can do so: From the Installer menu next to the Apple icon in the menu bar, choose "Quit Installer." A dialog box appears with buttons labeled "Restart," "Startup Disk," and "Cancel." Read the following before you make your choice.

Once you quit, your Mac will restart with the install disc again because it always looks first in a disc drive to see if it can find an operating system. So you need to force it to restart from the internal hard disk on your Mac. You can do either of the following:

- ▼ Choose "Restart." As soon as you hear the bong, hold the mouse button down *and keep it down.* This forces a CD or DVD to pop out (at which point you can let go of the mouse button). Without the disc, your Mac will start as usual.

- ▼ **Or** choose "Startup Disk." You will see at least two options to choose from—the internal hard disk that you've been using, or the DVD that is currently in the drive. Choose your hard disk and click "Restart."

If you absolutely *must* quit the installer while it's running, understand that all the files on your hard disk will probably be destroyed.

Choose an installation option

When you click the "Continue" button in the Installer screen, you will be asked (as usual) to agree to the software license agreement. If you don't, you can't install the operating system.

Once you agree, you see a screen where you can choose the hard disk to install Tiger on. If you have more than one choice, your Mac will usually choose the best one, but make sure it's the one you want. It must be an internal hard disk.

This screen has a **very important button!** Click the **Options...** button! You have several options for the installation process.

1. Upgrade Mac OS X *or* Install OS X for the first time

If your Mac is running an earlier version of OS X, you can choose to **upgrade;** the installer will **replace** your earlier version with this new one, Tiger. Your files, applications, preferences, and everything else will not be touched. Essentially, the next time you start your Mac it will look just like it always had but will be running the new system with the added features.

If you've never installed any version of OS X before, the option you have is to install it for the first time. If your hard disk is current running Mac OS 9, that operating system will be left intact—you'll now have both. If you want to keep and use both systems, see page 47 about Classic.

2a. Archive and Install

If you choose this option, the Installer will save your existing operating system and its related files into a folder called "Previous System." Then it will proceed to install a brand new operating system, but all of your own documents and applications and files will be left intact in case you need to copy them over later. You will not be able to start up your Mac from the "Previous System" folder.

This is a good choice if you're not sure about replacing your previous operating system. For instance, maybe you're not sure if you have copies of all the fonts in the various font folders or preferences that you need for different applications. By leaving the "Previous System" on your Desktop, you can work in the new system for a while and until you're sure you haven't forgotten anything important. Eventually, delete the "Previous System" folder.

2b. Preserve Users and Network Settings

Once you choose to "Archive and Install," another option is available *if your previous operating system was OS X:* **Preserve Users and Network Settings.** If you created multiple users on your Mac, this option will save them so everyone's Home folders and preferences will be intact.

Even if you have no extra users on your Mac, this option is still handy because you won't have to go through the Setup Assistant during the installation process—the Mac will pick up your Internet settings and automatically apply them. By the time you see your new screen, you will be connected to the Internet as usual.

3a. Erase and Install

If you have backups of all your important files and applications, you can choose *to completely erase your hard disk* and install a brand-new version of the operating system instead of updating the old one. This is called a "clean install." This is particularly great if, as I mentioned, your Mac is starting to act a little peculiar and you'd like to just start over, fresh and clean.

Of course, if you do a clean install, **every single thing on your entire hard disk will be destroyed!** So make sure you have backups of anything you want to keep. My favorite method these days for temporary backups is a little FireWire drive. I have one right now from SmartDisk.com, a little FireLite that fits in a shirt pocket, plugs into the FireWire port on the back of my flat-screen monitor, and holds 40 gigabytes. I love it.

3b. Format disk as

Once you choose to "Erase and Install," your Mac asks how you want to (re)format the hard disk. Your two options are "Mac OS Extended (Journaled)," which is most likely what you want, or "UNIX File System." If you want the UNIX File System, I highly doubt that you are reading this book. Trust your Mac that it is correct in already choosing Mac OS Extended for you.

Make your choice of installation option, and then click the OK button. The "Destination" screen confirms the option you just made, so click the "Continue" button.

Customize your installation

The next screen you see is the "Easy Install." But you can customize your installation, which lets you delete unnecessary printer driver files and language files. This can be useful if you don't have a lot of room on your hard disk. If you need *lots* more room, this won't help, but if you're close, try it.

Now, you can only customize this **if you did not choose to upgrade!** That is, you can only customize the installation if you previously choose to "Archive and Install" or "Erase and Install."

If you chose one of those options, or if the Installer tells you there is not enough room on your hard disk to install, click the button to "Customize."

▼ In the list that appears, check the "Languages" checkbox. This displays all the foreign languages your Mac is going to install in case you ever want them. If you feel pretty confident you're not going to be needing a number of those languages in the near future, uncheck their boxes.

▼ Then check the "Printer Drivers" box. You can safely uncheck the drivers for printers you've never heard of. If you ever need a driver for a printer you've unchecked, you can always find it on that vendor's web site.

Install!

Now you're ready to actually start installing. Click the "Install" button to continue. Actually, this button will say "Upgrade" if you chose to upgrade the previous system.

Customize the Setup Assistant

After your Mac installs the operating system, but before it takes you to your Desktop, you will go through the Setup Assistant. Well, as I mentioned on page 8, you will *skip* the Setup Assistant if you chose the options to "Archive and Install" and then "Preserve Users and Network Settings."

The Setup Assistant asks for information that will get you connected to the Internet and make sure the email program, Mail, can get your email for you.

VoiceOver option

During the Setup Assistant, one of the options you'll see is **VoiceOver.** This is part of the enhanced Universal Access capabilities of Mac OS X. VoiceOver provides a spoken user interface (English only), which means the *computer* speaks to the *user* and describes what is going on. People with visual impairments can access just about everything on the Mac using the keyboard instead of the mouse. It's quite amazing.

In this introductory process, VoiceOver walks a user through keyboard practice, moving around the screen using the keyboard, typing in text fields, as well as selecting items in pop-up menus, scrolling lists, and control panes.

If you choose not to practice VoiceOver at this point, you can always do it later at your leisure. Please see Lesson 17 for more details.

The welcome screen

Most of the next few screens are self-explanatory—choose your language, the time zone, etc.

You will be asked if you want to **transfer your files** from another, separate Mac or from a separate partition on the same Mac. This feature, called migrating, transfers over most of the files from your old machine to your new one; please see Lesson 2. You can either follow the simple, on-screen directions and migrate your files right now. **Or** you can skip to Lesson 2 and read about migrating before you do it. **Or** you can skip the entire process right now and do it later at your leisure, using the Migration Assistant; see Lesson 2.

The network setup

You will be asked how you connect to the Internet. If you know how you connect and you know all the pertinent data that needs to be entered (it's not much), follow the on-screen directions. If you run across information you don't know, call your Internet Service Provider (the one you pay your monthly connection fee to) and ask them what to enter.

If you don't know the information at the moment, **you can skip this part** of the process altogether. You can always set your connection up later; it only takes few minutes. If you want to do it later, check the button, "My computer does not connect to the Internet."

If you want to set it up now, select your connection method and then follow the directions. If you run across places where you need to enter information and you don't know the information, call your ISP or click "Continue." Either it will work without that particular information, or you can fill it in later (see Lesson 10 for details on filling it in later).

Your Apple ID

You will be asked to enter your Apple ID. If you have a .Mac account (which is explained in Lesson 11), your email address and password is considered your Apple ID. Use your entire .Mac email address, including your member name, the @ symbol, and mac.com.

If you do not have a .Mac account or any other Apple ID that you know of, leave the fields blank and click the "Continue" button.

Other details

There are a few more screens asking for information from you, like personal details and where you will use this computer. It's easy.

Create your account

This is **very important!** What you are creating here is your **Administrator account** as the primary user, as well as your **Administrator password.** Write down this password because your Mac will not let you install new software or upgrades or make certain system changes unless you can provide this password. The hint you provide is important, also—if you forget your password and enter the wrong one three times, the hint will appear on the screen.

You can leave the password field blank if you have no worries about anyone using your Mac. But I suggest you write down that you left it blank; it is just as easy to forget that you did *not* enter a password as it is to forget which one you used. You might spend hours trying all kinds of different passwords only to finally realize you didn't give it one. Guess how I know this.

Make sure the **short name** is something you want to keep because you will never be able to change it. When asked for your Administrator name, you can usually use either the long name or this short name.

Done!

It takes just another minute or two to finish it up. Apple will try your modem connection and register you instantly. (If it can't register because your connection is not set up yet, it will save the information and do it the first time you connect.) Continue on and you will see your new Desktop!

Take Advantage of the Utilities in the Installer

When you run the Installer and get to the first screen, you'll see a menu item called "Utilities." This menu gives you access to a number of troubleshooting features on your Mac. If you like, you can stop here before installing Tiger and use the Disk Utility to partition your Mac.

All of the utilities mentioned below, except "Reset Password," are in your Utilities folder, which is in your Applications folder. You don't need to use the Install disk to access them. **But if your Mac has totally crashed** and you can't get anywhere at all, insert the original Tiger install DVD, then restart your Mac. Immediately hold down the C key to make sure it boots from the DVD. Do not click any of the installation buttons, but use the tools that are available here.

From the Utilities menu, choose the appropriate tool:

▼ **Reset Password:** Here you can reset not only the Administrator password, but the passwords for every user on the Mac. You do not need to know the original passwords to set new ones.

▼ **Startup Disk:** Choose which disk you want your Mac to check first when starting up. Only disks that contain operating systems can be used as startup disks.

▼ **Disk Utility:** Select your hard disk and use the "First Aid" pane to see if anything's wrong with the hard disk. The "Repair Disk Permissions" feature has solved some odd problems for my Macs. This is where you can partition the hard disk before you install.

▼ **Terminal:** The Terminal lets you use UNIX commands to do all sorts of things. If you don't know anything about UNIX or how to use the Terminal, skip this altogether.

▼ **System Profiler:** The System Profiler tells you all the gory details about your Mac, the CPU type, the audio, what kinds of devices are attached to your Mac, the speed of everything you can think of, and oh so much more. It will even tell you the serial number of the computer.

▼ **Network Utility:** This utility has a number of great tools. If you know what it means to finger someone, ping your modem, run a lookup or a port scan, or when to use whois, then you'll have fun with this utility.

What You've Learned

▼ The system requirements for installing Tiger.

▼ What to do and what information to have on hand before you install.

▼ Whether to upgrade, archive, or clean install.

▼ In which format to reformat the disk.

▼ How to customize the installation.

▼ How to go through the setup process.

▼ The importance of the Administrator password.

▼ The numerous utilities available from the startup disk.

Keyboard Shortcuts

Restart, hold C	Restart and boot from a DVD or CD that's in the drive

> **TIP** Do not unplug the FireWire cable before you unmount the icon of your old Mac from your new Mac running Tiger! Even though it's "hot swappable," which means you don't have to shut down, it's still possible to lose data if you unplug it while the icon is still visible on the screen.

Find the hard disk icon of your old Mac on the Desktop of the Tiger computer. Drag it to the Trash before you unplug the FireWire cable.

Migrate Additional Users

At any time you can migrate additional users and their files from other computers. Just follow the directions on the previous pages.

What to Do After Migrating

It's a good idea to do a quick check of the files on your new Mac after migrating. Open every application to make sure it works okay—make a quick file and try to save it. If an application doesn't work, you will just have to reinstall it from the original disks.

Open sample files by double-clicking on them to make sure they can open in the correct application and that their fonts appear correctly.

Connect to the Internet, check your mail, and take a peek at your System Preferences to make sure things are really how you like them.

Other Ways to Transfer Files from Mac to Mac

The migration process can take quite a long time because it gathers up thousands of files. If you want to transfer just selected files, you might want to consider these other options.

Use an external disk

You can use a Zip drive with a USB connection, a portable hard disk with a USB or FireWire connection, or a floppy disk drive that connects to your new Mac. Just copy the files onto the disks as you usually would from your old machine (drag them from the hard disk of your old Mac onto the disk icon). Then connect the drive to the new machine and copy them onto your hard disk. If you have a very old Mac, the trouble, of course, is finding drives that work on both an old Mac and the new one. If you have a drive for your old machine and a different drive for your new one, the actual disks should go between the Macs just fine.

Burn a CD

If your old machine can burn a CD (or a DVD) you can transfer quite a few files that way.

Send attachments in email

If you don't have huge files, send them as attachments through email. It's kind of funny to send your files around the world to get to the machine sitting two feet away.

Use your .Mac account

If you have a .Mac account, put the files from your old Mac onto your iDisk (see Lesson 11). On your new Mac, download them from your iDisk.

Send files through the network

If both machines are on a network, connect the two computers and copy files directly from one to the other. See Lesson 10 for some minimal details.

What You've Learned

▼ An overview of the migration process.

▼ What sorts of files will transfer from an old Mac using the Migration Assistant.

▼ How to prepare your Mac before migrating.

▼ How to make sure iTunes can migrate songs that you bought from the iTunes Music Store.

▼ How to safely disconnect the FireWire cable.

▼ Other ways to transfer files.

Keyboard Shortcuts

Restart, hold T	Boot an OS X Mac in Target Disk Mode

Mac OS X Basics for New Users

3

Goals   Become familiar and comfortable with the Desktop and Finder.

Understand the Finder windows and how to use them.

Learn to use the Dock.

Work with contextual menus and keyboard shortcuts.

Burn a CD or DVD.

Learn to watch for tool tips and other visual clues.

Know where to go for more information.

Introduction to Mac OS X

Tiger is the latest and greatest version of the Mac OS X operating system. But even though it's the latest and greatest, it's still Mac OS X. In this section you'll become familiar with the basics of using your Mac in general, and the following sections will deal more specifically with the changes that appear in Tiger.

If you haven't yet installed Tiger, please see Lessons 1 or 2. Once you've got it installed and have gone through the setup process, you're ready to start using it!

Get to Know Your Desktop and Finder

When you turn on your Mac, you'll always see your **Desktop,** shown below. This is also called the **Finder,** although technically the Finder is the application that runs the Desktop. Whenever you see a direction that tells you to go to the Desktop or to the Finder, this is where you need to go.

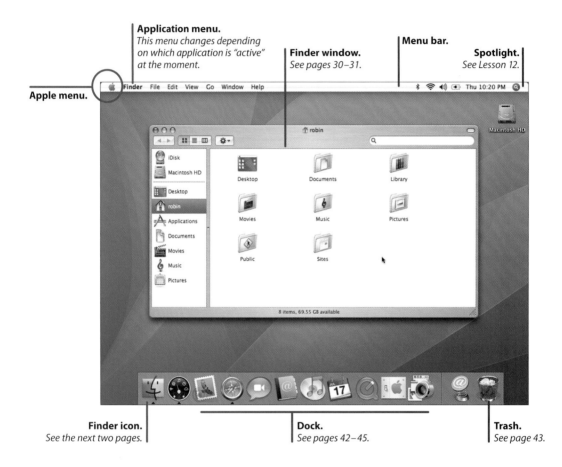

Application menu.
This menu changes depending on which application is "active" at the moment.

Finder window.
See pages 30–31.

Menu bar.

Spotlight.
See Lesson 12.

Apple menu.

Finder icon.
See the next two pages.

Dock.
See pages 42–45.

Trash.
See page 43.

> **TIP** ▶ Because of the way the computer works, you might *see* the Desktop but not actually *be* in the Finder. Get in the habit of checking the application menu, as shown top-left. When you are really in the Finder or at the Desktop, the application menu will show "Finder."

Make sure you can get to the Desktop or Finder when necessary

As you work on your Mac, you will be using a number of applications in which you'll create your documents, but you'll often want to go back to the Finder, which sort of acts like home base. The name of the *active* application, the one that's currently open and available to use (including the Finder), will always be displayed in the application menu. Keep an eye on that menu.

To go to the Finder at any time, do one of these things:

- ▼ Single-click on any blank area of the Desktop.
- ▼ Single-click on any Finder window (shown below) that you see.
- ▼ Single-click the Finder icon in the Dock (shown on the opposite page).

Check to make sure the application menu says "Finder."

Get to Know Your Finder Windows

Below, you see a typical **Finder window.** This is called a Finder window to distinguish it from similar (but different) windows you will use in your applications. The following pages go into further detail about this window.

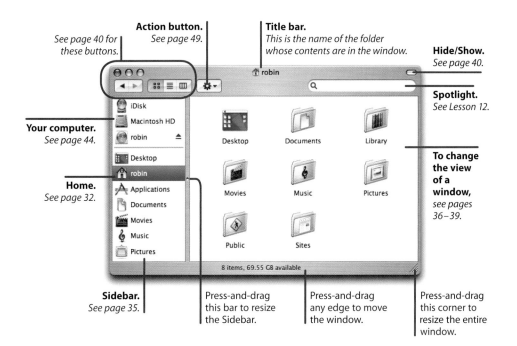

Action button.
See page 49.

See page 40 for these buttons.

Title bar.
This is the name of the folder whose contents are in the window.

Hide/Show.
See page 40.

Spotlight.
See Lesson 12.

Your computer.
See page 44.

Home.
See page 32.

To change the view of a window,
see pages 36–39.

Sidebar.
See page 35.

Press-and-drag this bar to resize the Sidebar.

Press-and-drag any edge to move the window.

Press-and-drag this corner to resize the entire window.

Get to Know Your Home and its Folders

When you open a Finder window, it usually opens to the Home window, as shown below. You can tell it's Home because your user name and the little house icon are in the title bar.

▼ **To open a Finder window,** single-click on the Finder icon (shown to the left) in the Dock.

If the window that opens doesn't display your Home folders, single-click the Home icon you see in the Sidebar.

Your Home window displays a number of special folders. I suggest you do not change the names of these folders or throw them away unless you are very clear on what you're doing and why you're making that choice! For now, just let them be.

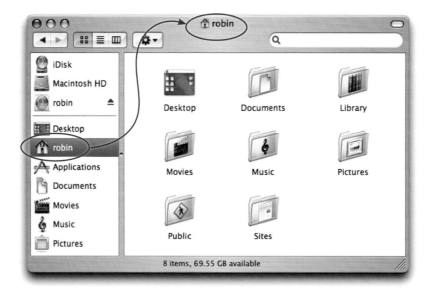

TIP If several people use one Mac, you can create individual Homes for each user. See Lesson 9.

What each folder is for

Desktop Although this doesn't look like a typical folder icon, it really is a folder. The Desktop itself is a place where you can store items, sort of like keeping them on your office desk instead of putting them in a filing cabinet. Any file you store directly on your Desktop also appears in this folder.

Documents Your Mac will make sure every document you create is safely tucked into this Documents folder. Later you can create your own folders, as described on the following page.

Library This folder is used by the operating system. *Do not rename this folder, do not throw it away, do not take anything out of it, and do not put anything in it* unless you know exactly what you are doing. Just ignore it for now. For more details, see page 46.

Movies iMovie uses this folder to automatically store the files necessary for creating the movies you make.

Music iTunes uses this folder to automatically keep track of all the music files you buy and all of your playlists.

Pictures iPhoto uses this folder to automatically keep track of all your photos and albums.

Public You'll use this folder to share files with other people who also use your Mac, as explained in Lesson 9.

Sites You can create a web site, store it in this folder, and share it with anyone on the Internet.

TIP You can have as many Finder windows open as you like. This makes it easier to move files from one window to another. To open another window, make sure you are at the Finder, then go to the File menu and choose "New Finder Window." Or press Command N.

Create your own folders

At any time you can create your own **folders** where you can **store** your documents and **organize** your files. For instance, you might want a folder in which to store all your financial documents. And another folder for all your newsletter files. And yet another for the screenplays you're writing. All of these documents *could* go inside the Documents folder, but to find the individual items that belong together would soon become unwieldy.

Use digital folders on your Mac as you would use paper folders in a metal filing cabinet. See page 128 for a tip on how to save files directly into your custom folders.

▼ **To open a folder,** double-click on it.

▼ **To go back** to the contents of the previous folder, single-click the left-pointing triangle, called the Back button (circled, below-left).

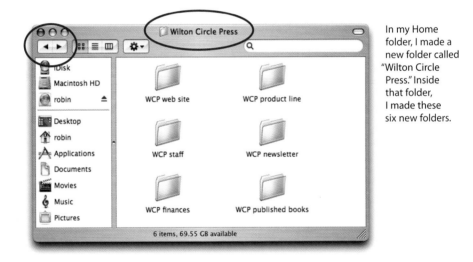

In my Home folder, I made a new folder called "Wilton Circle Press." Inside that folder, I made these six new folders.

To make a new folder:

Shift Command N	New folder	The new folder will appear inside the window whose name is in the title bar. Click on its name, then type to rename it.

If you're not sure how to use keyboard shortcuts yet, see pages 50–51.

Take Advantage of the Sidebar

The lower portion of the **Sidebar** of every Finder window is customizable—you can add or remove any folder as often as you like.

When you **add a folder** to the Sidebar, you make the folder easier to get into, not only on the Desktop, but also when you are working in an application and want to open or save a file (Sidebar folders are accessible in Open and Save As dialog boxes).

Remove folders that you don't use to make room for the ones you do. Don't worry—removing the picture of a folder from the Sidebar does not throw away the original folder nor anything in it!

▼ **To add a folder or document to the Sidebar,** simply drag the icon from any window or from the Desktop and drop it into the Sidebar.

▼ **To remove an item from the Sidebar,** simply press on it with the mouse and drag it out of the Sidebar. Let go when the mouse pointer is on the Desktop. As you can see above, the icon disappears in a puff of smoke. Notice that although I removed the Movies folder from the Sidebar, the original folder is still safe and sound in the Home window.

Change the View of the Finder Window

You can change how the items inside any window are displayed. Experiment with the **three different views** and you'll decide for yourself how you like to work. You might prefer one view for certain things and a different view for others—with the click of a button, you can switch from one to the other.

▼ **To change views,** single-click one of the three little view buttons.

 From left to right, the view buttons display icons, a list, or columns.

The Icon View

Obviously, this displays every file as an **icon,** or small picture.

In the Icon View, double-click to open files:

 Folder icons: Double-click a folder to display its contents in the window. (But *not* in the Sidebar; single-click those icons.)

 Document icons: Double-click a document to open not only that document, but also the application it was created in.

 Application icons: Double-click an application icon to open that application, ready for you to create wonderful projects.

The List View

As a **list,** you can see the contents of more than one folder at once. You can organize the list alphabetically by names, by the dates the files were last modified, by what kind of items they are, and other options.

The **blue column heading** is a *visual clue* that the contents are organized by that heading; single-click any other column heading to organize the contents by something else.

The **tiny triangle** in the column heading is a *visual clue* that tells you whether the information is sorted from first to last or last to first. Single-click the triangle to reverse the order. Try it.

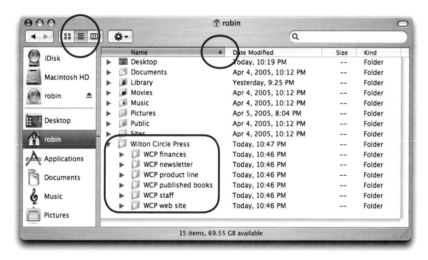

In the List View, single-click vs. double-click:

Folder icons: Single-click the **disclosure triangle** to the left of a folder to display its contents as a sublist, as shown circled above. You can view the contents of more than one folder at once.

Double-click a tiny **folder icon** to display its contents in the window, which will *replace* the contents you currently see in the window.

Document icons: Double-click a document to open not only that document, but also the application it was created in.

Application icons: Double-click an application icon to open it.

The Column View

Viewing the Finder window in **columns** allows you to see not only the contents of a selected folder or hard disk, but you can easily keep track of where each file is located. You can also view the contents of another folder without losing sight of the first one. This view helps you understand where everything is kept in your computer.

If you have photographs, graphic images, or movies in your folders, the last column displays **previews** of the items. You can even play a small movie in this preview column. Some documents can display previews as well.

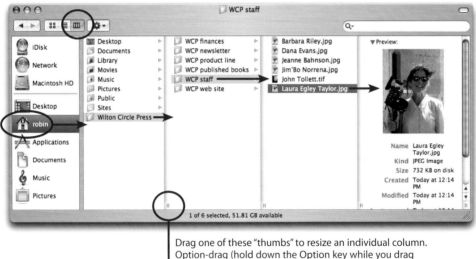

Drag one of these "thumbs" to resize an individual column. Option-drag (hold down the Option key while you drag with the mouse) to resize all columns.

In the example above, you can see that the "top level" folder is my Home folder, "robin." In "robin," I selected the folder "Wilton Circle Press" (I clicked once on it) and in that folder I selected "wcp staff," and in that folder I selected "Laura Egley Taylor.jpg," and that file displays a preview.

You won't see a column to the right until you **single-click** a folder or a file—then a new column to the right appears to display the contents of that folder or a preview of the file. The triangles indicate the file is a folder that can contain other files.

In the Column View, single-click files to display columns:

Folder icons: Single-click a folder to display its contents in the column to the right. If there is no column to the right, one will appear.

Document icons: Single-click a document to see a preview in the column to the right. Not all documents can provide picture previews, but the preview will at least give you information about that file.

Double-click a document to open not only that document, but also the application it was created in.

Application icons: Single-click an application icon to preview information about it, such as its version and date of modification.

Double-click an application icon to open that application.

TIP No matter which view you are in, you can always open a folder into a **new, separate window:** Hold down the Command key and double-click on any folder in any view.

TIP You can customize many features about the Finder windows, such as the font size, the icon size, even the color inside the window. You can organize the List View by different columns of information, choose to turn off the preview in Column View, and more. See Lesson 6.

Use the Buttons in the Finder Window

There are several more buttons in the Toolbar of every Finder window.

Red, yellow, and green buttons

- Single-click the **red button to close** the window.
- Single-click the **yellow button to minimize** the window, which sends a tiny icon down into the Dock, on the right side.

  To open that window again, single-click its icon in the Dock.
- Single-click the **green button** to make the window bigger or smaller.

Back and Forward buttons

These buttons go back and forward through the contents of windows you have viewed (just like the back and forward buttons on web pages). Every time you open a new window, these buttons start over.

Hide/Show the Toolbar and Sidebar

In the upper-right corner of every Finder window is a small gray button. Single-click this button to hide the Toolbar and the Sidebar, as shown below. When you double-click on a folder while the Toolbar and Sidebar are hidden, a new and separate window will open. Try it.

Select Multiple Items in the Finder

To select an individual item in a Finder window, you simply single-click it.
To select multiple items, there are two ways to do it, as explained below.
Once items are a group, you can move them all, trash them all, open them
all, change all their labels (see page 140), and more, all at once.

In the Icon View

In the Icon View, hold down the **Command key** *or* the **Shift key** and single-
click on as many items as you want to group together. You can only select
items from one window while in the Icon View.

In the List View or Column View

In these views, using the Shift key is different from using the Command key.

Hold down the **Command key** and single-click on multiple items. In the List
View, you can select items from several different folders in the same window,
as long as their contents are showing in the list; in the Column View, you can
only select items from one column at a time. See below, left.

The **Shift key** lets you select a group of items that are *contiguous,* or next to
each other in the list. Single-click on the first item you want to select in a list.
Then hold down the Shift key and click on the last item you want in the list.
Everything between the two clicks will be selected. See below, right.

Command-click to select non-contiguous items.   Shift-click to select contiguous items.

To deselect an item from any group in any view: Command-click it.

Understand the Various Disk Icons

In the **top portion of the Sidebar,** you probably see something similar to the example shown below—you might see more icons and you might see fewer. These icons represent hard disks, networks, a CD, a DVD, an iPod, or any other type of removable media.

Display the contents of each item the same way you do any of the items in the lower portion of the Sidebar: single-click the icon.

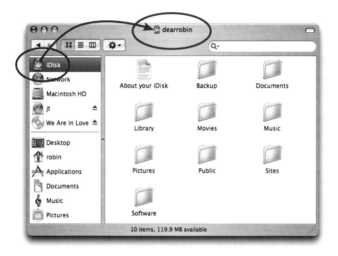

The **iDisk** is your personal storage space on Apple's computers, which is something you get when you sign up for a .Mac account (see Lesson 11). A single click on the iDisk icon connects you to that storage space, as shown above.

The **Network** icon is useful when you have multiple computers linked together, either with cables or wirelessly. Use this icon as one way to connect to the other computers. See Lesson 10.

The **Macintosh HD** is your main hard disk, the one that holds the operating system. See the details on the opposite page. You can rename your hard disk at any time, so yours might not be called "Macintosh HD" anymore.

When you see the **eject symbol** to the right of an icon (the triangle with a bar under it), that means it is a removable disk of some sort. It might be a CD, a DVD, an iPod, or even another computer that you are connected to over the network. Click on the symbol to eject or disconnect the item.

Use Mac OS X Together with Mac OS 9

It is possible to use Mac OS 9.2 with Tiger. If you have the entire OS 9.2 operating system installed on your Mac, it's called Classic. Applications that need it will automatically open it for you.

It's best, if you actually plan to use really ancient software that needs OS 9.2, that you open the Classic preferences, shown below, and have Classic automatically start up whenever you turn on your Mac. You will have fewer problems. Really, though, you need to let go of OS 9 and move on. It's okay.

To open the Classic preferences, go to the Apple menu and choose "System Preferences...." Single-click on the "Classic" icon.

Look for Contextual Menus

These are great. A **contextual menu** is one that pops up and is specific to the item you Control-click on, as opposed to menus that appear in the menu bar or in dialog boxes that are always the same.

To display a contextual menu, hold down the Control key (not the Command key) and click on an object, on a blank spot on the Desktop, inside a Finder window, or anywhere. A little menu will pop up. What this menu displays depends on what you clicked on, as you can see by the examples below.

If you have a **two-button mouse,** you don't need the Control key—just use the right-hand button to display a contextual menu.

There is *no visual clue* that any item has a contextual menu—just keep checking. You'll find them in applications, on web pages, in toolbars, in the Sidebar, and elsewhere.

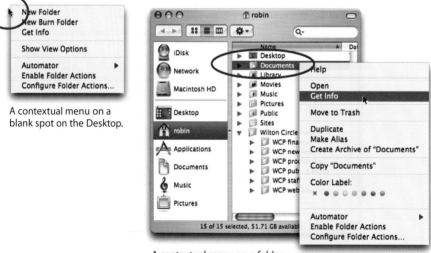

A contextual menu on a
blank spot on the Desktop.

A contextual menu on a folder.

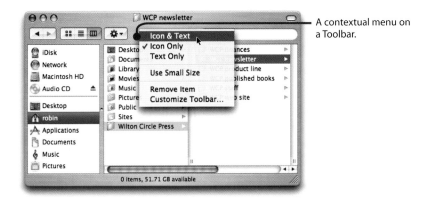

A contextual menu on a Toolbar.

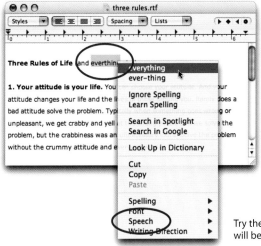

This is an example of a contextual menu in an application.

Control-click on a misspelled word to get a contextual menu with possible spellings. Select the correct word, let go of the mouse button, and the misspelled word is instantly replaced with the correct one.

Try the "Speech" option—your text will be read out loud to you.

 TIP In Finder windows, the **Action button** does many of the same things as the contextual menu. Try it: Single-click to select an icon, then click the Action button to see what the contextual options are.

Work with Keyboard Shortcuts

Most actions that you can do with the mouse and menus can also be done with a **keyboard shortcut.** Often this is not only faster, but more convenient because you don't have to take your hands off the keyboard to pick up and maneuver the mouse. You will see lots of keyboard shortcuts in the menus across the top of the screen, such as the ones shown below in the illustration of the Window menu. You'll use a keyboard shortcut *instead* of going to the menu.

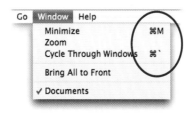

Take careful notice of which modifier keys are used and which character keys are used.

Recognize the common modifier keys

Keyboard shortcuts work with **modifier keys,** which are those keys that don't do anything by themselves. For instance, the Shift key doesn't do anything when you press it down by itself, *but it changes the behavior of other keys.*

Each key has a **symbol** by which it is known. These are the key symbols you will see in menus and charts:

⇧	**Shift**	↺	**Escape (esc)**
⌘	**Command**	⇞ ⇟	**PageUp or Page Down**
⌥	**Option**	⌫	**Delete**
^	**Control**	↑↓←→	**Arrow keys**
↵	**Return**	⌤	**Enter**

Fkeys are those keys across the top of the keyboard that are labeled with the letter F and a number, such as F2 or F13.

The **fn** key is on a laptop in the bottom-left corner. It helps individual keys do more than one function.

Keyboard shortcuts typically use one or more modifier key(s), plus one number, character, or Fkey, as you can see in the example of the Window menu above: the keyboard shortcut to minimize the selected window (to send its icon down to the Dock) is Command M.

Use a keyboard shortcut

The trick to using a keyboard shortcut is this: *hold down* the modifier keys all together and keep them held down, then *tap* the associated letter, number, or Fkey just once for each time you want to perform an action.

For instance, the keyboard shortcut to close a window is Command W, so hold the Command key down and then tap the letter W just once. If there are three windows open on your Desktop, you can hold the Command key down and tap the letter W three times and it will close three windows.

Notice gray vs. black commands

When commands in a menu are gray instead of black, that indicates an important visual clue that the Mac is giving you.

1 Click on an empty spot on the Desktop.

2 Now take a look through the Finder menus and notice the shortcuts for different actions, or commands. Notice how many commands are gray.

 If a command is **gray,** that means you cannot use that command at the moment. Often this is because you have not selected an item first, an item to which the command should apply. For instance, you can't use the command to close a window unless an open window is selected.

3 So open a Finder window and *select* a folder (click once on it).

4 Now look at the File menu again, and notice how many more commands are available.

5 Find the keyboard shortcut to "Open," but don't choose it. Click somewhere off the menu to make the menu go away.

6 Make sure the folder is still selected. Now use the keyboard shortcut to open it.

Navigate the Desktop and Finder windows

If you so choose, you can get around your entire Desktop and inside Finder windows using the keyboard. For instance, you can get to every menu across the top of the screen and choose commands, without ever touching the mouse.

Access the menus on the Desktop or in any application:

1 Press Control F2 to focus on the menu bar across the top of the screen.

2 Use the left and right Arrow keys to select menu items across the menu bar, *or* type the first letter of the menu you want to select. When a menu is selected, you'll see it highlight.

3 When the menu name you want is highlighted, press the Return key to drop down its menu.

4 Press the down and up arrows to choose a command in the list, *or* type the first letter or two or three. (If there is more than one command that starts with the same letter, type the first two or three letters quickly to select a specific one.)

5 Hit Return to activate the selected command.

To put the menu away without activating a command, press Command Period (Command .).

Try these shortcuts in a Finder window:

▼ Type the first letter or two or three to select files.

▼ When you're in the list or Column View, use the Arrow keys to select the columns to the right or left, then use the letter keys to select files.

▼ Select a document, hit Command O to open it, and get to work!

If you are interested in using more of these kinds of keyboard shortcuts, go to the "Keyboard & Mouse" preferences, as explained on page 149 and 403–404. There you will find an extensive list of keyboard shortcuts for getting around your Mac.

Keyboard shortcuts in dialog boxes

You can use keyboard shortcuts in the **Open** and **Save As** dialog boxes. Use the Tab key to select different areas of the dialog box and the Arrow keys to select items in the columns. When you Save As, you can title your document, select the folder in which you want it stored, and save it—without using the mouse.

Notice the blue border around this Save As edit box, and the blue highlight. The edit box and text are selected. Simply type to replace the highlighted text.

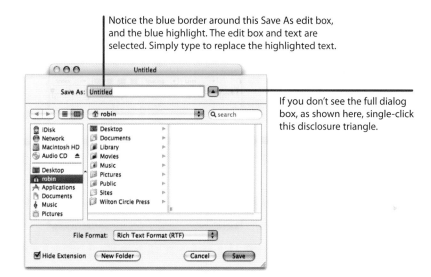

If you don't see the full dialog box, as shown here, single-click this disclosure triangle.

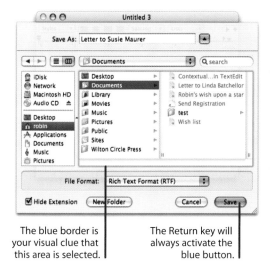

Use the Tab key to select the other parts of the dialog box:

The first Tab will select the Search field.

The next Tab will select the Sidebar. Use the up and down Arrow keys to highlight the folder or disk you need.

Hit Tab to select the columns. Use the up and down arrows to select a file in the first column, then hit the right Arrow to select the next colum.

When you select the folder into which you want to save the file, hit the Return key.

The blue border is your visual clue that this area is selected.

The Return key will always activate the blue button.

Burn a CD or DVD

To burn a CD or DVD is a simple process. You'll want to burn backups of your important work. Be sure to also burn backups of any applications or fonts or other files that you download straight from the Internet.

The steps below describe how to burn data files (as opposed to music or movies) onto a disc. A CD holds about 650 megabytes; a DVD holds about 4.3 gigabytes, even though the package might tell you it holds 4.7. (To burn a music CD from iTunes, please see page 108.)

To burn a disc, of course, you must have a computer with a built-in drive that is capable of doing this! You can buy an external CD or DVD burner, but you won't be able to use the process below to burn the discs; you'll need other software, such as Roxio Toast.

To burn a CD or DVD:

1 Insert a blank CD-R (do not use the CD+R discs!) or a blank DVD-R (the latest models of SuperDrives can burn the DVD+R or DVD+RW discs).

2 A message pops up asking what action you want to take. The option to "Open Finder" will let you do anything. Click OK.

3 You can name the CD at this point. Select the CD, then click on its current label, "Untitled." Type the new name.

TIP If you change your mind and want to take the unburned disc out of the Mac, Control-click on the icon and choose "Eject 'untitled CD.'" "Untitled" will be replaced with whatever name you gave it.

4 Drag the files from the Finder to the disc and drop them right onto the disc. You can drag as many individual files as you want—the Mac will tell you when the disc is full.

This does not burn the files onto the disc! At this point, you are merely telling your Mac which files you are going to burn. You will see the files copy to the disc.

Using Apple's built-in software, you will not be able to add more data to a disc once you've burned it, so be sure to drag everything you want onto the disc at this point.

5 When you're ready to burn, do one of these things:

 This is the Burn icon.

> **Either:** Drag the disc towards the Trash. As you drag, you'll notice the Trash icon turns into the Burn icon. Drop the disc onto this icon and let go.

> **Or:** Control-click on the disc to get the contextual menu. Choose "Burn Disc."

> **Or:** In the top portion of the Sidebar, you'll see the newly named disc. To its right is a Burn icon. Click that.

> **Or:** Click once on the disc to select it. From the File menu, choose "Burn Disc."

6 You'll get a message asking to confirm the process. Click "Burn." It can take several minutes.

7 After the burning process is complete, double-click the disc icon to make sure the data you want is on the disc. Then you can eject the disc (drag it to the Trash, or Control-click on it and choose "Eject Disc").

Learn Simple Troubleshooting Techniques

When things go wrong, here are a few simple troubleshooting techniques you can try.

Restart

It's amazing what a simple **restart** will fix. Especially if you rarely turn off your Mac, sometimes little things may start acting a bit quirky. Perhaps your Mac can't find the printer you've been using for months, or icons for new files don't appear. For little unexplainable things, restart.

▼ **To restart,** go to the Apple menu and choose "Restart...."

If for some reason you can't get to the Apple menu, try the **Restart button** that is on most Macs. It's a tiny little round button with a triangle on it.

On laptops, you can press the **Power button for one second** and you'll get a little message with a button to restart.

If you **can't restart,** then Shut Down. Either use the Apple menu command, if you can, or as a last resort hold down the Power button for five seconds.

Force quit an application or relaunch the Finder

Sometimes just one application has trouble. You can **force quit** any application and it doesn't affect any other application or the system. It's great. You can't force quit the Finder, but you can **relaunch** it, which only takes a minute.

▼ **To force quit,** hold down the Option key and **press** *(don't click)* on the application's icon in the Dock. A menu pops up with a choice to "Force Quit."

▼ **To relaunch the Finder,** hold down the Option key and **press** *(don't click)* on the Finder icon in the Dock. A menu pops up with a choice to "Relaunch."

Delete the preference file

Another tip to troubleshoot an application that isn't acting right is to delete that application's **preference file.** This is perfectly safe—when the application opens up again, it will recreate a new preference file from scratch. You will lose any preferences you had personally changed in the application, but it can be worth it because this works pretty well to solve inexplicable annoyances.

1 Quit the application.

2 Open a Finder window and view it by columns, as shown below.

3 Single-click your Home icon in the Sidebar.

4 In the column that appears to the right, single-click the "Library" folder.

5 In the next column to the right, single-click the "Preferences" folder.

6 In the next column to the right, find the ".plist" file for the application that's giving you trouble. That is the preferences file.

7 Drag the application's preference file to the Trash. Empty the Trash.

8 Restart the application and hope it works better.

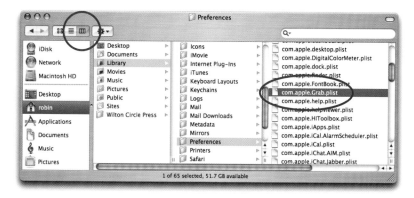

Check the Network preferences

If you are having trouble with your **Internet connection** (that is, connecting to the Internet, not email issues), check your Network preferences. One particular feature to check is the "Network Port Configurations." Also see pages 263–265.

1 Open the System Preferences: single-click its icon in the Dock.

2 In the System Preferences pane, single-click the "Network" icon (it's in the third row).

3 From the "Show" menu, choose "Network Port Configurations."

4 In the list of "Port Configurations," make sure there are no checkmarks in connections you don't use.

5 Also make sure that your primary connection is at the top of the list. If it isn't, just press-and-drag it up to the first position.

```
●  ○  ○                    Network
◀  ▶    Show All                              Q

              Location:  Automatic              ◆
                 Show:  Network Port Configurations  ◆

        Check a configuration to make it active.
        Drag configurations into the order you want to try them when
        connecting to a network.

          On  | Port Configurations
        ☑  AirPort                          ┌──  New...  ──┐
        ☐  Internal Modem
        ☐  IrDA                             ┌──  Rename  ──┐
        ☐  Built-in Ethernet
        ☐  Built-in FireWire                ┌──  Delete...  ──┐

                                            ┌──  Duplicate  ──┐   (?)

    🔓  Click the lock to prevent further changes.   ( Assist me... )   ( Apply Now )
```

6 If you've made changes, click the "Apply Now" button in the lower-right.

If you **can't get your dial-up connection going,** check the settings for "Internal Modem." Keep in mind that the account name and account password are not necessarily the same as your email name and email password! Call your provider and ask them to verify your account name and account password.

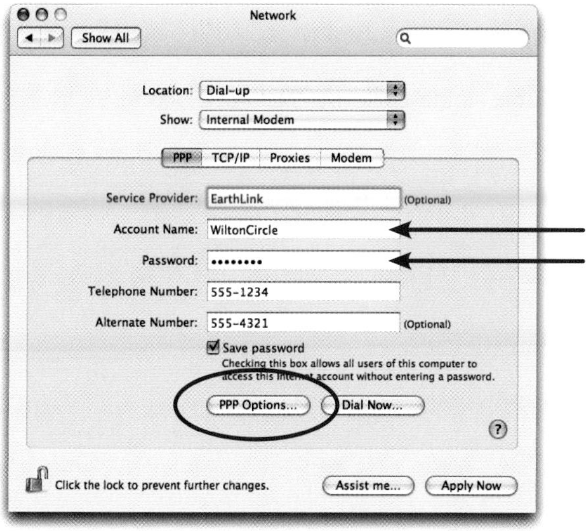

If you keep getting **disconnected from your dial-up connection,** check the "PPP Options" (circled, above, shown below). Uncheck the box, "Disconnect if idle for ____ minutes." Click the blue OK button, then click "Apply Now."

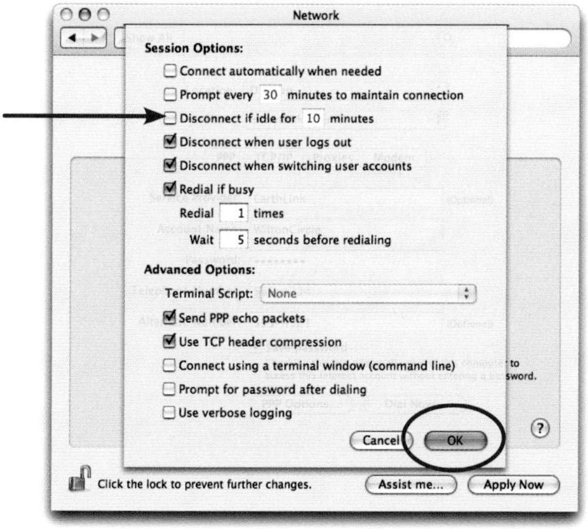

Check for software updates

Software
Update

Make sure you are using the latest versions of all your software. For your Mac OS software, use the Software Update preferences to see if everything is up to date (open it in the System Preferences, as described on the previous pages).

TIP If your connection to the Internet is a dial-up through a telephone modem, it's best *not* to check the box to "Download important updates in the background" because it may tie up your phone line for hours. Check for updates manually (click "Check Now" when necessary).

It's especially important to check for updated application software when you update your operating system, like when moving from any other OS to Tiger.

Create another user and test

If you install new software and it just won't work, like it won't even open, create another user (see Lesson 9 for details). Install the software in the new user's Home and see if it works. If it doesn't work for the new user, the software itself has a problem—check with the package it came in or the vendor you bought it from to make sure it is the corrrect version for your operating system.

If the software does work for the other user, that indicates there is something in your system that is conflicting. Try throwing away the preferences, as explained on page 57. If it still doesn't work, you may need to contact the vendor to find out what sorts of cache files or other files may be conflicting with that particular software.

If you forgot your password

If you forgot the password you entered when you first set up your new Mac or installed your new system (called the Admin password), you'll have to use the original install CD to fix the problem. (I think someone told you that you should have written down your password.) If you have created more than one user for your Mac, you can use these steps to change the password of any user.

1 Get the original CD. Put it in and double-click the "Install" button. Follow the directions to restart. No, you are not really going to re-install the entire system.

2 All you need to do is wait until the install screen appears. Then go to the Utilities menu and choose "Reset Password...."

3 Enter your new password—twice. And write it down where you can find it again. Click OK.

4 Quit the installer from the Installer menu. Your Mac will restart.

If you did not enter a password when you first set up your Mac, then you can leave the password field empty and just hit the blue "OK" or "Continue" button and it will work just fine.

Report crashes

Most of the time when an application crashes, an alert box appears and asks if you want to send a report to Apple. Now, Apple is not going to write you back—this is just an anonymous report you send in so Apple can figure out if there are common issues among many users, enough to warrant looking into. It's good to go ahead and send in the report.

Learn More About Mac OS X

There are a number of ways to learn more about your Mac and how to use it, all available right from your Desktop. Keep these tips in mind as you spend time on your Mac—you will learn a lot from them.

Tool tips

Most applications and dialog boxes provide little **tool tips** that pop up when you "hover" your mouse over an item. They tell you what the items do. Just hold the mouse still over a button or icon for about three seconds and if there is a tool tip, it will appear, as shown in the examples below.

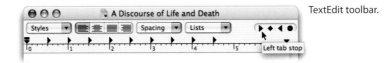

TextEdit toolbar.

Font Panel toolbar.

Preview toolbar.

Visual clues

Keep a constant eye out for the **visual clues** that the Mac is always providing. Every little visual extra you see means something! When the pointer turns into a double-headed arrow, that's a clue. When you see a little dot in a divider bar, that's a clue. When you see a triangle anywhere, that's a clue.

You are probably already aware of visual clues such as the underline beneath text on a web page to indicate a link, or the little colored dots in your word processor that indicate a word is misspelled. Here are a few others that will help you start noticing what your Mac is telling you.

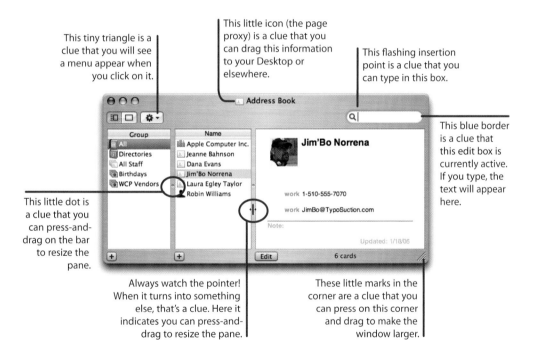

This tiny triangle is a clue that you will see a menu appear when you click on it.

This little icon (the page proxy) is a clue that you can drag this information to your Desktop or elsewhere.

This flashing insertion point is a clue that you can type in this box.

This blue border is a clue that this edit box is currently active. If you type, the text will appear here.

This little dot is a clue that you can press-and-drag on the bar to resize the pane.

Always watch the pointer! When it turns into something else, that's a clue. Here it indicates you can press-and-drag to resize the pane.

These little marks in the corner are a clue that you can press on this corner and drag to make the window larger.

Sometimes our eyes glaze over because there is so much visual stimulation on the Mac screen. Just keep in mind that everything means something and slowly get to know the visual clues.

Below you see a typical title bar of a document. There are two visual clues in this title bar: the **red button** has a dark dot in it, and the **tiny icon** next to the title is gray. Both of these visual clues mean the same thing: this file has unsaved changes. Once you save the document, the dark dot goes away and the tiny icon is no longer gray.

You might see a **dot** next to a document name in an application's Window menu—that's another visual clue that the document has not been saved recently. The **checkmark** indicates the active document, or the one that is in front of all the others and that you're currently working on.

Everywhere on your Mac you will see buttons to save a document, not save, cancel a process, etc. One of these buttons is always **blue.** The blue is a visual clue that you can hit the Return or Enter key to activate that button instead of picking up the mouse to click on it.

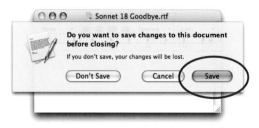

Help files

No matter where you are on the Mac or what application you are working in, you'll always find **Help** just a click away. At the Finder, go to the Help menu to look up tips and techniques on just about anything.

Every application has a Help menu, and it's always at the far end of the menu choices, as shown below. Choose the Help option for that particular application, type in a word or two that you want to look up, then hit Return.

Support pages

The Apple web site has a huge number of **support pages.** Here you can find manuals that you can view on screen or download (copy) to your computer. There are discussion pages where users talk about different products and software packages on the Mac, ask questions, and answer questions. You can sign up for training at a local Apple store, read the product question-and-answer pages for hardware and software, and more. Go to **www.mac. com/support.**

.Mac Learning Center

If you are a .Mac member, take advantage of the **.Mac Learning Center** where you'll find dozens of tutorials and movies to help you learn more about all sorts of features of your computer. Log in to your .Mac account and then find the link called "Learning Center."

To be a .Mac member costs $99.95 a year and includes lots of perks. Please see Lesson 11 for more details.

What You've Learned

▼ What all those items on the Desktop are.

▼ How to make sure you are at the Finder.

▼ What the Home folders are.

▼ How to use Finder windows.

- How to create new folders.

- How to add or delete folders from the Sidebar.

- How to change the views of windows and open items in those views.

- How to use all the little buttons in the Finder window Toolbar.

- How to select multiple items in a Finder window.

▼ How to use the Dock; how to add, delete, and rearrange items in the Dock; and what all the icons represent.

▼ How to throw items in the Trash and remove items from the Trash.

▼ What the various disk items are.

▼ Where on the hard disk the Home folders are located.

▼ What the icons on the Desktop indicate.

▼ What the Library folders are.

▼ How to use Mac os 9 with Mac OS X.

▼ How to use contextual menus.

▼ How to work with keyboard shortcuts.

- What the modifier keys do.

- Why some commands in menus are black and some are gray.

- How to navigate the entire Desktop and Finder windows with the keyboard.

- How to navigate the Save As and Open dialog box with the keyboard.

▼ How to burn a CD or DVD.

▼ How to use simple troubleshooting techniques.

- When to restart and how to restart.
- How to force quit an application.
- How to delete a preference file.
- When and how to check the Network preferences.
- How to check for software updates.
- When to create another user to test software problems.
- What to do if you forgot your administrator password.
- How to report crashes to Apple.

▼ Where to learn more about Mac OS X.

- Where to find tool tips.
- How to recognize visual clues.
- How to access the Help files for Mac OS X and for applications.
- Where to find Apple's support pages.
- Where to find the .Mac Learning Center.

Keyboard Shortcuts

Shift Command N	Make a new folder
Command W	Close the active window
Command Option W	Close all open windows
Command M	Minimize the active window
Command O	Open the selected folder, document, or application

4

Goals   Learn about the common features and tools available
in most Mac applications

Discover the key features of the Mac applications

Learn how the applications are integrated with each other

Introduction to Mac OS X Applications

One of the greatest things about Macintosh applications is that they are consistent, which makes them easy to learn and easy to use. What you learn in one application applies easily to just about any other application.

In this lesson, I'll show you the consistent features and tools you'll see in every Mac application that is bundled along with Mac OS X. And I'll present a very brief overview of the major apps that you'll find in your Applications folder and the Dock. Be sure to take notice of how all of these applications are so integrated with each other!

To learn specifically about the new features in Tiger, please see the second half of the book. But I recommend skimming through this chapter even if you are familiar with the applications—you might be surprised by what you don't know about your favorite software!

Know Your Applications Folder

In the Sidebar of any Finder window is an icon labeled **Applications.** Single-click this icon to display the contents of the Applications window. These are the programs you will use to create your work on your Mac.

At any time, you can put the application you use most often **in the Dock** so you'll have easy access to it: Just drag the application icon from this window and drop it on the Dock. If you accidentally lose something from the Dock, you can come back to this Applications window to drag the item back in.

Some applications that you buy will display their folders here in the Applications window. If so, open the folder and find the actual "application" icon to drag to the Dock.

Keyboard shortcut

Command Shift A	Opens the Applications folder even if there is no other Finder window open.

Know the Common Elements of Mac OS X Applications

Most Mac applications have these features in common.

Windows and window controls When you open an application, you'll actually be working in a **window.** If you worked through Lesson 3, you already know all about windows, even ones you haven't seen before. You see the same red, yellow, and green buttons to close, minimize, and resize the window. The document name and a tiny icon appear in the title bar. You can drag the title bar or any edge to move the window.

Application menu The application menu (directly to the right of the blue Apple menu) always tells you the name of the currently **active application,** the one you're working in (even if there is no document window open on the screen). You'll always find the Quit command at the bottom of this menu.

File and Edit menus You'll always find File and Edit as the first two menus to the right of the application menu.

Although each application includes specific features in its menus, in the **File menu** you'll always find the commands to **open** an existing document or create a **new** one, **save** the document or **save as** with another name, **close** the active window, and **print** the active document.

From the **Edit menu** you can always **undo or redo, cut, copy, paste, select all,** and check the **spelling.**

Preferences Every application has its own preferences where you can **customize** the application to suit yourself. You'll always open the preferences from the application menu (see the previous page). Typically you'll see a Toolbar across the top of the preferences pane; single-click an icon in that Toolbar to set the preferences for that particular feature.

Safari preferences. The Tabs pane is selected.

Toolbars Many applications have a Toolbar across the top of the window. Usually you can **customize** this Toolbar: check the **View menu** for a command called "Customize Toolbar…." In Safari, it's called "Customize Address Bar…."

Search Just about every application has a search feature. You might find it in the upper-right corner of the window or, as in iCal, at the bottom of the window (*or* press Command F). Just exactly what the search feature searches depends on the application. See the individual overviews on the following pages.

Sidebars or drawers Many applications have a sidebar, a drawer, or some other sort of pane on the side of the window. Single-click the icons you see in a sidebar-like feature to display its particular contents in the window.

Open and Save As dialog boxes Whenever you open an existing document or save a new one, the dialog boxes you see always look familiar. See page 53 for tips on how to get around these dialog boxes.

Help files Every application has a Help menu with Help files specific to that application. You can either use the menu you see on your screen or press Command ? to bring up the files. You'll find a search box where you can type in key words, then hit Return to display the answers.

Special collections Several applications use collection metaphors such as Albums in iPhoto, Playlists in iTunes, Bookmark collections in Safari, and Mailboxes in Mail. Use these to store and organize your stuff.

Action button and menu In many applications, you'll see the Action button (shown to the left) that displays the Action menu. Every application has different options—always click on it to see what is available.

Preview before you print At the bottom of the Print dialog box is a button called "Preview." Click this to open your document in the Preview application where you can see what it will look like when printed.

Smart Folders Many applications have some version of Smart Folders that automatically update themselves according to your specified criteria. For instance, the Address Book has Smart Groups that will add appropriate contacts to themselves, and iTunes has Smart Playlists that will add music to themselves. Mail has Smart Mailboxes. See Lesson 12 on Spotlight to learn how to take advantage of this great feature.

Use the Common Tools You'll Find in Every Mac App

In the Mac OS X applications, you'll find a number of common tools that operate in the same manner in all the programs.

Spell Checker

The spell checker is at the bottom of the Edit menu in Mac OS X applications. You have several options, as shown in the menu below:

Spelling... This brings up a dialog box. The spell checker runs through your entire document, giving you options for each word it thinks is misspelled. It provides possible alternatives for words it's not sure of.

> **To replace a misspelled word with an alternative,** just double-click the alternative you think is correct. Or you can type the correct spelling in the edit box, then click "Correct."

Learn Spell checkers typically don't recognize most people's names, as shown above. If you often use a particular word this is not in the spell checker's dictionary, click the "Learn" button while the word is selected. The spell checker will add that word to its dictionary and not whine about it being misspelled again.

Check Spelling Use this keyboard shortcut (Command ;) to skim through the spelling in your document without opening the dialog box.

Check Spelling as You Type This marks words that are misspelled as you type them—little red dots appears beneath words it thinks are misspelled. Any words not in its dictionary are considered misspelled, such as all names of people, most towns, and most specialized jargon.

To change a misspelled word quickly without bringing up a dialog box, Control-click (or right-click) on a misspelled word (you don't need to highlight the word first). A contextual menu appears, as shown below. At the top of this menu is a short list of alternative spellings for the word you clicked on. Just single-click on the correct spelling in the menu—the word is instantly corrected and the menu automatically disappears. (If the correct word is not offered, you can either type the correction yourself, or choose "Spelling" from this same menu to run a spell check.)

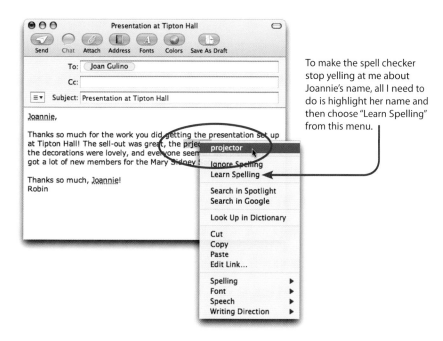

To make the spell checker stop yelling at me about Joannie's name, all I need to do is highlight her name and then choose "Learn Spelling" from this menu.

Font Panel

Press Command T in any Mac OS X application and the Font Panel appears, as shown below. If yours doesn't look like the one below, it might be because the Preview or the Effects are not showing.

▼ **To display the Preview and/or the Effects,** single-click on the Action button (circled, below). Choose "Show Preview." Click again on the menu and choose "Show Effects."

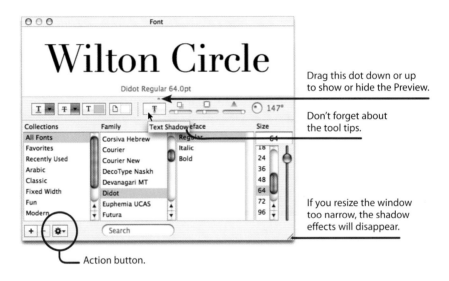

Drag this dot down or up to show or hide the Preview.

Don't forget about the tool tips.

If you resize the window too narrow, the shadow effects will disappear.

Action button.

In any Mac OS X application, open this Font Panel to choose the typeface family, the particular style (called "Typeface," above, hidden beneath the tool tip), and the size of type. Whatever you choose here will change the *selected* characters in your document. Note that you must **first select the text** you want to change, *then* choose the font and size. *Or* select the font and size right *before* you start typing.

Preview

Preview your own words Double-click the preview words shown at the top, and type your own. Then choose a different family, typeface, and size to see how your text looks in a different font.

Effects

You can apply **shadow effects** to selected text with these five controls, as shown below. Select text on the page, click the "Text Shadow" button (the button with the T), then experiment with the sliders on the other four tools.

Penshurst

When this button is blue, that's a visual clue that the *selected* text has a shadow effect applied to it.

Collections

The Font Panel has a number of **collections,** which are simply sub-groups of fonts from the main list. Making a collection doesn't disable or enable any fonts, it just makes it easier for you to choose a typeface—you don't have to scroll through a long list of fonts you don't care for.

To create a Collection, single-click the plus sign at the bottom of the Collections pane. Rename the collection. Drag font families from the "Family" pane into the new collection—drop the family name directly on the collection name.

Favorites

If you find you often use a particular family, typeface, point size, and color, turn that combination into a Favorite and keep it in the Favorites collection for easy access. Just select the text on the page that is formatted as you like it, or choose your favorite combination in the Font Panel. Then go to the Action button and choose "Add to Favorites."

When you want to use that typeface, single-click on the Favorites collection to display the combination. Select your text, then choose your favorite.

Action button options

Color option: See the following page.
Characters option: This displays the Character Palette; see pages 80–81.
Typography option: Choose sophisticated options for certain typefaces.
Manage Fonts option: This opens the Font Book; see pages 112–115.

Colors Panel

When you click on one of the color buttons (as shown below) in the Font Panel or the "Colors" icon in a toolbar, you get a deceptively powerful Colors Panel. Select text in Mail, TextEdit, and other applications, then choose a color.

Text color | | Paper color behind the text

Experiment with the Colors Panel to discover the possibilities

▼ Click one of the icons across the top of the panel to choose a color mode.

▼ Click the magnifying glass and your pointer turns into a magnifying glass. Drag it around the screen and when you find a color you want to "pick up," click on it and that color is added to the panel.

▼ In the "Color Wheel" mode, drag the dot around the circle to choose a color, and drag the slider up and down to change the tone.

▼ In the "Color Palettes" mode, shown below-left, use the List menu to choose "New." Use the Color menu at the bottom to create new colors.

▼ In the "Image Palettes" mode, shown below-right, click the "Palette" button, choose "New from File…," then choose a graphic or photo. Move the cursor around the photo to pick up colors you need. You can also drag any image from the Finder and drop it on the palette.

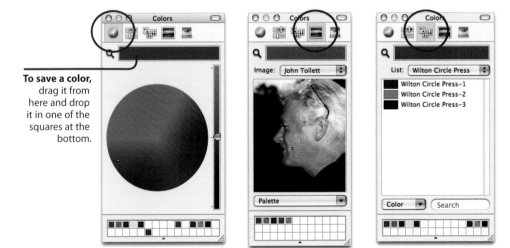

To save a color, drag it from here and drop it in one of the squares at the bottom.

Speech

In applications where there is typically a lot of text, **your Mac can read selected text to you.** You'll find a command for "Speech…" towards the bottom of the Edit menu in applications such as Mail and TextEdit, and you can use the Services menu option for "Speech" in iChat and Safari. (The Services options are in the application's menu.)

Have your email read out loud

1 Open an email message in Mail.

2 Click in the main body of text.

3 Go to the Edit menu, slide down to "Speech…," and choose "Start Speaking."

4 The entire text message will be read out loud to you.

   If you want just a portion read, select that portion before you go to the Edit menu.

5 The voice that's used is the one selected in the "Speech" preferences (see page 402).

To use the Services menu, first *select the text* in iChat or on a web page in Safari, then go to the application menu and choose the Speech option.

Character Palette

Many fonts have a lot of characters you don't know about but might like to use if you did. And different fonts have different sorts of **extra characters.**

For instance, these are the ampersands available in the font Zapfino:

How do you know which characters are available? Use the **Character Palette.**

At the bottom of most Edit menus is an option called "Special Characters…." This displays the Character Palette, as shown below.

Add special characters to your document:

1 Open TextEdit (it's in the Applications folder). A new, blank document appears on your screen. You'll see the insertion point flashing—that's where new characters will appear.

2 From the "View" menu on the palette (circled on the opposite page), choose "Glyph."

3 From the two "Font" menus, choose the typeface family and the individual style that you want to look at. In the example on the opposite page, you see the font "Skia." (Later, experiment with Zapfino!)

4 Scroll through the character pane to find the glyph you want. ("Glyph" refers to any individual variation of any character. For instance, above you see seven different *glyphs* for the ampersand *character.*)

5 Double-click the glyph you want to see on your page.

> **TIP** To reduce the Character Palette to a tiny box that is out of the way, but accessible, click its green Zoom button.

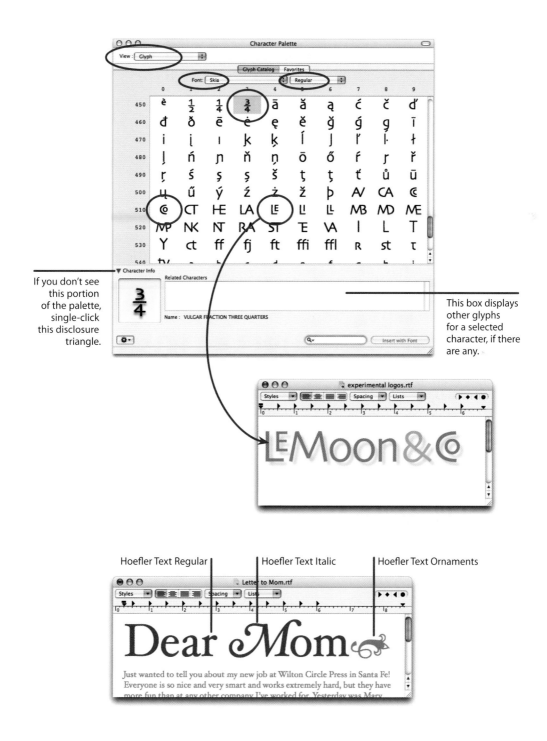

If you don't see this portion of the palette, single-click this disclosure triangle.

This box displays other glyphs for a selected character, if there are any.

Hoefler Text Regular

Hoefler Text Italic

Hoefler Text Ornaments

Learn the Key Features of Mac OS X Applications

TextEdit

TextEdit is a **word processor.** Use it for writing memos, letters, diaries, novels, grocery lists, memoirs, or any other text documents. You'll find TextEdit in your Applications folder. If you use it regularly, drag its icon to the Dock.

Open Word docs and save as Word docs

Do you work with people who send you **Microsoft Word files,** but you prefer to keep a Microsoft-free environment on your own computer? TextEdit can open Word files and save as Word files. Some of the advanced features will be missing, but this works great for basic text documents, now including those with tables or numbered/bulleted lists.

To open a Word document, drag the file and drop it on the TextEdit icon.

To save a TextEdit file as a Word document:

1 Go to the File menu and choose "Save As…."

2 In the File Format menu at the bottom of the Save As dialog box, choose "Word Format." This automatically adds the Word extension, .doc, to the end of your file name.

If you don't see the extension at the end of the file name—and you want to—make sure there is no checkmark next to "Hide Extension."

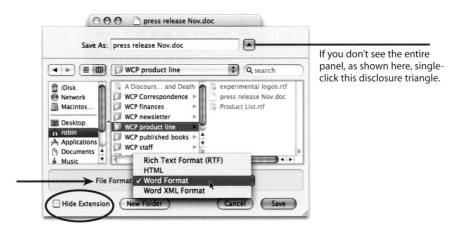

If you don't see the entire panel, as shown here, single-click this disclosure triangle.

Find and replace words or phrases

Did you write your entire story using your boyfriend's name, Joe, as the hero? And now you've broken up and want to **change** the hero's name to Heathcliff? No problem—go to the Edit menu, slide down to "Find," then choose "Find…," *or* press Command F. Find "Joe" and replace with "Heathcliff." It will be worth your time to experiment with the options you see in the Find dialog box—they're self-explanatory. Also see page 206 for an extra tip.

Paste in copied text to match the existing text

Let's say you're writing a term paper and you copy a quote from a web page to add to your paper (properly cited, of course). Typically the copied text pastes in with the typeface, style, size, and color that were originally applied to it. But to add this quotation to your term paper, you want it to look like the rest of your page. Use this great feature instead of the regular paste: **Paste and Match Style,** found in the Edit menu. The pasted text will pick up all the formatting *from the character to the left of the flashing insertion point.*

Use your favorite text styles easily

TextEdit doesn't have the powerful style sheets of an expensive word processor, but it does make your writing life much easier by letting you create **favorite styles** of basic type features so you can apply them quickly. These styles are saved with TextEdit, not with an individual document, so you can use the same styles in different documents.

To create your own favorite style:

1 Set up the typeface, size, color, and the ruler the way you want it. Click anywhere in the text you like.

2 From the "Styles" menu in the toolbar, choose "Other…"

3 Click the button, "Add To Favorites."

4 Name your new favorite style and choose your options. Click "Add."

To apply a style, select the characters, then choose the style name from the Styles menu.

Complete your word automatically

The **Complete** command in the Edit menu pops up a menu of possible comple-
tions for an unfinished word, as shown below. The list learns new words—type
a word once, then next time you start to type it, that word appears in the list.
Frequently used words appear at the top.

1 Start to type a word that you're not sure how to spell or one that is long
and you don't want to type the whole thing.

2 From the Edit menu, choose "Complete," *or* press Option Escape. A menu
like the one shown below will appear. Either double-click on the word you
want, *or* use the Down arrow key to select a word and then hit Return.

Standard Mac OS X application features

Don't forget that TextEdit includes all of the standard Mac features as
explained on the previous pages, such as spell checking, shadows for text,
color, special characters, previewing before you print, creating PDFs (see
pages 230–231), and more.

Tabs and indents

Drag tab markers from the Tab box to the ruler; drag them off the ruler to remove them. Drag the indent markers shown below.

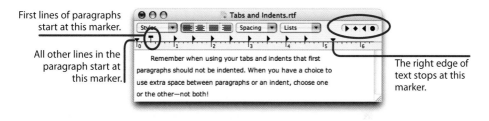

First lines of paragraphs start at this marker.

All other lines in the paragraph start at this marker.

The right edge of text stops at this marker.

TIP ▶ Tabs and indents apply to the *selected* paragraphs only. So select the text *before* you move the indent markers or the tabs!

TextEdit is integrated with:

- **Safari:** Web address links open in Safari.
- **Mail:** Email address links open a pre-addressed email message in Mail.
- **Preview:** Create a PDF in TextEdit that opens in Preview (see page 230–232). You can also annotate the PDF in Preview (see pages 214–215).
- **Speech:** Have your text read out loud to you; see page 79.

New in Tiger's TextEdit (see pages 201–206):

- TextEdit can now open Word files that include tables and numbered or bulleted lists.
- Create simple tables right in TextEdit.
- Create lists that automatically number themselves with a variety of number styles or bullets.
- Create more robust style sheets.
- Create live web address links.
- Create live email address links.
- Add page breaks to documents.

Mail

Mail is Apple's application for sending and receiving **email.** If you have more than one email account at more than one server, Mail can check them all at the same time. You can send mail from any of your accounts right through Mail.

Check your Dock icon

When email is received, your Mail icon in the **Dock** displays a little red tag telling how many messages are unread. Press (don't click) on the Dock icon to pop up a menu with options to get new mail and to create a new message (among other things).

Create mailboxes to organize your mail

Organize your mail with mailboxes in the same way that you make folders in a Finder window to organize all the files on your Mac. (In fact, most of the mailboxes look just like folders.) Use the "Mailbox" menu to create new ones, or Control-click in the Mailboxes drawer. If you Control-click directly on an icon in the Drawer, the new mailbox will be a subset of that icon.

Click "New" to compose and send a message.
Enter the recipient's email address, plus a subject.

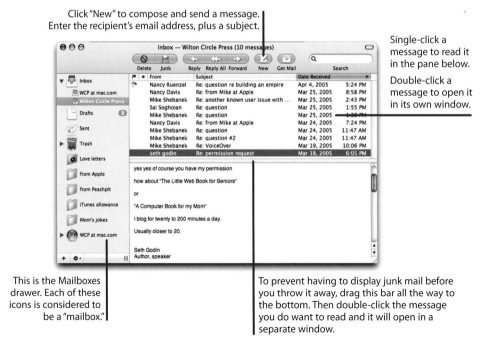

Single-click a
message to read it
in the pane below.

Double-click a
message to open it
in its own window.

This is the Mailboxes
drawer. Each of these
icons is considered to
be a "mailbox."

To prevent having to display junk mail before
you throw it away, drag this bar all the way to
the bottom. Then double-click the message
you do want to read and it will open in a
separate window.

Filter your incoming mail

Create rules, or filters, to **sort incoming mail** into the appropriate mailbox. First, create the mailboxes you want for organizing (see opposite page). Then:

1 From the Mail menu, choose "Preferences…."

2 Single-click on the "Rules" icon. Single-click "Add Rule."

3 Choose your parameters for the type of mail coming in and what to do with it. (If you forgot to make a special mailbox for something, you can actually do it while the preferences pane is open on your screen; use the Mailbox menu.)

In the example below, I first made a new mailbox called "Edits." Then I created a new rule to find any incoming mail from my editor, Nancy Davis. When found, I want that message to go straight into the "Edits" folder and play a little sound so I know it arrived.

Delete junk mail without ever seeing it!

Mail has a **junk mail filter** that can toss your spam automatically. Actually, while in "training," it will put spam in a special brown "Junk" folder where you can check to make sure messages really are garbage before you toss them. Once you are confident it's doing a good job, use the rules described above to delete junk mail immediately.

To turn on Junk Mail filtering, go to the Preferences pane (in the Mail menu), click the "Junk Mail" icon, and check the box to "Enable junk mail filtering." Carefully read the other choices in the pane and choose your options.

Add signatures to your messages

An **email signature** is the little blurb you can automatically add to your messages. A signature might include your contact information, promotion for your upcoming art show or book publication, your favorite quote, or even a small graphic. You can make more than one signature, then choose which one you want for a particular email message.

To make a signature, go to the Preferences (from the Mail menu), then click the "Signatures" icon. As is typical for many Mac applications, click the **+** button, name the signature, then in the right-hand panel, type it up. See pages 192–193 for more details.

To use a signature, put the menu in your message window:

1 Open a new message as if you're going to write a letter.

2 Single-click on the Action button to get the menu; choose "Customize…."

3 Put a checkmark in the box next to "Signature."

4 Click ok. Now you will see the Signature menu in every new mail message, as shown below. Choose the one you want to use for each individual message, or set a default in the Preferences pane.

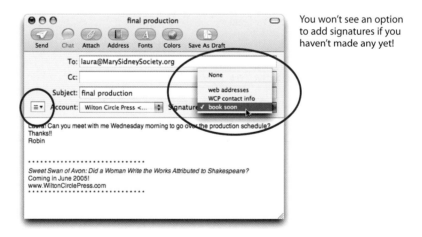

You won't see an option to add signatures if you haven't made any yet!

TIP If you can't do what you want with the text in a message, such as color it or even make words bold, go to the Format menu and choose "Make Rich Text."

Use the standard Mac OS X application features

Mail includes all of the **standard Mac features** as explained on the previous pages, such as spell checking, shadows for text, text in color, special characters, creating PDFs, previewing before you print, reading text aloud, and more.

The "Complete" feature, as explained on page 84, can be used in email messages. Any styles you created in TextEdit, as described on page 83, are also available in Mail messages—from the Format menu, slide down to "Style," then out to "Styles…."

Mail is integrated with:

- **Address Book:** Click the "Address" icon to bring up a minimalized Address Panel.

- **iChat:** A green dot in a column in your Viewer window indicates an iChat Buddy is online and available. If you don't see that column, go to the View menu, select "Column," then choose "Buddy Availability."

- **Photo:** Image attachments can be saved directly into iPhoto. See page 190.

- **iCal:** Email announcements to all attendees of an event.

- **.Mac sync:** Synchronize your .Mac email account with the .Mac mail web site so you have access to your mail on any computer in the world.

- **TextEdit:** Click on an email link in TextEdit to open Mail and automatically address the email.

New in Tiger Mail (see pages 184–197):

- Organize your email into Smart Mailboxes automatically, even after it has come in through filters.

- Organize multiple mailboxes of information with Smart Mailbox groups.

- Create different signatures for different accounts.

- Print email messages with new specifications.

- Format your email messages faster with enhanced style sheets.

- Troubleshoot your connections to different email accounts with the Connection Doctor; see page 267.

Address Book

The Address Book is a great **contact list** integrated with so many other parts of your Mac. It's much more complete than its simple appearance might lead you to believe—take the time to explore its possibilities!

Make and edit new cards

To make a new card, (sometimes called a vCard), click the **+** sign at the bottom of the "Name" pane, which displays the new card in the right pane, ready for you to add information.

A **+** sign in a green circle indicates you can add another field for that particular type of information, like another phone or email address.

The **–** sign in a red circle indicates you can click it to delete that field.

To change the existing field labels, click the tiny triangles.

To add a photo, double-click the photo space. Then drag any type of image into the pane, *or* click "Choose…" to find a photo on your hard disk, *or* click the camera icon to take a picture of someone with a connected camera, even someone you are iChatting with.

To edit an existing card, select the card in the "Names" column, then click the "Edit" button. When you're finished, click "Edit" again.

Search

In the search field, enter any type of data to search for. See pages 308–309 to learn how to take advantage of the Spotlight search right here.

Designate your own card

Enter a **card** for yourself in the Address Book. Then go to the Card menu and choose, "Make This My Card." Other applications, Safari and iChat in particular, will use that information in various ways, such as filling in forms online and accessing your email address. To keep some of the information **private** so it won't show up if you send your card to someone else, go to Preferences, click "vCard," then edit your own card and uncheck the boxes that you want to be private.

Customize one card or all cards

The fields for data only appear on the card if there is data in them. Select a card and click the "Edit" button to see what your current options are.

To add a field to one card, such as "Nickname," first select that card. Then go to the Card menu, slide down to "Add Field," and make a choice.

To add a field to every card, such as "Birthdate," go to the Card menu. Choose "Edit Template…." Click the "Add Field" button and make your choice. You can also go straight to the Address Book preferences to do this (click the "Template" button in the preferences).

Create group mailing lists

After you've made a group mailing list, you can **send email to the name of that group** and your message will go to everyone in the group.

To make a new group, click the **+** sign at the bottom of the "Group" column. Change its name. Then click the "All" group, and drag names from the "Names" column and drop them on the group name. You can put the same name in as many different groups as you like.

To prevent everyone's address from appearing in everyone else's email:

1 Open Mail (not Address Book).

2 From the Mail menu, choose "Preferences…."

3 Click the "Composing" icon.

4 Uncheck the box, "When sending to a group, show all member addresses."

Print in a variety of ways

From Address Book you can **print** mailing labels, envelopes, customized lists, and even pages that fit into a standard pocket address book. First select the names or the group that you want to print, then press Command P. It's a good idea to click the "Preview" button before you actually print to make sure you are getting what you expect.

You can save the job as a PDF and then send that PDF to someone else to print.

Backup your entire digital database

You have several options for backing up everything you have taken the time to enter into the Address Book. One way is to select everyone in the Name column, then drag that block to the Desktop to create a file.

Or go to the File menu and choose "Back up Address Book…."

Also see Lesson 11 about syncing your Address Book with your .Mac account so you have your contact list no matter what happens to your computer.

Address Book is integrated with:

- **Safari:** Put your Address Book in the Bookmarks Bar and you have instant access to any web sites listed in the Address Book. In the Safari Preferences, in the Bookmarks pane, check the box to "Include Address Book."

    You can also go to web sites directly from within the Address Book.

    The AutoFill feature in Safari uses the data you enter in your own card.

    Map: Click on an address and choose "Map Of." Try it

- **iCal:** iCal creates a Birthday calendar from your Address Book so everyone's birthday is automatically placed on its appropriate day; see page 218.

- **iPod:** Transfer your entire contact list to your iPod using iSync (see pages 298–299).

- **Mail:** Send email to a selected contact with a contextual menu, or use the Action button. The photos you put in the Address Book will appear in other Mac users email messages when they send you mail.

    To automatically add someone's email address to your Address Book, select a message in Mail, then press Command Y.

- **iChat:** iChat will pick up the data and picture you add here. And when a Buddy is online and available, his address card displays a green dot.

- **iSight:** With an iSight camera connected (or any camera), you can add a photograph of someone you are chatting with through iChat; see page 105.

- **.Mac:** Synchronize your other Macs and your .Mac account so you have your entire Address Book accessible on the web, anywhere in the world.

- **Spotlight:** Send your Address Book search out to your entire computer through Spotlight. See pages 322–323.

New in Tiger's Address Book (see pages 198–200):

- Share your Address Book with others.

- Print with enhanced options (as shown on the opposite page).

- Synchronize with an Exchange server.

- Create Smart Groups that automatically add new contacts to the appropriate groups; see pages 310–311.

- Beam a card to a mobile device with one click.

Safari

Safari is Apple's browser for **viewing web pages.** It's got lots of great features, both large and small.

Customize the icons you see in the Address Bar; use the command from the View menu.

Drag this icon to the right side of the Dock or to the Desktop to make a web location file you can click on.

This is the Bookmarks Bar.

The first button will "Show all bookmarks" in the Bookmarks Library.

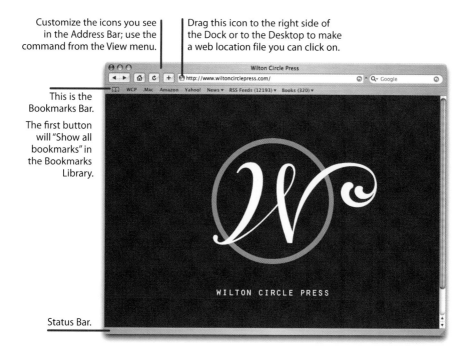

Status Bar.

Make a quick web address change

This is actually my favorite feature in Safari: If you double-click between www and .com, it selects *just* the domain so you can change it. This means you don't have to drag the mouse across tiny little letters when you want to change the address. Try it.

And don't forget you never need to type "http://." If it's a .com address, all you need to type is the main word. For instance, to go to www.apple.com, just select everything in the location bar, type *apple,* then hit Return.

Find a word or phrase on the current page

To find a word or phrase on the page you are looking at (as opposed to searching the Internet for it), press Command F.

Fill in online forms and passwords automatically

This is wonderful. Safari will **fill in online forms** with the information you have entered into your Address Book; it takes the data from the card you have designated as "My Card" (use the Card menu in Address Book to do that). You can also tell Safari to remember your **user ID and password** for specific sites, which is great if no one else uses your Mac (or if you have set up different users).

To enable Safari to fill in forms and passwords, go to the Safari Preferences and click the "AutoFill" icon. Check the appropriate boxes.

Next time you start to fill in a form, Safari will fill it for you. Next time you go to a page that needs an **ID and password,** go ahead and fill them in, then Safari will ask if you want to save that information. Try it on your .Mac page.

To delete saved user names, passwords, or forms, go back to the AutoFill preferences. Click the "Edit…" button. Select and remove items.

Quickly enlarge or reduce text

Make the **text on a web page** larger or smaller with Command **+** (larger) or Command **–** (smaller). You don't have to select anything first.

Block pop-up windows!

Go to the Safari menu and choose, "Block Pop-Up Windows." Woo hoo! Only pop-up windows that you click on will appear—none of those obnoxious ads.

SnapBack to a results page or other page

Do you see those little **orange arrows** in the location field and the Google search field on the opposite page? Those indicate "SnapBack" pages.

When you do a search in Google, either at Google.com or through the Google search field in the upper-right corner of Safari, you get a page of results. As soon as you click on a link on that page, the SnapBack arrow appears. Wherever you surf, you can always click the SnapBack arrow to return to the original results page.

You can mark any page you want as a SnapBack page: Go to the History menu and choose "Mark Page for SnapBack." As soon as you leave that page, the arrow appears in the location field, ready for you to click to return.

Tabbed browsing

Instead of clicking on a link that takes you to another page and loses your original page, Command-click on a link and it opens in a **tab,** as shown below. Command-click on lots of links and they will all load themselves in individual tabs. Then when you're ready, click any tab to display that page, while leaving your original page still available.

To use tabbed browsing, first go to the Safari Preferences, click the "Tabs" icon, and check the box to "Enable Tabbed Browsing." While you're there, check out the other options.

Tabs.
Click a tab to
display that page.
Click the **X** to
close that page.

Bookmarks

The bookmarks in Safari are extremely powerful.

The **Bookmarks Menu** is what drops down from the menu bar across the top of your screen.

The **Bookmarks Bar** is that strip in the browser window you see above, just below the address field. To display it, go to the View menu and choose, "Show Bookmarks Bar."

The **Bookmarks Library** and the various **Collections** you create let you organize hundreds of bookmarks, but you don't have to keep them all in the Bookmarks Menu, making your list a yard long. Click the "Show all bookmarks" button (shown on page 94) when you want to make new folders for **organizing your bookmarks.**

When you hit Command D to **create a bookmark,** a little sheet drops down and asks you where you want to store it. You can rename the bookmark at that point and choose any folder you have made in which to store it.

Safari is integrated with:

- **Address Book:** Put your Address Book in the Bookmarks Bar and go to the web site of any contact in your Address Book. In the Safari preferences, in the Bookmarks pane, check the box to "Include Address Book."

  The AutoFill feature uses the Address Book contact you have designated as "My Card."

- **Mail:** Email a web page or just the contents to someone; see page 225.

  Email links open a pre-addressed message in Mail.

- **TextEdit:** Web links on a TextEdit page will open in Safari; see page 205.

- **Dock:** Drag the tiny icon that you see to the left of a web address and drop it on the far right side of the Dock to create a web location.

New in Tiger's Safari (see pages 223–226):

- View PDF files on a Safari page. Just drag a PDF and drop it in the middle of the page—not in the address field!

- Use private browsing to prevent the History menu from keeping track of sites you've visited.

- Organize RSS feeds (news and blogs) right in Safari.

- Feel safer with enhanced parental controls.

- Send an email to a friend or colleague with the contents of a web page or the address to a page.

- Print web pages and display the web page information as headers and footers.

iCal

iCal is a **calendar** program that keeps track of events, creates an electronic To Do list, and pops up reminders to you, among other things. You can publish your calendar over the Internet for other iCal users (publicly or privately), and they can subscribe to it and get automatic updates. Amazing. Or publish it to a web page and anyone on any computer can view it.

Every calendar has its own events and To Do list.

Check one or more calendars to display those events and To Do lists.

Set an alarm so iCal will notify you of an upcoming event.

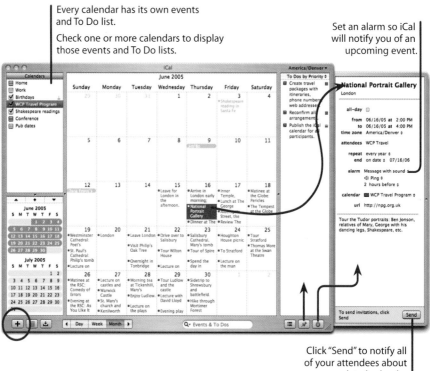

Click "Send" to notify all of your attendees about an updated calendar.

Create multiple calendars

To create a new calendar, go to the very bottom of the Calendars pane, click the **+** sign, then name it and choose an identifying color.

You can have lots of different calendars. The checkmark next to a calendar name indicates those events are displayed. Thus you can have a calendar for each one of your kids' activities, plus your work calendar, and choose to see all the events at once or just selected ones. This helps determine if you have any overlapping events.

Create events

You can **create events** in a variety of ways.

▼ In the "Month" view, double-click on a day to create a new event. The Info drawer opens and you can add your information. iCal arranges multiple events on one day according to the times you enter.

▼ In the "Week" or "Day" views, press-and-drag over the times for your event. The Info drawer opens and you can add your information.

▼ To stretch the event out across multiple days, be sure to click the "all-day" button in the Info drawer.

▼ To create a recurring event, use the "repeat" feature in the Info drawer. iCal automatically fills in the event throughout the years. For instance, my Shakespeare readings repeat every first Friday of each month.

These little icons indicate there is a note associated with this event, plus there is a list of attendees.

Click the "Info" button to see that information.

Preferences

Check the preferences (in the iCal menu) for **important options** for your calendars, including when to automatically delete events.

Detach the Info drawer

From the Window menu, choose "Detach Info." This is particularly handy on smaller screens, such as laptops.

Create a To Do list

Each calendar can have its own **To Do list.** So select a calendar first, then click the To Do list button (bottom-right, pushpin icon).

To add an item to the list, Control-click (or right-click) and choose "New To Do" from the contextual menu. *Or* double-click anywhere in the To Do list.

Open the Info drawer to **prioritize** your item, add a note, give it a due date, and more.

When the item has been **completed,** check the tiny checkbox next to it.

Publish your calendar

If you have a .Mac account (or a private server), you can **publish** your calendar of events, including the alarms and To Do list if you choose, to a web page and anyone in the world on any computer can view it. It's really amazing.

To publish, just select the calendar in the list, then go to the Calendar menu and choose "Publish...." A little dialog box (shown below) drops down. Make your choices, then click "Publish."

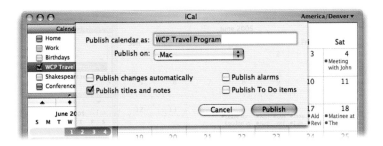

A message appears telling you the web address and asking if you want to email people with the address.

To notify other people at any time, select the calendar, go to the Calendar menu, and choose "Send Publish Email...."

In the Info drawer for the selected calendar, you can choose to have **notices** sent automatically every time you make a change to the calendar.

Subscribe to calendars

There are many public calendars you can subscribe to, such as calendars for the PGA tours, NASCAR races, musician's tour dates, and many more.

To subscribe to a public calendar, go to the Calendar menu and choose "Find Shared Calendars…." This takes you to an Apple web site with dozens of public calendars.

To subscribe to a private calendar, go to the Calendar menu and choose "Subscribe…." Enter the web address you have been given.

iCal is integrated with:

- **Address Book:** Use the cards and Groups to invite people to events.

   Any birthdays you enter in Address Book can automatically appear in iCal (go to the iCal preferences and check "Show Birthdays calendar").

   When you add attendees names in the Info drawer, iCal will pick up their email addresses from the Address Book.

- **Address Book** or **Panel:** Open it from the Window menu. Quickly add people to the attendee list—drag them to the "attendee" button.

- **Mail:** iCal will mail invitations and notifications of calendar updates, and Mail can automatically send notifications to iCal. See page 219.

- **iPod:** Transfer your iCal information to your iPod; see page 298.

- **iSync:** Synchronize the calendar on one computer with all the other computers in your office, as well as with your .Mac account; see Lesson 11.

New in Tiger's iCal (see pages 218–222):

- Create Calendar Groups to organize related calendars.
- Let Mail send a notification to iCal to keep you apprised of updates.
- Create an automatic Birthday calendar.
- Backup the entire database of calendar information.
- Sort your To Do list by due date, title, calendar, priority, or manually.
- Search your calendar.
- Change the time zone to reflect another part of the world.
- Print with great new options.

iChat

Using iChat you can **communicate** with others around the world using text messages, audio chatting, or video conferencing—free. A typical text chat is shown below.

This is a Buddy List. Double-click a Buddy name to open a text chat. Names in grey are not available at the moment.

Customize your IM (instant message) chat view through iChat Preferences, in the "Messages" pane.

Set up iChat

When you first open iChat, it will ask you to fill in certain information to get started. If you have a .Mac account, that will be your "screen name." You can get a 60-day free .Mac trial account, and keep the screen name after the free trial is over, even if you quit. Or go to www.AIM.com and sign up for a free AIM account; you can use that as your Buddy name. If you already have a Jabber account, you can use that name as well.

Create a Buddy List

To iChat with people, first set up a **Buddy List** of names.

1 If you don't see the Buddy List when you open iChat, go to the Window menu and choose "Buddy List."

If the title bar of the Buddy List says you are "Offline," click on the tiny triangle and choose "Available."

2 To add a new Buddy, single-click the **+** sign at the bottom of the list and choose "Add Buddy."

3 In the dialog box that appears, **either** choose someone in your Address Book whose screen name you have already entered. That person is now in your Buddy List and you can skip the rest of these steps.

Or choose someone in the Address Book whose screen name you have *not* entered yet. **Or** click "New Person."

4 In the new dialog box, enter the information. This will be automatically entered in the Address Book for you.

5 If you have a photo or image you want to use to identify that Buddy, drag the image from the Finder and drop it in the "Buddy Icon" well.

6 Click the "Add" button.

Add or change a Buddy's photo

If a Buddy has chosen an image in his own iChat on his Mac, that's the image you will see in your Buddy List. You can **override that image,** if you like.

1 In your Buddy List, single-click on a Buddy to select her (she doesn't have to be online), go to the Buddies menu, and choose "Get Info."

2 Double-click on the picture well (the little square) to get the "Buddy Picture" pane.

3 Drag a photo or graphic from the Finder and drop it in this well, or click the button to "Take Video Snapshot" with an attached camera. Adjust the size of the image using the slider, if necessary. Click the "Set" button.

4 Check the box to "Always use this picture." Click OK.

Chat with one other person

To have a **text chat** with someone around the office or around the world, simply open your Buddy List and double-click the name of the person you want to chat with. A chat window opens. Type a message, then hit Return.

Save a hard copy transcript of your chat

To save a **hard copy** of your chat, go to the iChat Preferences. In the "Messages" pane, check the box to "Automatically save chat transcripts." This creates a

Preview

Preview **opens PDFs and images** of all sorts. It's a great way to quickly view your images and preview them before printing.

Open an image or folder of images

Depending on how you have customized your Mac, you can often just double-click on images and they will open in Preview. *Or* Control-click on an image, select "Open With," and choose "Preview" from the list.

You can put Preview in your Dock (see pages 42–43), then drag an image onto the Preview icon to open it. You can drag an **entire folder** of images to Preview and they will all open and display themselves in the drawer, as shown above.

Check the Preview preferences for options on displaying your images.

Rotate, reduce, or enlarge the view

If an image appears sideways, just click one of the curly arrows in the Toolbar.

If an image looks bitmapped and blurry and too large, reduce its view: click on the magnifying glass with the **–** sign in it.

Enlarge an image, of course, with the **+** magnifying glass.

Save as another format

If you know you need a particular image in another **file type,** use the Save As menu (from the File menu). Cick the "Format" menu, as shown below, to make a choice.

```
                    ○ ○ ○   ◆ Tyler.gif      ⬭

      Save As: | Tyler                    |  ▼

      Where: | 📁 Flags            |  ⬍

       ───────────────────────────────────
                    ┌─────────────────┐
                    │   BMP           │
          Format ✓  │   GIF           │
                    │   JPEG-2000     │
                    │   JPEG          │
                    │   PDF           │
                    │   Photoshop     │
                    │   PICT          │
                    │   PNG           │
                    │   SGI           │        Save
                    │   TGA           │
                    │   TIFF       ▖  │
                    └─────────────────┘
```

Preview is integrated with:

- **Printing:** In the Print dialog box in any Mac OS X application, click the button "Preview." The file will open in the Preview application and display what the printed document will actually look like when printed.

New in Tiger's Preview (see pages 208–217):

- Preview a bunch of photos as a full-screen slideshow.
- Print with more options.
- Annotate PDFs. You can write notes on a PDF, circle items, crop the page, and more.
- Fax from Preview.
- Bookmark images so you can get to them again quickly.

Font Book

Font Book allows you to install new **fonts** you acquire, disable fonts in your font menus that you never use, and view fonts before you install them.

Preview fonts you haven't installed

If you acquire new fonts or if you just have some fonts on a disk and you don't know what they are, simply double-click on the font file. Font Book will open automatically and display the font. If you want to install it, click the "Install Font" button.

Install fonts

You can use the step above to install fonts. You can also:

1 Open Font Book (it's in your Applications folder).

2 In the Collection pane, single-click on "User" (if you want the fonts available only to you as the user) or "Computer" (if you want the fonts available to every user of this particular computer).

3 Go to the File menu and choose "Add Fonts...."

4 Find the font you want to install and double-click it. Font Book moves the font from its enclosing folder and puts it in the Library Fonts folder. You might have to quit and re-open your application before the fonts appear in the application Font menu.

The default location for installing fonts is determined in the Font Book preferences.

Preview fonts you have installed

Single-click on any typeface name in the Font pane of Font Book. A preview appears on the right. Use the slider to enlarge or reduce the typeface, or type in a point size.

Go to the Preview menu and choose:

"Sample" to display the upper and lowercase letters, as well as the numbers.

"Repertoire" to see every glyph in the font.

"Custom," and then type your own words to see them displayed in this typeface. Use the slider bar to enlarge the font.

To disable an individual font, find it in the Font list. Single-click to select it, then click the little checkmark button at the bottom of the Font list.

Create your own Collections

A **Collection** is simply an easy way to look at fonts you like instead of having to grope through a lengthy font list of typefaces you don't know or want.

To make a new Collection, single-click the **+** sign at the bottom of the Collection pane, then name it. Click the "All Fonts" collection, then drag font names from the Font pane to the new Collection name.

To disable (turn off) an entire Collection, select it in the Collection pane. Then go to the Edit menu and choose, "Disable 'CollectionName.'"

Font Book is integrated with:

- **Font Panel:** From the Action menu, you can choose to "Manage Fonts…," which will open Font Book.
- **Finder:** Font Book will add or remove fonts from your Library Fonts folders.

New in Tiger's Font Book:

- Differentiate clearly between managing fonts for the entire computer or just one user, as explained on page 112.
- **Export a Collection** for others to use (this actually makes copies of the original fonts): Select a Collection, then go to the File menu and choose "Export Collection…."
- **Validate fonts** to make sure they are not corrupt or damaged in any way: Select a font in the Font list, then go to the File menu and choose "Validate Font."
- Show **more complete font information** for each file: Select a font in the Font pane, then go to the Preview menu and choose "Show Font Info."
- **Create your own Libraries** of fonts: From the File menu, choose "New Library." Rename this Library and add fonts to it just as you would to a Collection. This Library folder can be stored anywhere you like. You can make many Libraries and turn their fonts on or off through Font Book.

What You've Learned

▼ The common features and tools of many Mac applications.

- Windows and window controls, toolbars, search, drawers or sidebars, Help files, Action button, and more.
- The application menu and its importance.
- The File and Edit menus and their importance.
- The preferences for every application.
- The spell checker and how to use it.
- The Font Panel and how to use it and preview fonts.
- The Colors panel and how to use it.
- The Speech feature to read text out loud to you.
- The Character Palette to find extra characters.

▼ The key features of most Mac OS X applications that come with the Mac.

▼ How each application is integrated with other applications.

▼ Search and replace, tabs and indents, and how to complete typing words automatically.

▼ Create mailboxes for organizing email, get rid of junk mail automatically, and add signatures to outgoing messages.

▼ Create a contact list in Address Book and print the list in a variety of ways.

▼ Fill in online forms automatically, organize web bookmarks, block pop-up windows, and save web search results for a quick "snap back."

▼ Create calendars, events, and to-do lists, then publish the information to share with others.

▼ Chat with other computer users around the world, change a Buddy's photo, exchange files, have an audio chat or a video chat.

▼ Import music, create Playlists, and burn a CD of your own collection.

▼ Preview images, rotate and enlarge their views, and save files in different formats.

▼ Preview and install fonts.

5

Goals   Learn various keyboard shortcuts for making Mac life easier

Control your windows with Exposé

Drag and drop between applications

Take advantage of Services

Lesson **5**

Working between Mac OS X Applications

Now that you've had an overview of the main applications that come with Mac OS X and how they are all integrated, let's carry it one step further and work *between* all the applications—pop between windows, drag-and-drop content and files, use the Services, and more.

Once you realize how easy it is to move data between applications and windows, you'll find more and more uses for it. Plus you'll feel like a Power User.

Work with Multiple Applications at Once

In Mac OS X, you can keep lots of applications and windows open at once. You can always just single-click an application icon in the Dock to switch to it, but there are a couple of great shortcuts to switch between multiple applications quickly and easily.

Switch between all applications

No matter which application you are currently using, you can bring up a floating palette like the one shown below, then select the application you want to switch to—without ever having to reach for the mouse.

To get a lovely palette that displays icons for all the *open* applications, press Command Tab and *hold down* the Command key.

To cycle through the icons from left to right, tap the Tab key (keep the Command key down).

To cycle through the icons in the other direction, right to left, keep the Command key down, but also hold down the Shift key while you tap the Tab key.

Or press Command Tab to display the palette, then use the mouse to select an icon (you don't have to actually click on the icon—just hover over it to highlight it).

However you choose to do it, when the application icon you want is highlighted in the palette, **let go of the keys** and that application will come forward as the active application.

Remember, if there is no window open in that particular application, it might look like nothing happened—always check the application menu to see which one is currently active! You might need to hit Command N to open a window in that application once it's active.

Switch back and forth between two applications

Most of us probably spend the greater part of our time between our two favorite applications. There's a shortcut that will switch you back and forth between just those two, instead of having to bring up the palette.

While in one of your favorite applications, switch to the other one using the method on the previous page, or just click on its icon in the Dock. Now you can press Command Tab **to switch between those two applications.** I know it sounds too similar to the shortcut for switching between all applications, but the trick is to hold down the Command key, hit the Tab key *just once,* then let go of both keys right away.

Quit or hide applications

Don't forget that Command H will **hide** all of the windows of the active application, and Command Q will **quit** the active application. Use these shortcuts in combination with the switching shortcuts to quit or hide selected applications.

To hide all other applications except the one you're currently using, press Command Option H.

Control Your Windows with Exposé

When you use more than one application at a time and also use the Finder windows, you can end up with lots of windows that stack on top of each other on the screen. That's where **Exposé** comes in handy.

With the click of a button or a key, Exposé will display **All windows,** meaning all Finder windows that are open and every window in every application—all neatly arranged on the screen so you can see every one clearly.

If you prefer, you can tap a different key and Exposé will display just the open **application windows** in the currently active application. This is great when you're working on several documents at the same time and want to get back and forth between them quickly.

Or tap a different key and all visible windows disappear to the outer edges of the screen with just a window border showing, making everything on your **Desktop** immediately available.

To set active screen corners, keyboard shortcuts, or mouse actions to work with Exposé, use the **Exposé preferences,** as explained below.

Exposé preferences

First, open up a bunch of windows so you can experiment with this. Open several Finder windows (Command-click on folders to open them in separate windows). Also open an application or two, and open at least two windows in each application. Now you've got a good mess to work with.

1 Open the System Preferences: Single-click its icon in the Dock.

2 Single-click on the Exposé icon in the System Preferences pane.

3 In the Exposé preferences, shown below, choose the various ways you want to enable the Exposé actions. You can set actions for as many or as few of the options as you like, depending on how you prefer to work.

Active Screen Corners: Choose what will happen (if anything) when you shove your mouse into one of the corners. A dash (–) means nothing will happen. (Because the Apple menu is in the upper-left corner and Spotlight is in the upper-right corner, I usually assign actions to the bottom corners.)

Keyboard: Choose which keyboard shortcut you want. To maximize your options, hold down any combination of the Shift, Control, Option, or Command keys to add that modifier key to the shortcut. For instance, if you have already assigned F9 to some other shortcut on your Mac, you can assign Option F9 or Shift F9 to an Exposé action.

Mouse: If you have a two- or three-button mouse, you can assign actions to the extra buttons.

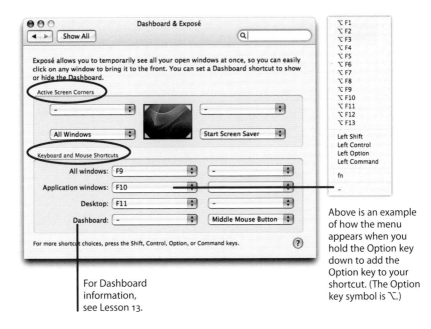

For Dashboard information, see Lesson 13.

Above is an example of how the menu appears when you hold the Option key down to add the Option key to your shortcut. (The Option key symbol is ⌥.)

4 You don't have to close the Exposé preferences to experiment with your choices—just use the shorcuts you have created and see what happens. Try these experiments:

- Since you made a mess of windows earlier, use the action you set for "Desktop" to make all windows go away (if you didn't change the existing shortcut, hit the F11 key). Try it—you should see just your Desktop.

  Use the same action to display everything again.

- With that mess of windows on your screen, use the action you set for "All windows." (If you didn't change the existing shortcut, hit the F9 key.) Every window becomes small and visible. As you mouse over windows, a little label appears to tell you the title of that window.

  If you have a movie playing or the iTunes visualizer on, it will continue playing even while small.

- While all windows are visible (see above), tap the Tab key: every tap of the Tab key brings a different *group* of windows forward—each application's open windows are a group, plus the Finder windows are another group.

● Select one of the open applications in the Dock, one of the applications in which you earlier opened several windows. Use the action you set for "Application windows" (if you didn't change the existing shortcut, hit the F10 key). This brings forward all the windows that are open in that application, sized small and tiled across the screen. Single-click the one you want to work with.

Spend a few minutes to familiarize yourself with Exposé so it becomes a natural way to work. You'll wonder how you lived without it!

Simplify Your Work with Drag-and-Drop

You probably have lots of applications open on your Mac. Often you'll need to move data from one open application to another. Your Mac makes this so easy with **drag-and-drop:** drag the information you want from one application and drop it into the other application. Below are some examples. Experiment with these, and then try dragging and dropping in all sorts of other ways! If it doesn't work, nothing bad will happen—it just won't work.

Move text around in a document window

In TextEdit or Mail messages, you don't have to cut-and-paste to move text, you can simply drag-and-drop it.

1 First select the text you want to move: with your mouse, press-and-drag over the text so it is highlighted. Let go of the mouse button.

2 Once the text is highlighted, press anywhere in the text and hold it for a second or two, then drag.

3 Watch for the insertion point! It's that thin, flashing, vertical bar. As you move the mouse and pointer, the insertion point moves too. When the insertion point is positioned where you want the new text to appear, let go of the mouse button. Text will aways drop in or paste in at the flashing insertion point!

Don't forget to use that great option in the Edit menu of applications like TextEdit and Mail to "Paste and Match Style."

To move a copy of the selected text, press the Option key and hold it down while you drag the text.

If you drag text from one document window to another, you don't need to hold down the Option key because it will automatically make a copy.

TIP Often you'll find it works best to select the text or items, then *press and hold and count to three* before you drag.

Move text from one application to another

Not only can you drag-and-drop within one application, you can drag text from one application window and drop it in another. Let's say you wrote a nice essay in TextEdit—select it and drag it into an email message in Mail.

This automatically makes a *copy* of the text (instead of deleting it from the first application), so you don't need to hold down the Option key.

Make a text clipping on the Desktop

Have you ever wanted to save a quote from a web page or a statement from an email message? Just select the text, then drag-and-drop it onto the Desktop or into any folder or window. This makes a small file on your Desktop with an extension called ".textClipping" (if your extensions are visible; see page 141).

The clipping names itself with the first few words of the text.

The lights burn blue.textClipping

Anytime you want to see what the text clipping says, just double-click on it. And you can drag-and-drop that clipping file into most text windows, such as TextEdit or a Mail message, and the actual text will drop onto the page.

Add email addresses to Mail message

Drag a person's name from the Address Book or the Address Panel and drop it into any of the To fields in an email message to automatically address a message. You can drag addresses from one field to another.

To add more than one name at a time, select more than one name in the Address Book or Panel: Hold down the Command key and click on the names you want to add. Then let go of the Command key and drag *one* of the names to the email To field—*all* of the selected names will come along.

To add a Group name, drag the Group name and drop it into one of the "To" fields.

Send contact information through email

You can send a person's Address Book data (his card information) to anyone who uses Mac OS X. Drag a person's name from the Address Book or Address Panel and drop it into the body of a Mail message. You'll see a "vCard" icon, as shown below.

Amy Meilander (2.2 KB)

The recipient can then drag the vCard to her Address Book where it will be added automatically. *Or* she can double-click the icon in the email message and all of the Address Book data will be added.

Make a web location file

In Safari, you can make a web location file that will take you to a specific web page. There is a tiny icon that appears in the location field, directly to the left of the web address, shown circled, below. Drag that tiny icon and drop it in the Dock (on the right side of the dividing bar), onto the Desktop, or into any folder. This creates a web location file, shown below.

If you dropped the icon in the Dock (shown below), single-click it to open that web page.

If it's in the Finder (the icon looks different, shown below), double-click the icon, or drag-and-drop it into the middle of any open web page.

ApplePro Tip of
the Week.webloc

Send a file to a Buddy

Drag a document to a Buddy name in the Buddy List of iChat and drop it. Hit Return or Enter and the file will go straight to that person. This is a great way to quickly send a photo or a document.

You can also use your iChat instant message window—just drag the file into the field where you type your message. Hit Return and both your text message and the file will go to your Buddy. All he needs to do is click the link in the iChat window and the file downloads to his Desktop.

Also send Address Book data this way—to send the information from a person's card, drag his name from your Address Book and drop it on the Buddy List name or in the message field (see the previous page for more Address Book information).

Invite people to an iCal event

Drag a person's name from the Address Panel or Address Book (from the Window menu) to an iCal event to automatically add that person as an "attendee." Be sure to drop it on the "Attendee" item in the Info drawer. You can drag a Group name as well. Once you have the names in here, you can click the "Send" button at the bottom of the Info drawer (circled, below) to send everyone on the list an email update of the calendar.

Save into a particular folder

When you are saving a file, drag a folder from the Finder and drop it in the window of the Save As dialog box. Your Mac will save the document into that particular folder.

Take advantage of the page proxy

You may not have noticed the tiny page icon that is in the title bar of every document you create (it appears after you save the document). It's called the "page proxy." You can do a lot with this tiny icon.

Make sure the document has been saved recently before you experiment with any of the following techniques. If there is a dark dot in the red button or if the page proxy is gray, that means you need to save the document first.

To create an alias of the document on the Desktop or in any folder or window, drag the page proxy and drop it on the Desktop, on top of any folder icon, or directly into any window. You'll see the telltale sign of alias's tiny curved arrow as you drag the page proxy. (See page 408 about aliases.)

Methinks I scent the
morning air

To create a copy of the document, hold down the Option key and drag the proxy. Drop it on the Desktop, on top of any folder icon, or directly into any window. You'll see a plus sign as you drag, indicating your Mac is making a *copy* of the document.

To send the document through iChat or Bonjour, drag the page proxy and drop it on a Buddy name in your iChat Buddy List or on any name in your Bonjour list.

Or drag the page proxy into the text field of an iChat instant message. The recipient will get a message with a button to "Save File."

To email the document, drag the page proxy to an email message and drop it anywhere in the body of the message.

To drop the entire document into another application, drag the page proxy and drop it into the window of the other app. For instance, you can drag a Microsoft Word page proxy into a TextEdit page or onto a web page. Remember to watch for the insertion point—that's where the new text will drop in.

Open documents in other applications

Drag documents (or page proxies, as explained above) onto application icons in the Finder or Dock to open those documents in the targeted applications; if an application is capable of opening the document, the application icon will highlight. This is great for when you want to open a document in something that isn't the default.

For instance, **open Microsoft Word files in TextEdit**—just drag and drop the file onto the TextEdit icon, either in the Dock or in the Applications folder.

Or **drag a PDF** and drop it in the middle of a Safari window or directly on the Safari icon and Safari will open and display the PDF.

Take advantage of spring-loaded folders

Combine drag-and-drop with spring-loaded folders to organize the Finder. A spring-loaded folder opens as you hover your mouse over it. You can use this technique to dig down into folders with a file you are dragging: Hover over a folder, its window pops open, hover over the next folder, its window pops open, etc. As soon as you drop the file, all of the previous folder windows close.

You can set the parameters for how long you have to hover the mouse to open a spring-loaded folder—use the Finder preferences, under the Finder menu. Or you can always use the Spacebar instead, even if the option for spring-loaded folders is unchecked: Whenever you want a folder to open instantly, hover over the folder and hit the Spacebar.

Drag content, images, or files between applications

Try dragging anything and everything!

Drag an image from the web onto a TextEdit page or an email message.

Drag a graphic file from the Desktop or a folder and drop it into the text area of your application. This works in lots of other applications, not just the ones from Apple. For instance, I'm using Adobe InDesign to create this book—I dragged the image you see below from the Finder and dropped it on this page, like so (and it's linked):

Drag text content and/or images from any application and drop them into other applications. Not everything will work, or it might work but not quite as you expect, but you will discover some wonderfully useful ways for working in your favorite applications.

Take Advantage of System Services

Every application in its application menu has an item called "Services." Exactly which services are available at any moment depend on which application you have open and what you have selected within that application, if anything.

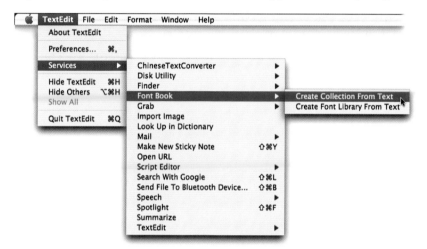

You might find some text in a file that you want to keep in your Sticky Note collection—select the text (and a graphic, if you like) and choose "Make New Sticky Note" from the Services options.

Or you might be viewing a photograph in Preview and decide you want to email it to someone—go to Services, choose "Mail," and then choose "Send To."

Perhaps you are reading the synopsis of a Shakespeare play online and you want to have the synopsis in TextEdit—select the text, go to Services, choose "TextEdit," and then choose "New Window Containing Selection."

Perhaps the synopsis is lengthier than you care to read at the moment, and you'd like to skim it—select the text, go to Services, and choose "Summarize" to open a new window where you can view as much or as little of the summary as you like. Then don't forget about drag-and-drop—drag the selected summary into a TextEdit page.

Keep the Services menu in mind while you work. You'll be surprised how often it comes in handy!

6

Goals

Discover how you can customize your Mac to suit your work style

Understand the differences between System settings and settings for specific applications

Learn about the security options you can customize

Lesson **6**

Personalize Your Mac to Meet Your Needs

Now that you've learned all the basics of the various applications and system settings on your Mac, discover how to customize them to suit your particular way of working. Would you prefer to have your Dock on the side of the screen instead of at the bottom? Do you like a brightly colored Desktop? Do you want to customize the insides of certain windows? Color-code your files? Make the icons and text bigger? Or perhaps you want to work with the security options to make your computer a little less accessible to anyone who walks by (or steals your laptop). It's all do-able—and more.

Customize the Dock

When you first turn on your Mac, the **Dock** is sitting along the bottom at a certain size. But like everything else on the Mac, you can customize it to suit yourself. Would you prefer the Dock along the side of your screen? Would you like it to disappear altogether and only appear when you need it? Are the icons too small or too big? You can adjust everything.

There are three ways to customize the Dock: You can use the System Preferences, the Dock options in the Apple menu, or the secret pop-up menu in the Dock itself.

Customize the Dock using the System Preferences

1 Single-click on the System Preferences icon in the Dock.

2 Single-click on the Dock icon. You'll get the Dock preferences.

3 Here you can resize the Dock, turn "Magnification" on or off (see the next page), adjust the size of the magnification, reposition the screen, and other options.

Magnification If you turn on "Magnification," then the icons in the Dock will enlarge as you run your mouse over them. Just how big they enlarge is up to you—move the slider to "Max," then hover your mouse over the Dock (don't click) and see how big the icons get.

Minimize using This option has two choices, and all it does is change how windows float down into the Dock when you click the yellow Minimize button in a window. Choose one of the options, then minimize a window to see the difference. (Hold the Shift key down when you click the yellow button to see the effect in slow motion.)

Animate opening applications This is what makes the icons in the Dock bounce up and down when you click to open them. You can turn it off.

Automatically hide and show the Dock Click this and the Dock will disappear. It will reappear whenever you move your mouse into that edge where it disappeared. As long as your mouse is hovering over the Dock, it stays visible. Move your mouse away, and the Dock hides itself again.

Customize the Dock using the Apple menu or Dock menu

▼ **From the Apple menu,** select "Dock," then choose your options.

▼ **In the Dock itself,** hold down the Control key and single-click on the dividing line, as shown below. A menu pops up; make your choice.

Resize the icons and the whole Dock

▼ Press-and-drag on the dividing line. Try it!

Customize the Finder

There are a number of features you can customize in the **Finder.** You might expect to find these in the System Preferences, but because the Finder is actually an application (it runs the Desktop), its preferences are in the application menu.

Customize the General preferences

1 From the Finder menu, choose "Preferences…." Click the "General" icon.

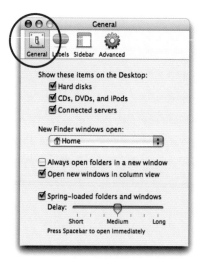

2 Because your Finder window can display the hard disk icons, removable disc icons, and servers in the top portion of the Sidebar, you can choose that these items do *not* also **show up on the Desktop.** Or if it makes you feel better to see the CD icons on the Desktop, you can choose to show only those. Whatever makes you happy.

3 Every time you open a **new Finder window,** it starts over—that is, it doesn't remember the last window you opened. From this menu, choose the window you want to see whenever you click the Finder icon in the Dock or press Command N to get a new window. For instance, I want to see my Home window every time I open a new Finder window. You might prefer to see your Documents folder or perhaps a project folder.

4 If it bothers you to have only one Finder window open to work in, you can choose to have a **new window open** every time you double-click a folder icon. Usually people who are recently converted from Mac OS 9 like to use this feature for a while, until they get used to working in one window.

Don't forget that you can always open a separate window for any individual folder: Command–double-click on it.

5 If you really prefer working in the **Column View,** choose to have all new Finder windows open to that view. See pages 38–39 for details about the Column View.

6 If you turn on **spring-loaded folders and windows,** then folders will automatically pop their windows open as you hover the mouse over the folder. This is great when you are dragging a file somewhere—you don't have to put it down to open the folder.

The "Delay" refers to how long your mouse has to hover before the folder pops open. If you find folders popping open when you least expect it, make the delay longer.

Even if you turn off spring-loaded folders, you can always hit the Spacebar to make a folder pop open, as long as your mouse is positioned over that folder.

Create labels for files and folders

Labels are colors that you can apply to any file or folder or application as a tool for organizing and searching.

1 From the Finder menu, choose "Preferences…." Click the "Label" icon.

2 Change the label names for any color label you want. You don't need to use them all.

3 **To apply the labels,** select a file, then go to the File menu and at the very bottom choose a "Color Label." As you mouse over the color dot, a tool tip appears to tell you the label name.

Or Control-click (or right click) on a file of any sort. From the contextual menu that pops up, choose a color label. **The "x" takes a label off.**

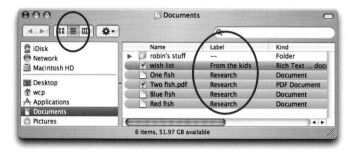

To add the "Label" column, see page 144.

Choose what appears in your Finder window Sidebar

1 From the Finder menu, choose "Preferences...." Click the "Sidebar" icon.

2 Check the items you want to see in the Sidebar of your Finder windows, and uncheck the items you don't want to see. Coordinate this with the "General" Finder preferences shown on page 138—you don't want to eliminate the hard disk icon, for instance, from both the Desktop *and* the Sidebar!

Choose file extensions and turn off the Trash warning

1 From the Finder menu, choose "Preferences...." Click the "Advanced" icon.

2 **File extensions** are those three- or four-letter abbreviations at the ends of file names; see page 408.

3 If that **warning** you see whenever you **empty the Trash** makes you crazy, turn it off here.

Customize the Inside of Finder Windows

Are the icons too big? The text labels too small? Do you want more columns of information available? Fewer columns? In the List View, would you like to rearrange the columns? In the Column View, do you want to turn off the preview column? You can do anything you want.

Customize the Icon View

1 Open a Finder window. Click the "Icon View" button, as circled below.

2 From the View menu, choose "Show View Options."

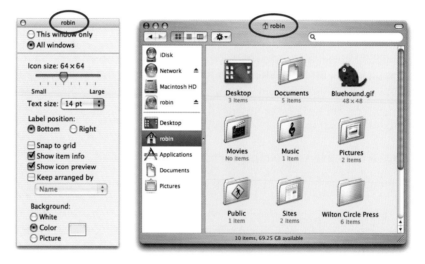

3 First of all, in the top portion of the preferences window, make a choice of whether you want these changes to apply to "This window only" or to "All windows."

Notice the title bar of the preferences pane shows you the name of the currently active window, the one to which these changes will apply.

4 Experiment with these options.

Use the slider to change the **size of the icons.**

Use the **Text size** menu to change the size of the text that labels each file.

And use **Label position** to put the labels (file titles) to the right side of the icons (they're generally on the "Bottom").

5 If you check **Snap to grid,** every time you add or move an icon in the window, it will "snap" into a certain position on the invisible, underlying grid. This makes sure your icons are always lined up neatly.

TIP ▶ If "Snap to grid" is turned on, you can override it: Hold down the Command key as you move an icon in the window, and it will stay right where you put it—it WILL NOT snap to the grid.

If "Snap to grid" is TURNED OFF, you can override it: Hold down the Command key as you move an icon in the window, and it WILL snap to the nearest spot on the grid.

6 **Show item info:** This displays information about some icons. For instance, the window will display how many items are in each folder. It will also display the size (in pixels) of graphic files.

Show icon preview: This displays tiny versions of the actual images for graphic files and photos.

Keep arranged by: This combines "Snap to grid" with an arrangement determined by you—choose an arrangement from the menu (the menu is only available after you check the box). For instance, if you choose "Name," any file you drag into or save into this window will automatically snap to the underlying grid AND alphabetize itself. If you choose "Kind," all items will be grouped by what kinds of files they are—applications, folders, text files, photos, etc. "Labels" is also an option, but in this case it refers to the colored labels, as explained on page 408, not the labels (titles) mentioned in Step 4!

7 **Background:** Click the "Color" button to make a tiny color box appear; click the color box to get the Colors Panel to choose a background color for the window, as shown on the opposite page.

Click the "Picture" button to select a graphic image. Click "White" to remove all color and images from the window background.

Customize the List View

1 Open a Finder window. Click the "List View" button, as circled below.

2 From the View menu, choose "Show View Options."

3 First, in the top portion of the preferences window, choose whether you want these changes to apply to "This window only" or to "All windows."

4 Choose the **icon size** you want, the **text size** for the labels, and which **columns** you want visible. This is where you can choose to display the "Label" column if you like to use labels (see page 140).

5 **Use relative dates:** Under the "Date Modified" and "Date Created" columns, you will see "Today" or "Yesterday" instead of the actual date.

Calculate all sizes: With NO checkmark in this box, the Size column will display the file sizes of documents and graphic images, but NOT folders or applications. Displaying the sizes of folders and applications can take an extra minute or two.

Organize the columns in List View

1 To organize the items in your list by any column, just click on a column heading to organize everything by that. For instance, if you want all the different sorts of files grouped together so you can clearly see which ones are, say, Photoshop files, organize by the "Kind" column.

The column heading under which everything is organized is the blue one. For example, in the illustration on the opposite page, the items are organized by "Name."

2 To alphabetize, or sort, the items in the list backwards or forwards, click the heading triangle. That is, perhaps you want the items in the "Name" column to be listed alphabetically backwards: First click on the "Name" column heading. Then single-click the tiny triangle (the "sort" triangle, or arrow) you see on the right side of the column heading.

If you would like your items to be sorted by "Size" in ascending or descending order, first click on the "Size" column heading. Then, if necessary, single-click the tiny sort arrow to reverse the current order.

3 To horizontally rearrange the order of the columns (except the "Name" column), *press* on any column heading (except "Name") and drag it to the right or left. You will see the other columns move over to make room. Drop the column (let go of the mouse button) when it's positioned where you want it.

4 To resize the width of the columns, just *press* on the dividing line between any column; the pointer changes to a double-headed arrow. Drag the double-headed arrow to the left or right.

Customize the Column View

1 Open a Finder window. Click the "Column View" button, as circled below.

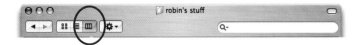

2 From the View menu, choose "Show View Options."

3 Choose the **text size** of the labels.

You can choose **not to show icons at all**—just a nice, clean list of items. Uncheck the box to remove the icons. (But keep in mind that the icon can tell you a lot about a file! If you can't see it, you'll miss its visual clues. This might not matter in a folder that contains nothing but photographs or nothing but text documents.)

If you uncheck **Show preview column,** the last column will NOT display a preview image of the selected file, such as a photograph.

To use a particular System Preference, single-click its icon. Most things are self-explanatory—poke around and see what your options are. We'll look at a couple of examples.

1 Open System Preferences as described on the previous page. Single-click the **Keyboard & Mouse** icon. Or if it's still open, click the "Show All" button.

2 What you see in this preferences pane depends on your computer. For instance, a laptop will have a "Trackpad" pane. A Bluetooth-enabled computer will have a "Bluetooth" pane.

Single-click any tab to see the preferences for that feature.

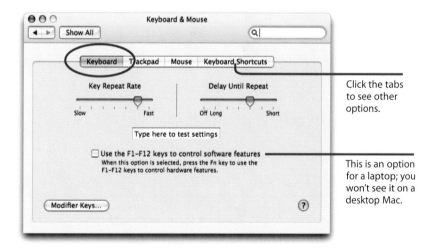

Click the tabs to see other options.

This is an option for a laptop; you won't see it on a desktop Mac.

3 In the "Keyboard" pane, you can adjust how fast any **key repeats** across the page as you press it down.

The **Delay Until Repeat** refers to how long your fingers can linger on the keys before they start repeating. If you find you type lots of double letters or spaces, choose a longer delay here. If your fingers are really heavy on the keys, slide the blue slider all the way to "Off" and the keys will never repeat automatically.

This is another fun and useful System Preference—use it to **change the color or image on your Desktop.**

1 Open System Preferences as described on page 148. Single-click the "Desktop & Screen Saver" icon. Or if the preferences are still open, click the "Show All" button in the upper-left.

2 Single-click the "Desktop" tab, as circled below.

3 In the list on the left, single-click each folder to see what's in it, displayed in the pane on the right.

4 Single-click any image you see in the pane on the right to view it on your Desktop. Use the little menu in the middle to adjust the image.

5 To use your own photo, first put it in the "Pictures" folder that is in your Home window. Then you can choose the photo from the "Pictures Folder" option in the list.

Or click "Choose Folder…," then find the folder where your photos are stored. The folder will then be placed in the list for easy access.

Correct the **date and time** on your Mac, change it when you go to a different time zone, make a regular clock float on your Desktop, and more.

1 Open System Preferences as described on page 148. Single-click the "Date & Time" icon. Or if the preferences are still open, click the "Show All" button in the upper-left.

2 Click each of the three tabs and see what your options are. You can't hurt anything, so poke around and experiment.

The option to "Set date & time automatically" is useful if you have a full-time broadband connection (don't bother if your connection to the Internet is a dial-up). This keeps your Mac in touch with a satellite so your time is always correct—it will even switch to daylight savings time for you.

Don't forget the Help files!

You can easily find specific details and help for every preference pane. Just go to the Help menu while System Preferences is active, and choose "System Preferences Help," *or* press Command ?.

Even though there is no underline, the colored text headings are links. Single-click any heading to get details.

Find the preference you need, then click the blue link.

Find the right System Preferences for your task

Sometimes you know you need a System Preference to customize a particular Mac feature, but you're not sure which one has the option you need. That's where Tiger's new Spotlight feature can help.

The search field you see in the upper-right corner of the System Preferences pane is not the typical search field you're accustomed to—it's Spotlight. You can read all about Spotlight in Lesson 12, but using it here is particularly easy.

Just type what you're hoping to find in the search field. As you type, you'll see certain System Preference icons highlight, and you'll see a list of possible options. The more you type, the more specific the results will be.

Try the example shown below. I was looking for all the preferences that give me an option to put a status icon in the menu bar.

Choose an option in the list, and the appropriate System Preference will slowly flash twice at you and then open.

Click the **X** to clear the search field.

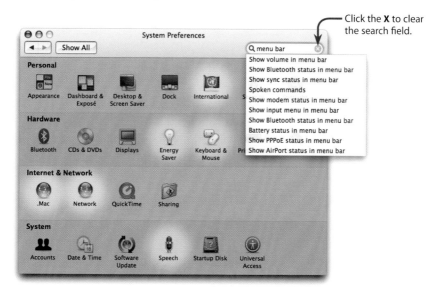

Know Your Security Options

There are several kinds of **security features** on your Mac. One set of features is to protect you from bad things that come in through the Internet or another network. Apple has installed lots of security stuff on your Mac, things like Kerberos, Secure Shell, Wired Equivalent Privacy data encryption, Virtual Private Network, firewalls, and other features. It doesn't matter to most of us what those are—they work behind the scenes. Your Software Update (one of the System Preferences) will automatically update security features as Apple releases them.

The above features work without you having to do anything. The features that require your participation are explained on the following pages:

- **Viruses** are another external threat (a minor annoyance on Macs, compared to devastation on PCs); please see page 164. A .Mac membership includes the software Virex to combat the evil buggers.

- You might need security from humans who walk past your desk when you're not there. Your Mac has a number of **low-level security features** to protect your information from the curious.

- **Keychain Access** stores many of your passwords in locked "keychains." This includes passwords to your .Mac account, servers, eBay account, PayPal, and more. Keychain Access also lets you store passwords and codes for other things, such as credit card numbers you might like to use while shopping online. Keychain Access does double-duty—it makes things easier for you and harder for thieves. Please see pages 160–161 for details.

- If you have highly personal or valuable stuff on your Mac, you can use **FileVault** for maximum security. If you have a laptop, this is especially important to prevent thieves from accessing your data.

- And don't forget about the feature to **Secure Empty Trash.** This deletes files from your trashcan in such a way that no one can retrieve them again. See page 159.

Passwords on your Mac

You have several different passwords on your Macintosh.

▼ **Administrator password:** When you first turn on your Mac, you are asked to create a password. Write this down in a safe place! You will need this password whenever you install new software or when you make certain system-wide changes.

You can choose *not* to have a password. Your Mac will still *ask* you to enter a password, however—if you never entered one, just leave the password field blank, and click the OK or "Continue" button.

If you forget this Admin password, you will need to reset it:

1   Insert the original Mac OS X installer CD.

2   Double-click the "Installer" icon to start the process of reinstalling. You are not really going to reinstall!

3   When you get to the Install screen, go to the Utilities menu. Choose "Reset Password…."

4   Enter your new password. Write it down in a safe place!

5   Quit the Installer from the Installer menu.

▼ **Login password:** If you have set up multiple users on one Mac, each user has her own password to log in. *An Admin password is also the login* *password for that Admin user.* By default, your Mac is set to auto-login the Admin so you don't need your password at startup (you can turn this off).

If a standard user forgets his password: The Administrator (or anyone who knows the Admin password) can reset the user password in the Accounts preferences.

▼ **Keychain Access password:** This is the same as the login password, whether you are a standard user or the Admin (you can change it to create a special keychain password). Keychain Access is the application on your Mac that keeps track of a variety of passwords for you. If you can remember your login password, then Keychain Access can show you the rest of your passwords. See pages 160–161.

▼ **Master password:** An Administrator can set up a computer-wide password in case he forgets the login password. Master passwords are usually used in conjunction with FileVault; see pages 162–163. The Admin's Master password can override a standard user's FileVault password.

What to do if you forget the Master password? Well, you can scream. It won't help, but you can scream. See page 162.

Password tips

▼ A password should be difficult for others to guess, but easy for you to remember.

▼ Don't use a word that can be found in a dictionary. Some hackers use software that tries every word in the dictionary in a matter of minutes.

▼ Combine caps and lowercase and numbers.

▼ Most passwords are case-specific, meaning a lowercase "r" is completely different from an uppercase "R." Take advantage of this and put capital letters where someone wouldn't expect them.

Low-level security features

▼ **Turn off auto-login:** Auto-login lets your Mac start up without a password—it automatically logs in the person who has "auto-login" turned on in the Accounts preferences (click "Login Options" at the bottom of the list of accounts).

Then be sure to **log out** before you leave your computer for a while. This ensures that people walking by will need a password to log back in to your account, even if they restart your Mac. Laptops should always require a login password.

▼ **If you don't want to turn off auto-login,** you might want to take the extra step to uncheck the box to "Show the Restart, Sleep, and Shut Down buttons." Because if auto-login is on and you log out, the login screen appears. But someone can just click the Restart or Shut Down button, and the computer starts back up again and automatically logs into your account.

This precaution isn't going to help much if your laptop is stolen because someone can just reboot the computer. Nor will it help if the Restart button is accessible on your desktop machine!

▼ Mac OS X lets you have multiple users on one computer, and each user has a separate, private Home area (see Lesson 9 for details). Even if you are the only one using this Mac, you can **create another user,** a standard user who has no administrative privileges, and log in as the standard one. This is a simple step that just makes it one level more difficult for someone to get into your main account and make system-wide changes.
It won't protect any data that you create as that user, but it will make it more difficult to get to any data you create as the Administrator.

To prevent access to anyone walking by your computer, you can use these simple yet effective features:

▼ Use the Security preferences to **require a user/Admin password to wake up the Mac** from sleep or from the screen saver. Remember, to get to a system preference such as Security or the ones mentioned below, go to the Apple menu and choose "System Preferences...."

Then go to the "Desktop & Screen Saver" preferences to choose a screen saver and tell it when to start.

Then go to the "Energy Saver" preferences to tell your Mac to put either the computer and/or the display (the screen) to sleep after a certain amount of time.

▼ An alternative to the above technique is to set up your Mac so you can **lock it with a mouse click** whenever you choose, not just when the screen saver comes on or when it goes to sleep.

To lock your Mac with a click:

1 Open Keychain Access (first open the Applications folder, then open the Utilities folder; Keychain Access is in the Utilities folder).

2 From the Keychain Access menu across the top of the screen, choose "Preferences...."

3 Check the box to "Show Status in Menu Bar."

4 Quit Keychain Access.

5 You'll now see a tiny padlock icon on the right side of your menu bar across the top of your screen. Click that padlock icon to get the menu shown below.

6 Choose "Lock Screen." The screen saver will start and no one can access your Mac unless they know your login password.

Higher-level security features

▼ **Secure Empty Trash:** You might think that after you empty the Trash, it's gone. But it's possible to recover many deleted files using special data-recovery software. If you are selling or giving away your Mac, you might want to make sure no one can recover your old, trashed files. To completely overwrite files so no one can ever get to them, go to the Finder menu and choose **Secure Empty Trash.** This might take several minutes, depending on how much stuff you've thrown away since you got the computer!

▼ **Encrypt a disk image:** Using the Disk Utility (found in the Utilities folder, which is in the Applications folder), you can protect all or part of your hard disk by making a selected portion of it into a "disk image," which looks like a hard disk icon. It has its own password; if your Keychain is locked (see pages 160–161), this image is really safe from prying eyes and fingers because someone would need both passwords to access the disk. When unlocked, this disk image acts just like any other hard disk and you can move files in it, copy files to it, and delete files from it. I recommend you read all about this feature in the Disk Utility Help files before you start using it.

Use Keychain Access for Protection

Keychain Access provides a secure place to store information that can only be accessed with a user name and password. Keychain automatically and safely stores the passwords you create on your Mac, like those for web sites you go to, servers you connect to, email accounts, etc.

You can also add your own secure collections of Keychains to store your credit card numbers, PINs, bank card information, private notes or messages, and other things that you want easy access to, but you want them to be secure. They won't be entered automatically anywhere—it's just a safer place to store them than on a sticky note.

Keychain Access sets up your initial Keychain file, the one based on your user name and password, as the default Keychain. This default Keychain automatically opens when you log in. To make other Keychains more secure, such as your list of credit card numbers or banking passwords, be sure to make *new* Keychain files for them instead of *adding* them to your default file.

Click this button to show the list of Keychains, now showing at the top of the sidebar. Any new keychain you create will appear in that area.

To open Keychain Access, first open your Applications window. Inside there you'll find the Utilities folder. Keychain Access is inside the Utilities folder.

To access any password Keychain has been storing for you:

1 Find the item in the list of "Passwords," as shown on the opposite page.

2 Double-click that item. You will be asked for your Keychain password, which is the same as your login password. If you are the only user of the Mac, it's the password you assigned yourself when you first set up your Mac, the Admin password. A window like the one below appears.

3 Click in the box to "Show password." Your password appears!

You can create a new Keychain: Go to the File menu and choose "New Keychain…." Give it a descriptive name *and a password you will remember.* This Keychain will appear in the top portion of the sidebar, as shown on the opposite page. You will need to know that Keychain's password if you want to access things in it!

With that Keychain selected, go back to the File menu and choose to create a new password item or a new secure note to store in it.

Oh, Keychain is a very powerful and fairly complex application! To use it wisely and well, please study the Keychain Help files.

Consider FileVault for Heavy-Duty Protection

FileVault encrypts, or scrambles, the data in your Home folder so unauthorized people or software cannot get to it. While you are working on your Mac with FileVault turned on, you won't notice anything. But everything in your Home folder will be safely protected from prying eyes, both in your office and from remote connections. Don't ever forget the Master password, though, or you will never again see anything in your Home folder!

To turn on FileVault:

1 Before you begin, make sure you have the Admin name and password, as well as the password for this user (if it's separate from the Admin user).

2 Also before you begin, make sure all other users are logged out.

3 Check to make sure you have enough hard disk space available for the process—you'll need as much free hard disk space as there is data in your Home folder.

> To check the file size of your Home folder, single-click the Home icon in the Sidebar of any Finder window.
>
> Press Command Option I to display the Get Info window.
>
> Check the "Size" of the Home folder.
>
> Now check to see how much free hard disk space you have: Single-click the hard disk icon in the Sidebar. In the Get Info window (which has now switched to show you the info for the hard disk), find the amount "Available." About 1024 megabytes fit into one gigabyte, so unless you've been making movies on your Mac, you probably have plenty of space.

4 You must first set a Master password. Keep in mind that once you set a Master password, you can never get rid of it. *If you forget your login password and you also forget the Master password, everything in your Home folder is lost forever.*

> **To set a Master password:**
>
> **a.** From the Apple menu, choose "System Preferences…."
>
> **b.** Single-click the "Security" icon to get the Security pane shown on the opposite page.

c. Read the warning! Then click "Set Master Password…," enter your password and hint, and click OK.

5 Now click the button "Turn On FileVault…."

6 Read the warning! If this is what you really want, click the button to "Turn On FileVault." It may take a few minutes. Your Mac will log itself back into this account and FileVault will be on.

7 Close the Security preferences window.

Protect Your Mac from Viruses

A computer **virus** can erase your hard disk, send out millions of junk email messages in your name, steal your passwords, make your computer act stupid and worthless, and much more. A virus is software written by malicious little rat-like creeps who are among the most despicable scum of the universe. Can you imagine what kind of person uses his bright, inquisitive mind intentionally to make millions of people miserable and sad and creates a phenomenal waste of time and money and causes people to lose documents and images that are close to their hearts? A virus is not an accident—it is a mean and nasty intention from someone with a teeny little soul.

Well. Now you know how I feel about people who create viruses.

Although your Mac can't get most of the viruses you hear about (they are usually created to run on a Windows machine), we do get a few (mostly ones that come in through Microsoft products, another good reason to have a Microsoft-free environment).

Virus protection software comes with a .Mac account—see Lesson 11 for details about why and how to get a .Mac account. Once you're a member, you can download—for free—the software **Virex** that protects your computer. It scans new files for potential viruses that might infect you, diagnoses files on your Mac that might already contain viruses, and repairs files that have been infected. Your system preference called Software Update will automatically check for updates and when necessary, download and install them for you.

What You've Learned

▼ How to rearrange the Dock, hide and show it, resize it, magnify it, and more.

▼ How to make your Finder windows open to the folder you want.

▼ How to use spring-loaded folders.

▼ How to color-code your files with labels.

▼ How to customize your Sidebar.

▼ How to turn off the Trash warning.

▼ How to make sure file extensions show at the ends of file names.

▼ How to customize the Icon View, List View, and Column View of Finder windows: resize text size, icon size, color the backgrounds of windows, hide the hard disk icon, change the order of items, and more.

▼ How to use the System Preferences to customize many features of your Mac, such as the keyboard sensitivity, the color or image on your Desktop, the date and time, and much more.

▼ Where to access the Help files for the preferences.

▼ How to find the right preference for your task.

▼ Security options from low-level to maximum security.

▼ Password tips.

▼ Tips on viruses and what to do about them.

7

Goals

Provide new and experienced users with an understanding of the printing features in Mac OS X

Make sure users understand how to access the special features of their printers and software

Teach users how to fax to and from their Macs

Set Up Printing and Faxing

Printing and faxing has changed only slightly in Tiger. The biggest change is that you can now access all the printing features from the System Preferences instead of from a separate utility. Well, you can still use the Printer Setup Utility if you have come to know and love it, but now you also have another way to reach it.

Set Up Your Printers

To set up and manage your printers, use the "Print & Fax" pane in the System Preferences. You may never need to use this preference—try printing, and if it works, then skip this section! If it doesn't work, check these preferences.

Your Mac automatically finds printers that are directly connected to the computer or that are on your local network. If your Mac doesn't find your printer automatically, use the preferences, as explained below.

Choose which printers appear in the Print dialog box

1 Make sure your printer is turned on and tightly connected to your Mac with the proper cables.

2 Go to the Apple menu and choose "System Preferences…."

3 Single-click on the "Print & Fax" icon to get the pane shown below.

Print & Fax

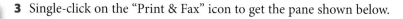

If you choose the name of a specific printer here, that printer becomes the default and its name will be gray in the list.

4 If you see the name of your printer in the list on the left, but it has no checkmark next to its name, check its box. Then close the preferences and try to print.

5 If you don't see the name of your printer in the list on the left, click the **+** button. (Also check again to make sure the cable between the Mac and the printer is snug on both ends, and that the printer is turned on.)

This opens the "Printer Browser," shown below, that lists every printer that is turned on and that your Mac is aware of. If you see your printer listed, single-click its name to select it, then click the "Add" button.

6 This takes you back to the "Print & Fax" dialog box, shown on the opposite page. Make sure there is a checkmark in the checkbox next to the printer's name. Close the preferences, then try to print.

7 If you did not see your printer listed in the "Printer Browser," maybe you didn't install the printer software that came with the printer. Install it now, then try these steps again.

Not all printers *must* have the software installed. Generally, the more expensive the printer, the more likely your Mac needs the software.

Access the Special Features of your Printer

If you installed the software that came with your printer, then you probably have special features that allow you to choose the correct paper, the quality settings, adjust the colors, and more. The difference in output between a setting for inkjet paper as opposed to glossy photo paper is quite amazing.

To access the specific printer settings, start to print the job (press Command P). In the Print dialog box, click on the menu circled below and choose "Print Settings." Here you will have lots of options, different options for each "Media Type" you choose.

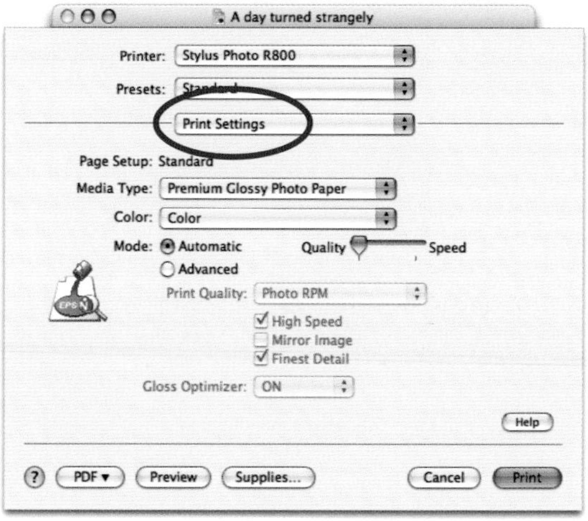

Buy ink cartridges for your printer

Apple has made it easier than ever to buy new ink cartridges for most printers and to buy them from Apple. Just single-click on the "Supplies…" button you see at the bottom of the Print dialog box (shown above). This takes you to an Apple website where you can buy the cartridges.

You can do the same thing in the "Print & Fax" preferences pane shown on page 168: Single-click the button called "Supplies for this printer…," found in the right-hand pane under the info for the selected printer.

Access the Special Features of your Software

Many software applications have special features for printing. For instance, Address Book lets you print lists and envelopes and several other great options, as shown on page 92. But some of your applications have their special features hidden away.

To access specific software settings, start to print the job (press Command P). In the Print dialog box, click on the menu circled below and choose the name of your application, if it's there. If the application name does show up in this menu, it usually provides you with print settings specific to that type of job.

Below you see the specific print settings for Keynote, which is software from Apple for creating digital presentations.

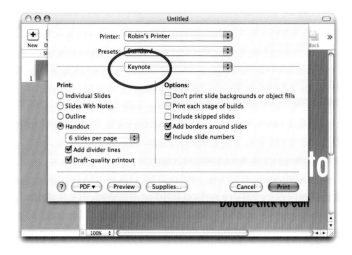

5 A dialog sheet will appear (shown below) where you type in the fax number of the person you want to send the fax to.

If necessary, the "Dialing Prefix" is where you enter any number that gets you "out" of the office building. Typically it's 9. If you need to wait a couple of seconds after the 9 before the phone starts dialing, put one or two commas after the 9. Each comma makes the Mac wait two seconds.

6 If you want a cover page, check the box to "Use Cover Page," then enter the subject and message. Click the "Preview" button if you want to see what you're sending.

This button opens your Address Pane so you can automatically enter the fax number. See the steps on the following page.

7 Click "Fax" and off goes your page. You'll see the Fax icon in the Dock.

Enter fax numbers in your Address Book

You must **enter the fax number into your Address Book** properly before the Address Pane shown on the previous page can supply it for you.

To enter a fax number into your Address Book:

1 Open your Address Book.

2 Find the person whose fax number you want to enter.

3 Single-click the "Edit" button at the bottom of the pane, as shown below.

4 There are two fields at the top of the card, both pre-programmed for phone numbers. This is where you will enter the fax number. If both of these fields are already used for numbers that are not faxes, add a new field, as explained on page 91.

5 Single-click on the tiny double arrows next to the field where you will enter (or have already entered) the fax number.

6 In the menu that pops up, choose "home fax" or "work fax."

7 Click the Edit button again to set your changes. Now when you click the little Address Pane icon when faxing, as shown on the previous page, this fax number will appear in the pane.

Receive a fax on your Mac

This process hasn't changed from the previous version of Mac OS X. Set up your Mac to **receive faxes** using the "Print & Fax" pane in System Preferences, as shown below.

Check the box to "Receive faxes on this computer," then enter your fax information. Choose which actions your Mac should take when you receive a fax.

Remember, if you use a broadband connection to get to the Internet, you'll need to connect a phone line to your Mac before you can send or receive a fax.

If you choose "Faxes" or "Shared Faxes," your Mac instantly makes that folder for you and puts it in your Home folder.

What You've Learned

▼ How to set up your printers.

▼ How to access the special settings for your printer software.

▼ How to access the special settings for your applications.

▼ How to share printers with other computers on your network.

▼ Some troubleshooting tips.

▼ How to fax from your Mac.

▼ How to receive faxes on your Mac.

Keyboard Shortcuts

Command P	Print

8

Goals   Provide a quick review of the Mac OS X applications.

Provide the experienced user with an overview of the lesser-known new features in Tiger.

Lesson **8**

Discover the Special Gems in Mac OS X Tiger

This chapter explains the new features in the applications you already know and love. If you are unfamiliar with any of these applications, please see Lessons 4 and 5 for overviews.

There are dozens and dozens of wonderful tips in this lesson, from improvements to email signatures, sharing your Address Book, automatic email notifications in iCal, private browsing in Safari, cropping images and annotating PDFs in Preview, and even making your own bookmarks and video clips in the DVD Player. Lots to explore and enjoy!

Burn Folders in the Finder

A great new feature in Tiger is the **burn folder.** You drag items into this special folder, and when you're ready, you burn the contents to a disc. The wonderful thing is that you can collect items you want to burn without having to actually burn the disc at that moment—you can collect files over the period of a project and when finished, you have a folder ready to back up onto a disc.

When you drag files into a burn folder, your Mac automatically creates **aliases** of those files (see page 408 for details on aliases). This means that after you burn the disc, you can throw away the entire folder without destroying any original files.

To create a burn folder, put files inside, and burn it:

1 Open a Finder window and select the window in which you want the burn folder to appear. For instance, single-click on your Home icon in the Sidebar, or single-click the Documents folder icon. Or click on the Desktop, if you want the folder to appear there. (You can always move the burn folder to wherever you like, of course.)

2 From the File menu, choose "New Burn Folder."

3 A folder with the "Burn" icon on it appears in the selected window.

Rename this folder just as you would any folder: Drag over the part of the name you want to replace, then type.

4 To put a file in the folder so you can burn it later, just drag the original file and drop it into the burn folder. Your Mac will put an *alias* of the file into the burn folder and the original will stay right where it was.

5 To burn the folder, first insert a blank CD or DVD.

6 Then single-click the burn folder; a bar across the top of the window appears with a "Burn" button, as shown on the opposite page. Click that "Burn" button.

Or Control-click (or right-click) on the burn folder icon and choose "Burn Disc" from the contextual menu that appears.

To check the amount of storage space used in the folder:

1 Single-click the burn folder icon.

2 Press Command I to display the Get Info window, as shown below.

3 Click the disclosure triangle next to "Burning."

4 Click the "Calculate" button to see how much you have collected in the folder.

It says there is no device available, even if there is one ready to burn.

New Features in Mail

Mail has a number of new features, plus a new look, as you can see below. But even though it looks a little different, everything you know and love is pretty much the same—on the surface.

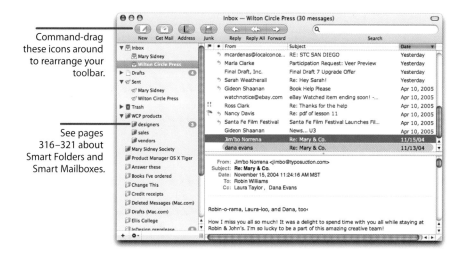

Command-drag these icons around to rearrange your toolbar.

See pages 316–321 about Smart Folders and Smart Mailboxes.

Customize the message window

It's now easier to customize the message headers. Open any new message (click the "New" button in the Mail toolbar). Click on the Action menu (shown below), and choose "Customize…" to get the pane shown below. Check the boxes of the items you want to see in your messages. Click OK when you're done.

Signatures, see page 192.

Priority, see page 194.

New Account Setup Assistant

It's easier than ever to add a new email account to Mail.

1 In Mail, go to the File menu and choose "Add Account...."

2 A window, shown below, appears. First choose the type of account.

If you don't know what kind of account it is, call your Service Provider and ask. *Generally speaking,* this is how to choose the type of account:

Choose .Mac if you signed up with Apple for a .Mac account and this is a new email address you want Mail to check.

Choose POP if you have an email account with your ISP, or if you have a domain name that you paid for and you opted for an email account with it (regardless of whether there are actually web pages for that domain name). This is the most common.

Choose IMAP if your account is the kind that you can use on different computers and always see your mail. This is usually with a paid service or a large company intranet (although most POPs can be set up as IMAP if you ask your provider).

Choose Exchange if your company uses the Microsoft Exchange server and the administrator has configured it for IMAP access. See your system administrator for details.

Most free webmail accounts, such as Hotmail or Yahoo, cannot be set up for Mail. If you buy the "plus" service, you might be able to do it; check with them.

3 Enter the other information necessary, then click "Continue."

The **Account Description** is any name you want to make up that reminds you what this account is for.

The **Full Name** is what will appear on the Mail messages that you send to people so they know it's you. You can enter anything you want.

The **Email Address** is the address of this particular account.

4 Each account type will have slightly different information to enter. For instance, if you choose a POP account, Mail wants to know the **Incoming Mail Server.** It's usually something like *pop.example.com* or *mail.example. com.* If neither of those work, call your email provider and ask for the "incoming mail server."

5 The **user name** for a POP account might be different from your email name, or it might be your entire email address (very often) or it might be something different altogether. If you don't know, ask your provider.

Enter your password as provided by your provider.

6 Successful creation of a new account is announced, as shown below.

To edit your account or add another account:
At any time you can edit an existing account or add another one by using the Preferences.

1 Go to the Mail menu and choose "Preferences…."

2 Click the "Accounts" icon.

3 **To add a new account,** single-click the **+** sign at the bottom of the Accounts pane. Fill in the information on the right.

   To edit an existing account, single-click the account name in the pane, then use the pane on the right to edit.

4 When finished, just close the preferences or click on another icon. A message will appear asking if you want to save these changes.

Attachments

One of the greatest aspects of email is the ability to send files and photos back and forth. Mail has some new features for attachments, making it easier than ever to share files.

To send an attachment:

1 Open a new message window and type your subject, message, etc.

2 To attach a file or photograph, single-click the "Attach" icon.

This opens the standard Open dialog box. Find your file, select it, and click "Choose File." You can hold down the Command key to click on and select more than one file to attach.

Or drag a file or photo from a window on your Desktop and drop it directly into the message window.

3 A file icon appears in your window, as shown below. If it's a one-page PDF or a photo, the actual image will probably appear instead of a file icon.

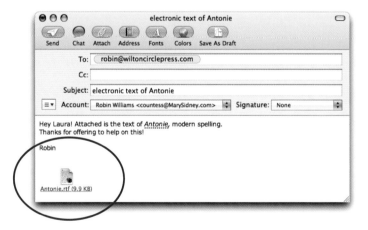

4 If the file in the window appears as the actual image, you can change it into an icon: Control-click (or right-click) on it. From the menu that pops up, choose "View as icon." This does *not* determine how the person who *receives* the file will view it.

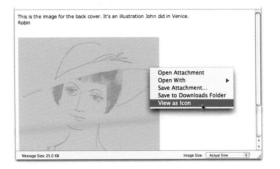

5 Send your email.

To receive and download an attachment:

1 The attachment shown on the opposite page appears in someone's Mail message, or yours, as a file icon or as an actual image, shown below.

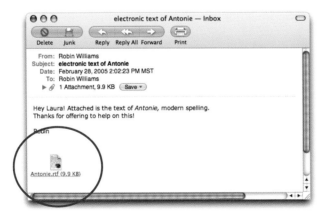

—*continued*

2 There are several ways to deal with this file:

If it's a photograph and you can see it in the window, then you see it and maybe that's all you want to do with it. So you're done.

If it's **one file or photograph,** you can do any of several things:

Note: *If the email went to your .Mac account, you might get a message that you need to download the file before you can save or open it. Just click the "Download Now" or "OK" button in the message that appears, and then try one of the following techniques again.*

Either: Drag the file to the Desktop or directly into any window or folder on your Mac.

Or: Single-click the "Save" button in the header information at the top of the message, then choose the folder where you want to save the file.

Or: Single-click the "Save" button and choose "Add to iPhoto" to save the image directly into your iPhoto collection.

Or: Go to the File menu and choose "Save Attachments…" to choose a folder in which to save the file.

Or: Control-click (or right-click) on the photo or file icon and choose any of several options, shown below.

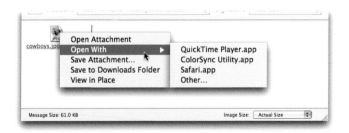

If it's a **series of photographs,** you have even more options. You can do everything mentioned above, plus:

Save only one file from the collection. *Press* (don't *click*) on the "Save" button and a menu appears, as shown on the opposite page. Choose the file you want to save.

You can view a **full-screen slideshow** of the photos. Simply click the "Slideshow" button in the header information.

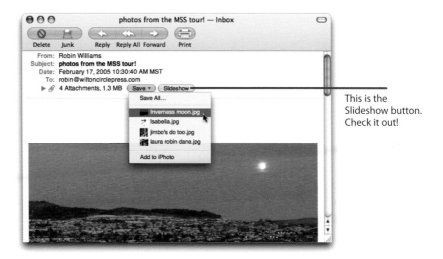

This is the Slideshow button. Check it out!

Downloads folder

Unless you've changed it, the place where files are automatically downloaded is in the **Downloads folder,** which is in the Library folder of your Home folder. That's a bit convoluted to find, so here is how you can choose where downloads automatically appear:

1 From the Mail menu, choose "Preferences…."

2 Single-click the "General" icon.

3 In the menu options for "Downloads Folder," choose a folder where you would like files to go automatically.

4 To close the Preferences, click the red close button.

Signature improvements

An email **signature** is any contact information or message or image that you designate to appear at the end of an email message you send.

In Apple's Mail program, you can create a number of different signatures and choose which one you want to use in any email message. You can choose to have one signature as a default signature that automatically appears, or let Mail randomly choose one for you.

You might have a business email address as well as a personal account with a different address. If so, each account can have its own signature or collection of signatures.

If you have created more than one signature, you can choose which one to use in the message.

If you don't see this option, see page 184.

This is a signature.

To create a signature:

1 From the Mail menu, choose "Preferences…."

2 Single-click the "Signatures" icon.

3 Choose an email account in the left-hand pane.

4 In the middle pane, single-click the plus sign (+). Name this new signature.

5 Single-click in the right-hand pane and type your signature. You can use the formatting menus at the top of your screen to choose a font, size, style, alignment, and color. You can use Returns and Tab keys.

Don't choose a font that you have bought or acquired along the way because most of your recipients probably won't have that same font installed. Use one of the fonts that came with your Mac.

6 If you want an **image** to appear in this signature, drag the image from the Finder and drop it into the right-hand pane. Keep in mind that this should be a very small image, both in file size and in visual size!

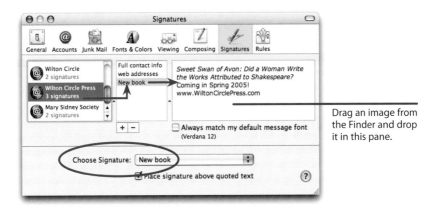

Drag an image from the Finder and drop it in this pane.

7 Each email account can have its own **default signature** that automatically appears in each email message you write: First select the account in the left-hand pane, then use the "Choose Signature" menu circled above. (In any outgoing message, you can still choose any signature you've created to override the default; see the illustration on the opposite page.)

To make a signature appear in a message:

Choose a default signature as explained in Step 7, above.

Or make sure the "Signature" menu is available in the message window, as explained on page 184. Then choose a signature from that menu.

Priority options

You can set one of three **priority** options in Mail messages so your recipient understands how urgent (or not) a particular message is—provided the recipient's email program can display the priority marker. If someone sends you a message marked as high or low priority, Mail will mark it as such.

To set a priority:

With an email compose window open, go to the Message menu in the menu bar, slide down to "Mark," and choose the priority option you want for this message.

If you would like to have the priority options handy, you can put this tiny menu in the message window. See page 184.

To check the priority of an incoming message:

If the Flag column is visible in Mail, you will see two exclamation marks to denote a message that has been labeled **High Priority.** A dash indicates the message is **Low Priority.** (One exclamation point means the message is **Normal Priority,** but you won't see any symbol for this kind of message.)

Parental controls

You can apply parental controls to a user's Mail access, which allows that person to correspond only with the email addresses that you choose. This control is applied to the individual **user** (users are explained in Lesson 9).

1 Go to the Apple menu and choose "System Preferences...."

2 Single-click the "Accounts" icon.

3 If the lock icon in the bottom-left corner is locked, single-click it and type the Administrator's password (which is your login password, if you are the Admin).

4 Select the user to whom you'd like to apply parental controls.

5 Click the "Parental Controls" button.

6 Put a check in the box next to "Mail.app."

7 Click the "Configure" button. Enter the names of people with whom this user is allowed to communicate. Click OK.

Purge individual messages from server

You've always been able to delete all the messages from the mail server, but in Tiger you can purge messages individually (or all at once, of course).

1 In Mail, open the Action menu at the bottom of the drawer.

2 Choose "Get Info."

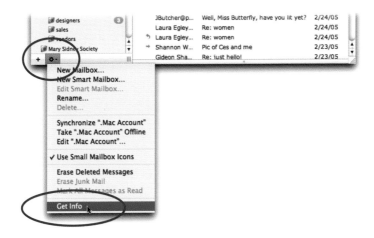

3 In the "Account Info" window that appears, choose the account you want to look at from the "Account" menu at the top of the window.

If you choose a .Mac account, your window will look like the one at the top of the opposite page, until you click "Show Messages."

If you choose a .Mac account, you can see any folders you have created
and all the messages in those individual folders. Once you choose to
"Show Messages" (circled, bottom-right) the window will look like the one
on the bottom of the opposite page.

4 Select messages and then click "Remove From Server," shown circled on
the opposite page.

5 Close the window (click the red button) when done.

Other relevant lessons for Mail

Search, Smart Folders, and Smart Mailboxes: See pages 319–321 for details
about how to search in Mail, create a Spotlight search, and create Smart
Mailboxes that automatically update themselves.

Troubleshooting: See page 267 for tips on using the Connection Doctor.

Address Book Enhancements

There are some great new features in the Address Book. If you are a .Mac member (see Lesson 11), you can **share your entire contact list** with other .Mac members. This can be useful for families, teens and their friends, organizations, businesses, and others. And you can **subscribe** to someone else's shared Address Book, provided that person has already put you on their shared list.

Share your Address Book contact list

Remember, you must have a .Mac account to share, and the only people who can share your Address Book are other .Mac members running Tiger. The people you want to share with must already be in your Address Book as contacts, so if they're not there yet, add them before you follow these steps!

1 From the Address Book menu, choose "Preferences...."

2 Single-click the "Sharing" icon.

3 In the window that appears, check the box to "Share your Address Book."

4 You must choose who is allowed to access and share your Address Book: Single-click the **+** sign at the bottom of the window.

5 This drops down a sheet displaying the people who are in your Address Book, as shown below. Select the names you want to share with; hold down the Command key to select more than one name.

6 Click OK. After you add names, you can send an email inviting someone to share your Address Book: Single-click a name (or Command-click several names), then click "Send Invite."

Subscribe to someone's Address Book

You can only subscribe to an Address Book that someone else has already set up as shared, as explained above. And that person must have already chosen you as someone who is allowed to access his Address Book. Once that's done:

1 In your own Address Book, go to the File menu and choose "Subscribe to Address Book…."

3 Enter the .Mac account name of the person whose Address Book you want access to. After you enter the account, click OK.

Sync with Microsoft Exchange Server 2000

If you know what Exchange 2000 is, you might want to sync your Address Book with it. This won't work with earlier versions of Exchange.

1 From the "Address Book" application menu, choose "Preferences."

2 Click the "General" tab, if it isn't showing already.

3 Check the box at the bottom to "Synchronize with Exchange."

4 Then click the "Configure..." button and fill in the information. It's not always necessary to actually configure it yourself, but if you need to and don't know the information necessary, contact your network administrator.

The Apple Help file has more details about this process: While Address Book is open and active, go to the Help menu and choose "Address Book Help." Then enter "exchange" in the search field and hit Return.

Other relevant lessons for Address Book

Search: Search your Address Book and, if you like, send that search out through Spotlight to find all files relating to that contact. See pages 322–323.

Smart Groups: Create Smart Groups that automatically update themselves as contacts fulfill the requirements. See pages 324–325.

Sync: Synchronize your contact information with your other computers and your .Mac account: See Lesson 11.

Dashboard: Pop up a mini-version of your Address Book for quick and easy access. See Lesson 13.

Printing: See page 92 for new options for printing mailing labels, lists, envelopes, and a pocket-sized address book.

TextEdit Grows Up

For such a small word processor, TextEdit is a little dynamo. (Except it *still* has no option for automatically typing true quotation marks. That's silly.)

Read Microsoft Word files

TextEdit can open just about any Microsoft Word file and hang on to most of the formatting, including simple tables. The default in Tiger is set up so when you double-click on a file whose name ends with .doc, **it automatically opens** in TextEdit.

You can also drag the Word file and drop it on top of the TextEdit icon. (The TextEdit icon might not be in your Dock. If not, it's in the Applications folder. If you want the TextEdit icon in the Dock, drag it from the Applications folder and drop it in the Dock.)

If you own Microsoft Word and want your **.doc files to open in Word,** not TextEdit, you can **change the default application**:

1 Control-click (or right-click) on the Word file to get the contextual menu.

2 While the menu is visible, also hold down the Option key.

3 Choose "Always Open With," then "Other…" from the pop-out menu.

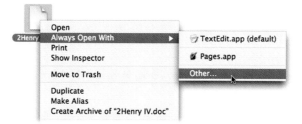

4 This takes you to your Applications folder in an Open dialog box where you can select Microsoft Word. Select Word, then click "Open."

To save ("write") TextEdit files as Word documents, please see page 82.

Create lists that automatically number themselves

If you have a list of items, TextEdit can number them for you with Roman numerals, regular numerals, capital or lowercase letters, or other options. When you add or delete items from the list, TextEdit automatically updates the numbering.

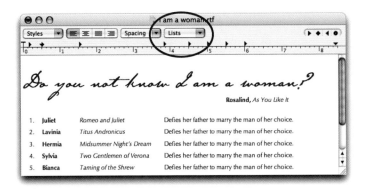

When you click on the Lists menu (circled above) and choose a numbering option, the numbers apply to **either** of the following:

If you **selected text** on the page before you went to the Lists menu, your choice of list numbering will apply to the selected text. Each time you hit a Return, TextEdit considers that the next item in the list.

If there is no selected text, the **insertion point** is "filled" with the list specifications, and everything you type from that point on will be in the list format. This is a good way to start a new list: Just make sure your insertion point is flashing where you want the list to begin, *then* go to the List menu and choose your numbering system, *then* start typing.

If you choose the "Other…" option in the Lists menu, you can set up the specifications of your choice, as shown below.

To end the sequencing of numbers in a list, hit the Return key twice at the end of the last item.

To delete the list numbers, single-click anywhere in the list. Open the Lists menu and choose "None."

Create tables

You can create simple tables in TextEdit. This table feature also helps ensure that tables created in a Word document will open in some form in TextEdit.

To create a table in TextEdit:

1 Position your insertion point where you want the table to begin.

2 Go to the Format menu, slide down to "Text," then choose "Table…."

3 The Table palette appears, as shown below. Choose how many rows and columns you want in the table. You can determine how the text is aligned vertically as well as horizontally in each cell, and more.

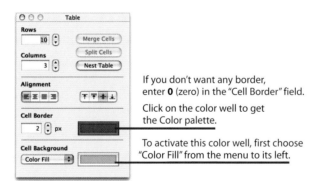

If you don't want any border, enter **0** (zero) in the "Cell Border" field.

Click on the color well to get the Color palette.

To activate this color well, first choose "Color Fill" from the menu to its left.

As you **type in a cell,** the cell expands downward to fit the text.

Change the formatting of the text as you do on a regular TextEdit page.

4 **To resize rows and columns,** position your pointer over the edge of a cell. The pointer turns into a two-headed arrow. With that two-headed arrow, press-and-drag on a cell edge to resize it.

Add breaks

You can add three different kinds of **breaks** to a TextEdit document.

Page break This tells TextEdit to start the next sentence at the top of the next page. This is handy for dividing chapters or sections.

Line break This is exactly the same as using the Shift Return. It ensures that your line will always end at that place, but it will *not* add any paragraph features that you may have added, such as space before or after, indents, etc.

Paragraph break This is exactly the same as hitting a Return. Your line of text will end at that point and a new paragraph will start. If your formatting is set so a new paragraph has an indent or an outdent, it will appear.

To add a break:

1 Position the insertion point where you want to make a break. The break will appear directly *after* the insertion point.

2 Go to the Edit menu, slide down to "Insert," and choose the break you need.

To delete a break:

1 Find the first line *after* the break. Position the insertion point right *before* the first character of that line.

2 Hit the Delete key.

Create live web links and email links

It's easy to create web links and email links on a TextEdit page. If you then send someone the TextEdit file, that person can click on a web link; her browser will open and go to the page you specify. An email link in the document will open her email program, preaddressed to whomever you specified.

If you make a PDF of your document (see pages 230–231), the links will still work in the PDF.

To create a web link on a TextEdit page:

1 Type the text that you want to apply a web link to. This text can be anything—it doesn't have to be the web address itself.

2 Select the text you want to apply the link to.

3 From the Format menu, slide down to "Text," then choose "Link…."

4 Enter the web page address. Make sure you include this code at the beginning of the web address: **http://**

5 Click OK.

To create an email link on a TextEdit page:

1 Type the text that you want to apply an email link to. This text can be anything—it doesn't have to be the email address itself.

2 Select the text you want to apply the link to.

3 From the Format menu, slide down to "Text," then choose "Link…."

4 Type into the field: **mailto:**

5 Immediately after the colon you typed (as shown above), enter the entire email address just as you would address it.   mailto:**name@domain.com**

6 Click OK.

Print automatic page numbers

You can add page numbers to a *printed* document (the numbers won't appear on the screen). This feature also automatically adds the name of the document in the upper-left corner (including the extension, probably .rtf), the date and time in the upper-right corner, and the words "Page ___ of ___" in the bottom-right corner. That is, in TextEdit you can't choose one or the other of these—they all appear on the page, or none.

To print the page numbers (and everything else), go to the TextEdit menu and choose "Preferences…." Single-click the tab "New Document," and then check "Number pages when printing."

Search and replace with options

TextEdit has surprisingly robust features for searching and replacing text. Press Command F to display the Find palette. In the fields, enter the text you want to search for and the text you want to replace it with. Click "Next" or hit the Return key.

To replace:

Only the **currently selected occurrence** of the text, click "Replace."

All occurrences of the text in the document, click "Replace All."

All occurrences of the text **in a block of selected text,** hold down the Option key and click "In Selection."

To simultaneously select (but not replace):

All occurrences of the text, hold down the Control key and click "Select All."

All occurrences **in a block of selected text,** hold down both the Control key and the Option key and click "In Selection."

Select non-contiguous text

This is really quite wonderful. It is very rare that you can select items that are not physically next to each other (contiguous). This technique lets you apply formatting or copy, cut, or delete separate sections of text all at once.

To select non-contiguous text:

1 Press-and-drag to select a section of text.

2 Hold down the Command key. Press-and-drag to select some other text that is not contiguous!

Extra tips and notes

Ruler: If the ruler isn't showing, press Command R. Without the ruler showing, you can't set tabs, indents, or margins.

Formatting: If text won't let you apply formatting, it's probably using "Plain Text." Go to the Format menu and choose "Make Rich Text."

Wrap the text: If the text is stretching the entire width of the window no matter how wide you open it, you might want to switch to the option where the text wraps according to the page it will be printed on. To do this, go to the Format menu and choose "Wrap to Page."

When the TextEdit page is using "Wrap to Window," your printer will reduce the size of the text on the printed page to match the line lengths on your screen. So if your text prints really tiny, follow the step above to "Wrap to Page."

Other relevant lessons for TextEdit

Miscellaneous: See pages 82–85 for lots of great information on a number of other great features in TextEdit.

Search: Besides the search-and-replace feature explained on the opposite page, you can also do a Spotlight search, as explained on page 328.

PDFs: All TextEdit documents can be turned into PDFs with the click of a button, as explained on pages 230–231.

Fax: You can fax any TextEdit page with the click of a button. See Lesson 7.

Crop a PDF

You can crop any part of a PDF. When you crop it, Preview actually keeps track of the part of the document you deleted and hangs on to it in case you want to uncrop the file, even after you've saved it.

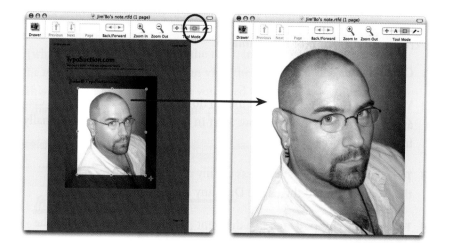

To crop a PDF:

1 Open the PDF in Preview.

2 Single-click on the "Select Tool," circled above. If the little tools are not visible in the window, drag the bottom-right corner of Preview to widen the window. *Or* go to the Tools menu and choose "Select Tool."

3 Starting in an upper corner, drag diagonally downward across the PDF to select the part of it you want to save. The light area is what you want to save.

4 If you need to resize the cropped area, position the mouse directly over one of the eight "handles" you see on the corners and edges of the cropped area (see the previous page). Drag a handle to resize.

5 If you need to move the cropped area to another part of the page, position the pointer in the middle of the crop box. You'll notice the pointer turns into a gloved hand. Press the hand in the middle of the crop box and drag.

6 If you have a multi-page document, it looks like the cropping will apply to every page. But don't worry—you have a choice in a minute. When you have the cropped area finalized, go to the Tools menu and choose "Crop," *or* press Command K.

7 You will be asked if you want to crop just the current page or all pages. Click the button of your choice.

To switch between displays of the full page or the cropped page:

1 **Display the entire contents of the PDF:** Go to the View menu, choose "PDF Display," and choose to see the "Media Box" (as shown below).

2 **Display the cropped image:** Go to the View menu, choose "PDF Display," and then choose to see the "Crop Box."

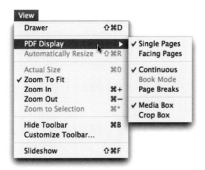

When you **re-open a cropped file,** it might open in the uncropped version. Just use the technique above to view the cropping again.

Search a PDF

The search feature in Preview is quite amazing. Use the standard keyboard shortcut for "Find," Command F. Once you have found an instance on the page, press Command G to find the next instance. These are the same shortcuts you've probably used in Safari to find text on a web page or in TextEdit to find text in your document.

To search a PDF:

1 With the PDF document open in front of you, press Command F.
 Or go to the Edit menu, slide down to "Find," then choose "Find…."

2 A search drawer appears on the side of the document window, as shown below. Type your search word or phrase into the search field.

3 As you type, Preview starts finding words that match. The more you type, the narrower the search becomes and the fewer words it finds.

4 In the list of results, double-click any one to go directly to that result. Preview will outline the word briefly, as shown below, and then the outline fades to a highlight so you can see the word.

5 To find the next occurrence of the word or phrase, press Command G, or double-click on any other result in the list.

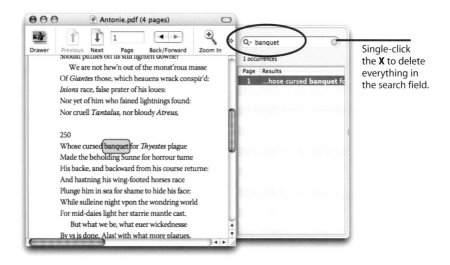

Single-click the **X** to delete everything in the search field.

Create bookmarks

The bookmarks in Preview are not bookmarks in individual multi-page documents. A bookmark puts the name of a file in the Bookmarks menu so you can open the document or photograph immediately without having to go look for it. It's like having a list of bookmarks in your web browser so you can instantly go to a favorite web page.

To make a bookmark for an open document or image, press Command D (the same shortcut as in Safari). You will be asked to name the bookmark. Give it a name that you'll recognize in a list.

If the PDF is a **multi-page document,** you can make several bookmarks for the same document, each one to a different page. Just make sure you are viewing the page you want to bookmark before you press Command D.

To open a bookmarked file, open Preview, go to the Bookmarks menu, and choose the file from the list in the menu.

To edit the name of or to remove a bookmark, go to the Bookmarks menu and choose "Edit Bookmarks…." In the dialog box that appears:

To delete a file, single-click the file name, then click the "Remove" button.

To edit the file name, double-click on its name, then edit.

View a slideshow

This is a fun feature: Drag a selection of images and drop them on the Preview icon in the Dock. This opens all of them at once in Preview. Then go to the View menu and choose "Slideshow." Each image will appear for three seconds, then switch to the next image. To stop, press Command Period.

Annotate a PDF

You can add comments and red oval highlights to PDFs to call out items for other readers. Unfortunately, the notes completely obscure the text and cannot be moved once the PDF is saved. They print in exactly the same places as they appear on the screen. So be judicious about where you place your notes!

There are **two tools** available for annotations, as shown here:

Press on the visible annotation tool to make the little menu appear where you can choose the other tool.

To create a text note on a PDF:

1 In an open PDF, select the Text Annotation tool, as shown above.

2 With that tool, press-and-drag anywhere on the page **to create a box** in which you can type a note. **To resize a note,** drag its bottom-right corner.

3 Double-click inside the note to start typing.

4 **To move a note,** first unselect it by single-clicking anywhere else on the page. Then *press* inside the note and drag it.

5 **To delete a note,** first unselect it by single-clicking anywhere else on the page, then single-click on the note. Hit Delete.

To draw a red oval annotation:

1 In an open PDF, select the Oval Annotation tool, as shown on the opposite page.

2 With that tool, press-and-drag anywhere on the page **to create a red oval.**

3 **To resize an oval,** single-click on it so you see the black box in the bottom-right corner. Drag that black corner to resize.

4 **To move an oval,** press inside of it and drag.

5 **To delete an oval,** single-click on it to select it. Hit Delete.

Copy text from a PDF to paste somewhere else

You can copy text from a PDF file and paste it into any other document as **editable text.** Or you can copy a section of text as a **graphic** and paste it into another document as a graphic image that can be resized as a unit.

To copy text:

1 Select the Text Tool, shown circled below, *or* press Command 2.

2 Press and drag over the text you want to select. To select just a vertical portion of text, as in one column, hold down the Option key as you drag.

3 From the Edit menu, choose "Copy," or press Command C. Open your other document and paste it in (Command V).

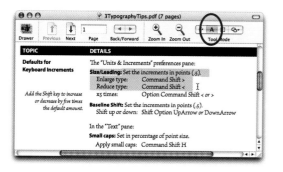

To copy any part of a PDF as a graphic, see page 209 to select a cropping area. Then, instead of cropping, go to the Edit menu and choose "Copy."

Enhancements for iCal

iCal, a delightful calendar program, just keeps getting better and better.

Groups of calendars

Create calendar **groups** to organize related calendars. You might want to group together the calendars that all have to do with your kids. Or perhaps a particular project has several different calendars associated with it.

To make a group, go to the File menu and choose "New Calendar Group." *Or* Shift-click on the **+** sign in the bottom-left corner of the iCal window. Name the new group, then drag other calendars into it.

Automatic Birthdays calendar

iCal can work with your Address Book to create a Birthdays calendar that automatically updates itself.

1 First you must add the Birthday field to your Address Book, as explained on page 91.

2 Then, in iCal, go to the iCal menu and choose "Preferences...."

3 Check the box to "Show Birthdays calendar."

Double-click any birthdate showing in the calendar to open the Info drawer. There you can click the link to go straight to that person's contact information in Address Book. You can't make any changes to the Birthdays calendar in iCal; in fact, you can't even add alarms to notify you of upcoming birthdays.

Email notification

If someone sends you an email invitation to an event, Mail can automatically put a notification in iCal. First you must make sure this option is turned on in the Preferences.

1 In iCal, go to the iCal menu and choose "Preferences…."

2 Click the "Advanced" icon. Make sure there is a checkmark next to "Automatically retrieve invitations from Mail." Close the Preferences.

3 When you get an email message from someone inviting you to an iCal event, the Notifications box appears in the bottom-left corner of iCal.

If the box isn't showing and you want to see it, single-click the Notifications button, as shown below.

4 When a notification comes in, click on it. The Info window will open. In the Info window:

To choose a reply, single-click on the "my status" pop-up menu.

To choose a calendar in which you want this event to appear, click on the "calendar" pop-up menu.

To choose an alarm to remind you of the upcoming event, click on the "alarm" pop-up menu.

Notifications button.

Sort (organize) your information

Automatically sort your To Do list by due date, title, calendar, or priority (see page 100 if you're not sure how to prioritize items). Just Control-click on the To Do list, slide down to "Sort by," and choose your option.

No matter how you've chosen to automatically sort items, once you manually drag an item into a different position, the sort order returns to "Manually" and is no longer an automatic arrangement.

Change time zones

You can change the time zone for selected events to reflect another part of the world. You don't want to do this while you're at home—it's only useful once you have arrived in the other country (otherwise all your events go catawampus). And you only need to do this if you choose *not* to change your computer's time zone while you're in another country.

So if you want to change the time zone, go to the iCal Preferences, click the "Advanced" icon, and check the box to "Turn on time zone support." Close the Preferences.

In the upper-right corner of the iCal window, click on the time zone shown there. If the time zone you want is not displayed, choose "Other…" to add it.

Now in each event Info window, you'll have an option to change the time zone for that event.

Backup the entire calendar of information

To make sure you don't lose the valuable information you have entered into your calendar, go to the File menu and choose "Back up Database…." You will be asked where to save the file. If you have a lot of information you don't want to lose, you should probably save that file onto a CD and store it in a safe place.

Search

Search your calendar for an event, a person, a To Do item, or other parameter. You can limit the search to specific parts of iCal, as shown below.

1 To search, enter the first several letters of the item or person you're looking for into the search field at the bottom of the iCal window. iCal instantly pops up the search results list you see below. As you enter more characters, the list narrows.

2 To limit the search to certain areas, click the tiny triangle in the search field and choose the area from the menu that appears, shown below.

3 To hide the list results, delete everything from the search field (click on the X), *or* single-click the List button, shown below.

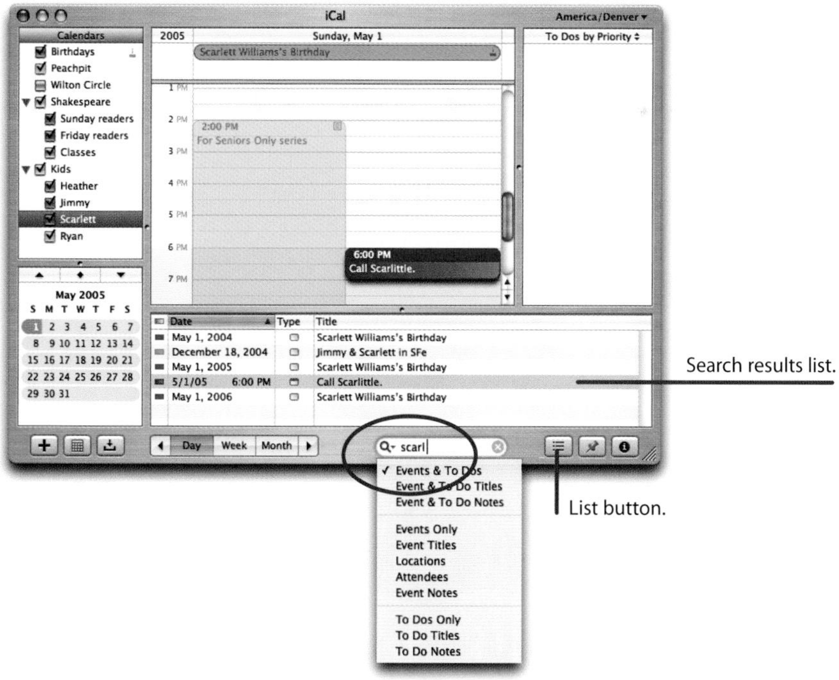

Search results list.

List button.

Don't forget that **Spotlight** can also search your iCal data even when iCal isn't open. See Lesson 12 for lots of details about Spotlight.

Print in a variety of ways

Check out the new features in the Print dialog box. Each "View" changes the options, so spend a few minutes here exploring the possibilities. You can choose to print the data from as many or as few calendars as you like. They are all color-coded, so just like in iCal itself, you can see how different events overlap.

Slide this bubble to resize the preview.

Other relevant lessons for iCal

Sync your calendar with your other computers and your .Mac account: See Lesson 11.

More Options in Safari

Of course Safari has a number of great Tiger enhancements!

Private browsing

You may have noticed that Safari keeps track of where you've been and what you've entered into search fields and what web pages you've asked to see. Safari's AutoFill feature even keeps track of user names and contact information you've entered on sites, as well as passwords and credit card numbers. If there are other people who use your computer, or if you are using Safari on someone else's Mac or at a school or an Internet cafe, you probably don't want Safari keeping track of all that information. That's where private browsing comes in handy.

When you turn on private browsing:

- None of the information you enter on any page is saved.

- Any searches you do will not be added to the pop-up menu in the Google search field.

- Web pages you visit are not added to the History menu. However, you can still go back and forward to pages you've viewed.

- If you downloaded anything, those items are automatically removed from the Download window when you turn off private browsing or quit Safari.

- Cookies are automatically deleted when you turn off private browsing or quit Safari.

To turn ON private browsing, go to the Safari menu, choose "Private Browsing."

To turn OFF private browsing, first close all Safari windows. Then go to the Safari menu and choose "Private Browsing" again to remove the checkmark.

When you **quit Safari,** private browsing is automatically **turned off,** even if you left it on before you quit. So each time you open Safari, you need to turn private browsing on again if you want to use it.

Parental controls

If you have a young child (or anyone acting like a young child), you can set up some serious parental controls to limit access to web sites. It involves multiple users, which are explained in detail in Lesson 9. You'll need an admin user (you) and you'll set up another user for the child. The child will be able to view only web sites you have placed in the Bookmarks Bar. He won't be able to enter web addresses in the Address field, modify any bookmarks, or use the Google search field in the toolbar.

1 Using the Account preferences, set up another user (details in Lesson 9). Do *not* give this user administrative privileges.

When setting up the user, click the "Parental Controls" tab, then put a checkmark next to "Safari.app."

Close the preferences.

2 Log in as the new/child user, and open Safari. Go to the Safari menu and choose "Preferences...."

3 Click the "Security" icon. **Uncheck** the box at the bottom, "Enable parental controls." You will be asked to enter your admin name and password.

4 **Remove all bookmarks** from the Bookmarks Bar that you do not want the child user to access. (If you don't see the Bookmarks Bar, which is a thin strip directly under the Address field, press Command Shift B to display it.)

Add bookmarks that you want to allow access to. The child user will be able to go to every page in the web site, not just the one page that the bookmark is set for.

Bookmarks Bar.

5 Go back to the Safari Preferences and check, "Enable parental controls." Close the preferences. In Safari, check the sites you enabled to make sure they work okay.

Note: This does not prevent the user from surfing the web with any other browser. If you want to limit the *applications* this user can use, do so in the Accounts preferences; see pages 253 and 254.

Email the contents of (or a link to) a web page

Safari makes it especially easy to **email an entire web page** to anyone, complete with images and links.

1 Open the web page in Safari.

2 From the File menu, choose "Mail Contents of This Page."

3 The Mail application opens with the name of the web page as the subject. The entire web page is in the body of the email. All you have to do is add the recipient's address and click the "Send" button.

Or you can **email just the link.** Follow the steps above, but choose "Mail Link to This Page."

View PDF documents

To view a PDF document right in Safari, just drag the PDF file and drop it into *the middle* of any Safari page.

To enlarge or reduce the size of the PDF on the screen, Control-click (or right-click) anywhere on the PDF page. From the menu that appears, choose "Zoom In" to enlarge or "Zoom Out" to reduce.

If the PDF has **more than one page,** but all you see in Safari is one page, Control-click (or right-click) and choose "Continuous."

Search your bookmarks

You can search the Bookmarks Library (see page 94) or the History list.

1 From the Bookmarks menu, choose "Show All Bookmarks."

2 At the bottom of the Bookmarks Library window is a search field. Enter the word or phrase you want to find.

To search the History, first single-click on "History" in the Collections pane, which is on the left side of the Bookmarks Library window.

Save a web page and all the graphics and links on it

Safari lets you save a web page and all the images and links and text on the page. It creates one file, an archive, that you can open at any time; all the links will work (as long as the destination pages haven't changed!). This is particularly handy for pages that you know aren't going to last long, such as online newspaper articles or purchase receipts. Keep in mind that some web pages can prevent you from saving items on the page.

1 Open the web page you want to save.

2 From the File menu, choose "Save As…."

3 In the Format menu in the dialog box, choose "Web Archive," as shown.

4 Choose the folder you want to save into, then click "Save."

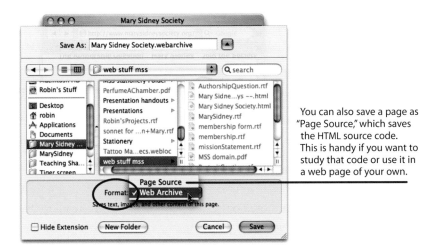

You can also save a page as "Page Source," which saves the HTML source code. This is handy if you want to study that code or use it in a web page of your own.

To save a frame of a web page, Control-click (or right-click) on the frame. From the menu that pops up, chose "Save Frame As…."

Other relevant lessons for Safari

RSS feeds: See Lesson 15 on bringing in RSS feeds straight to Safari.

Spotlight search: See page 328 for a quick tip on how to use Spotlight to search a word or phrase on a Safari web page.

DVD Player Improvements

The DVD Player has several nifty new tricks.

Create bookmarks to find specific points in the video

A bookmark lets you skip immediately to certain points in the video that you choose. That is, you are not limited to the chapter markers that were created when the DVD was made.

To create a bookmark:

1 Play a DVD. Then . . .

2 **Either** go to the Window menu and choose "Bookmarks." A palette appears. When you get to the point in the DVD where you want to insert a bookmark, click the + sign at the bottom of the Bookmarks palette.

   Or when you get to the point in the DVD where you want to insert a bookmark, press Command = (*or* go to the Controls menu and choose "New Bookmark…").

3 A sheet drops down where you can either leave the time code as shown, or you can rename the bookmark so you know exactly which one this is.

Once you have created bookmarks, you can go to the Go menu and choose to skip straight to any bookmark you made. These bookmarks are *not* stored with the DVD; that is, if you loan the DVD to anyone, it will not include your bookmarks. They are stored only on your Mac. If you make more than one bookmark, use the Bookmark palette to choose one of them to be the "default" bookmark.

Create your own clips with endpoints

Amazing. You can create individual video clips of selected segments of a DVD and then choose to play just those clips. This feature and the bookmarks feature are terrific for teachers or trainers who want to separate segments or start a scene in a DVD at a particular point. Or maybe there's a specific section of your dance or exercise video that you want to view over and over again—this makes it so easy!

To make a video clip:

1 While viewing the DVD, view until you get to the beginning of the section you want to save as a clip. Then press Command – (hyphen).

2 A little sheet drops down. Single-click the upper "Set" button, as circled below.

3 Now go to the DVD controller and click the triangle button ("Play") to continue playing the DVD (or hit the Spacebar to play). When you get to the *end* of the clip that you want to mark, click the lower "Set" button.

4 If you click "Add and Play," the clip is added to your collection of clips and the DVD Player replays just that clip.

If you click "Add," the clip is added to your collection and the video continues to play as usual.

Make adjustments

To adjust video color, sound, and zoom controls, go to the Window menu. Choose the adjustment you want to make and use the sliders.

Create your own personal disc jacket on the screen

This is great—you can add your own image to the DVD so whenever you stop the DVD, it displays the image of *your* choice.

To add your own disc image, open a DVD in the player. Go to the File menu and choose "Get Disc Info." Drag any image from your hard disk and drop it into the well. Click OK. Cool.

This is a DVD of *Richard III.* I added an image of the woman who I believe actually wrote *Richard III.*

This will only appear if I play the DVD on the computer on which I added the image.

Remember, changes like this don't really apply to the actual DVD—they are stored on your Mac. So the disc jacket will only appear if you show this DVD from the computer on which you added it.

Play a movie in the Dock

While a movie is playing, you can minimize it: click on the yellow button in the upper-left corner of the window. The window goes down to the Dock but continues playing. Useless trick, but interesting.

Create PDF Files

A PDF (Portable Document Format) is a file created in such a way that most people can open and read it, no matter what kind of computer they use. The graphics, the images, the fonts, and all the formatting is held intact in the document. And it's usually compressed into a smaller file size (not physical size) so it can travel through the Internet quickly.

To make a PDF in most Mac applications, have the document open in front of you. From the File menu, choose "Print...," then click the "PDF" button.

This option lets you add workflows that you might have created in Automator or AppleScript.

Save as PDF Saves a regular PDF that you can share with others. The graphics are at full resolution and the fonts are embedded.

Save PDF as PostScript This saves the document as a PostScript Level 2 file in ASCII format, meaning if you open it, it will look like a lot of code. But you can send it directly to a Postcript printer or run it through Acrobat Distiller. Don't choose this option unless you know you need it.

Fax PDF If you have set up your fax specifications as explained in Lesson 7, then your Mac will make a PDF of the document and open the fax dialog box where you can enter the fax number and a message. Remember, you must have a phone line connected to the Mac.

Compress PDF This makes a smaller file with compressed images. It's useful if you need to email the PDF, but the printed page won't look as good.

Encrypt PDF This lets you give the PDF a password. No one will be able to read the PDF unless she knows the password.

Mail PDF This creates a PDF of the file, opens Mail, creates a new message, and puts this PDF in the message ready to send.

Save as PDF-X The PDF-X standard from Adobe is designed for high-end printing. I don't suggest you choose this option unless you *know* you need a PDF-X file, and even then it would be best to create it in a high-end application.

Save PDF to iPhoto Your Mac will turn this document into a PDF, open iPhoto (if you have it installed, of course), ask you which album to put it into (or ask you to create a new one), and then put the PDF in that album.

Web Receipts

Save PDF to Web Receipts Folder I love this. Have you ever bought something on the web and you got that page that says, "This is your receipt"? And you know you should print it but maybe the printer isn't turned on at the moment or it's three pages long and you know they're going to send you an email receipt anyway, but what if they don't send you the email receipt and you need this web page receipt? Well, this is a great solution: The Mac will save this web page as a PDF and it will make you a folder in your Documents folder called "Web Receipts" and it will store this PDF (and all others you make like it) in that folder.

Grapher Takes Off

You'll find the **Grapher** (a graphing calculator) in the Utilities folder, which is in the Applications folder. When you first open it, you'll get the small window shown below. Make one of the choices in either the "2D Graph" or "3D Graph" tab, then click the "New" button to get the actual calculator. Be sure to check the preferences (found in the Grapher menu) and the Help files for this powerful tool.

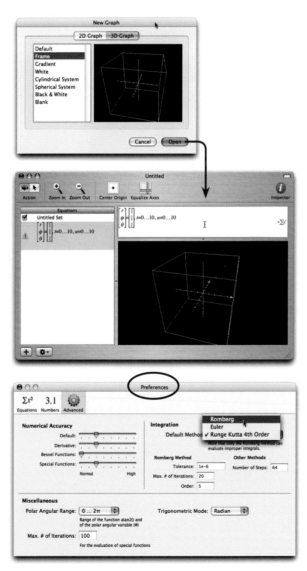

What You've Learned

▼ How and why to create a burn folder.

▼ The enhanced features of Mail, including how to display a slideshow of attachments someone sent you.

▼ The enhanced features of Address Book, including how to share your Address Book with other .Mac members.

▼ How to create automatically numbering lists and simple tables in TextEdit.

▼ How to save files as Word documents, and how to open Word documents in TextEdit.

▼ How to annotate PDFs in Preview, crop images, and make screenshots.

▼ The enhanced features of iCal, including group calendars, email notifications, and new print options.

▼ How to browse privately in Safari, apply parental controls, email the contents of web pages to friends, and more.

▼ How to create bookmarks in a commercial DVD, and create your own clips and a disc jacket.

▼ The new look of Grapher, the graphing calculator.

9

Goals

Develop an understanding of how Mac OS X takes care of more than one person sharing one Mac.

Learn how to set up your Mac so you have control over what another user can do and with whom they can communicate.

Lesson **9**

Share One Mac
with Multiple Users

Mac os x is specifically built for what's called a **multiple user environment;** that is, Apple expects that more than one person is probably using the same computer, whether it's in a school, office, or home.

If you are the only user who ever has or ever will use this computer, you can skip this lesson altogether. But are you really the only user? Perhaps your grandkids come over and want to use your Mac. Or maybe your husband uses your machine from time to time. Or sometimes you have relatives staying for a week who just want to use your Mac to get their email.

In all of these cases, you can set up another user so no one else can access your personal letters, change the sound level, poke around in your financial files, put up a dorky picture as the Desktop background, or change any of your settings.

If you ever use your computer for presentations or teaching, you can create a new user just for the presentation materials, making it easy to move back and forth between your normal workspace and a simplified presentation space in which it's easier to find and navigate your presentation files—and your personal files are out of sight.

Overview of Multiple Users

First, let me explain the **concept and advantages of having multiple users** on your Mac so you can decide if you need or want to create other users.

You already have one user, **you,** which was automatically created when you first turned on your Mac and went through the setup process. You are the main user known as the **Administrator.** The password you set up when you first turned on your new Mac or installed Tiger is your **Admin password.**

You might not have noticed that you are a "user" because Apple sets a default so when you turn on your Mac, you are automatically "logged in" without having to type in a password. Once you have other users set up, you can change this default so everyone must log in with a password. If others use your Mac only occasionally, like your grandkids, you can set it to automatically let you in daily; then when the kids come over, you go to the Apple menu and **log out,** which means they must then **log in** with their own settings and yours will be protected.

One user, the first one (which was you, if it's your own Mac), is automatically created as the original, main **Administrator (Admin)** of the computer. If you are the *only* user, you are still the Administrator.

Limitations of other users

So you are the **Admin** and other people are either **standard users** or **managed users.** All users are limited in certain ways:

- Applications can be made available to everyone, *or* limited to specific users. This means you could install a game in your child's Home folder and it won't clutter up your own Applications folder. If the game has to change the resolution of the monitor and the number of colors and your child cranks the volume way up, it won't affect what you see and hear when you log back in. You can install your financial program in your own Home/Applications folder so others cannot use it or access your files.

    You can create managed users for young kids and grandkids, where you can customize their Docks so they only have access to their own programs. You can seriously limit with whom they chat and email and which web sites they can go to.

- Even if an application is available to everyone who uses the machine, an individual user can set his own preferences because the preferences are stored in the user's personal Library folder.

- Every user can customize the Mail program, and all of a user's email is privately stored in each user's personal Library folder.

- Every user can set up her own screen effects. Fonts, window and Desktop backgrounds, Sidebar, Dock placement, and preferences are individually customizable. Preferences are also individual for the keyboard, mouse, web browser bookmarks, international keyboard settings, Classic, applications that start up on login, and QuickTime.

- The features that make the Mac easier to use for people with challenges can be customized by each user. This includes the Universal Access settings, full keyboard access, Speech preferences (talking to your Mac to make it do things), etc.

- Users who need international settings for such things as date, time, numbers, or for typing other languages, etc., can customize the Mac without bothering other users. If you have a laptop that you travel with, you can set up yourself as another user, such as "Carmen in Belize," and customize those settings for that country without affecting all your settings for home.

- **Standard users cannot** change the date or time (except for the menu bar settings), nor can they change the preferences for energy saving, file sharing, networking, or the startup disk. They cannot add new users nor can they change certain parts of the login process.

- **Managed users** have all of the above limitations, *plus* they have parental controls applied. You can severely limit a managed user, as explained on pages 253–256.

More than one Admin

As the Administrator, you can **assign Admin status to any other user** (see page 246). When that Admin user logs in, he can make system-wide changes that standard users cannot; he can create and delete other users, and do most of the things you can do. But your personal Home files are still protected from everyone else, including other Admins.

Create New Users

If you are the Admin (as explained on the previous pages), you can create standard or managed users (also explained on the previous page). You'll create the new user in the "Accounts" pane in the System Preferences, plus you'll assign a password and a login picture. In the "Login Options" pane, you can make adjustments to the login window.

To create a new user:

1 Go to the Apple menu and choose "System Preferences…."

2 In the System Preferences pane, single-click on "Accounts." You'll get the dialog box shown below, except it probably has only one user listed, you. This one user is also the **Admin.**

3 You will probably have to click the lock icon in the bottom-left corner. In the dialog box that appears after you click the lock, enter the Admin password (the one you chose when you set up your Mac), then click the OK button. The lock in the bottom-left corner should now be open, as shown below.

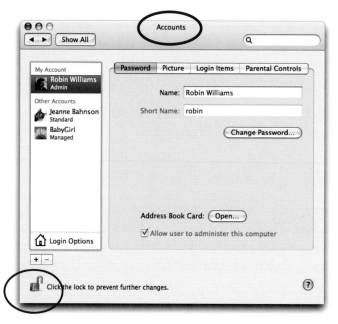

4 To add a new user, click the "plus" button. This makes a sheet drop down (as shown below) where you will add new user information.

Type the full name (or any descriptive phrase) in the "Name" edit box. A short name is automatically created for you, but you can edit it. *You will never be able to change the short name after you leave this pane!* The only way to "change" it is to delete the entire user and make a new one.

The short name should be short, you can't use spaces, and you should avoid non-alphabet characters (like * ! ? or /).

Mac OS X can use either the short name or long name. But the short name is necessary if you ever use FTP, Telnet, or other applications that let you log in to your Mac from some other location.

Click this to get secure password suggestions.

5 Enter a **password** for the user. **Write this down somewhere.** As you've probably seen before, you need to type in the password twice to make sure you've spelled it right, since you can't see it. If you like, click on that tiny key icon to get some suggestions for passwords that are very secure.

—continued

Passwords are "case sensitive." That means capital or lowercase letters change the password: "ChoCo" is not the same password as "choco." So be darn sure when you write down your password somewhere that you make note of any capital letters.

It is possible to leave the password blank, but that makes that user's Home easier to get into. If privacy is an issue, be sure to assign a password.

You can, if you like, enter a **password hint.** On login, if a user enters the wrong password three times, a message appears with this hint (see pages 242–243 to make sure the box is checked to make the hint appear).

TIP If you have a very young user or two, you can set them up as users with *no* passwords so all they have to do is click on their pictures to log in. Or make the password something like "xxx" so it's really easy for them.

6 **To choose a login picture,** single-click the "Picture" tab, circled below.

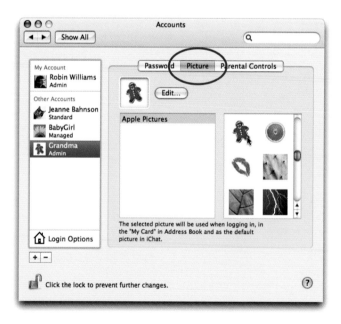

Then choose one of the following steps to add the picture:

- Single-click one of the "Apple Pictures" in the scrolling panel on the right.

- **Or** drag a photo or other image from a Finder window and drop it into the little picture "well" to the left of the "Edit…" button (where you see the gingerbread man on the opposite page). This will open the Images pane, as shown below.

- **Or** click the "Edit…" button to open the Images pane, shown below. Drag a photo or other image from a Finder window and drop it into the picture well in the Images pane, as shown below.

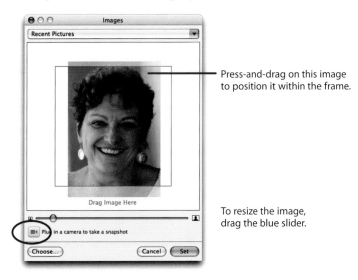

Press-and-drag on this image to position it within the frame.

To resize the image, drag the blue slider.

In the Images pane, shown above:

- To choose from photos you may have added recently in Address Book or iChat, click the "Recent Pictures" pop-up menu.

- To select an image from any location on your computer, click the "Choose…" button.

- If you have a video camera attached to your computer or if someone is sending video to you, click the video button, circled above. A beeping sound and a five-second delay precede the video camera snapshot.

7 Click the "Set" button when you're done and continue to the next step.

— continued

8 In the Accounts window, single-click **Login Options** to assign a user the ability to automatically log in, as explained below. This pane is available only to Administrators (that is, standard and managed users will not be able to change anything on this pane).

I just set up several new users, but my Mac will **automatically start up** with "Robin Williams," meaning I do not have to go through the login screen and enter a password whenever the Mac starts or restarts. This is good for me.

Because the Mac will automatically log me in, the only way the other users can get to their Home folders is if I go to the Apple menu and choose "Log Out...," *or* if I uncheck the automatic login on this pane. Which one you choose depends on how often the other user needs your machine; if it's infrequent, you can let yourself automatically log in daily, then log out when the other user arrives to log in.

Only one user can be assigned the automatic login. Any time you like, open this pane and choose another user from the menu shown above to give that person the automatic login privilege.

Display login window as:

The option "List of users" displays a list of all accounts. The pictures that were chosen appear next to the names of the users. It's really cute. At login, click a picture, then type your password. (If you have a very young user who can't type, do not assign a password; she can just click her picture to log in.)

The "Name and password" option displays a small window with two edit boxes, one for the user name and one for the password. A user will have to type in both name and password.

Show the Restart, Sleep, and Shut Down buttons: This adds a wee bit more security to your Mac. You see, when you log out, your computer does not turn off. It sits there with a little window where you can log back in again, and there are buttons in the window to "Sleep," "Restart," or "Shut Down." If your Mac is set to automatically log you in on startup, then an unauthorized user can walk by after you have logged out, click the Restart button, and your Mac will restart and automatically log you in. Or someone could shut down your Mac, insert an OS X CD, boot up the Mac, and get access to your whole computer. By disabling these buttons, an unauthorized user cannot click them, which makes your Mac one step closer to being protected.

However, there is nothing to prevent anyone from pushing the Restart button on the Mac, so if you really don't want people getting into your Mac, do not enable automatic log in, and do not leave your OS X CD laying around.

Show Input menu in login window: This gives you access to the language options that you may have set up in the International system preferences.

Use VoiceOver at login window: This turns on Apple's built-in spoken user interface so a visually impaired person can log in. It reads everything on the login screen out loud to you and tells you what is highlighted so you know where to type your name and password. See Lesson 17.

Show password hints: If a user enters the wrong password three times, the hint provided in the password pane (see page 239) is displayed.

9 To limit what the new user can access, see pages 253–256. Otherwise, close the Accounts preferences pane.

Log Out and Log In

Automatic login allows *one* selected user to use the Mac without having to enter a password. If automatic login is enabled (page 236), then you must make sure to **Log Out** (*not* restart or shut down) before another user can log in. This is because the computer will automatically log you in again when it starts up.

If automatic login is *not* enabled, then it doesn't matter how you turn off the Mac—it will always display a **Log In** screen where every user, even Admins, will have to enter a password.

When you log out, all of your documents will close and your applications will quit. If this is inconvenient, read about "fast user switching," opposite.

To log out, go to the Apple menu and choose "Log Out *User*...."
"*User*" is the name of the currently active user. All applications will quit, the current screen will disappear, and the login window will appear waiting for the next user to log in.

To log in, click your name and then type your password. If the password is incorrect, the login window shakes back and forth, as if it's saying "No! No! No!" After three wrong passwords, it will show you the hint you assigned (see page 239).

Switch Users with a Click

The Mac has a feature called **fast user switching** that allows multiple users to stay logged in at the same time without having to close files or quit applications. If you're working on a newsletter and your teenager needs to do her homework, she can switch to her personal user environment, do her work, then you'll switch the Mac back to your user space—with your newsletter sitting there waiting for you. The important thing is that you didn't have to close your documents and quit your applications to log out.

When fast user switching is turned on, all users are listed in the top-right corner of your screen, next to the menu clock. The currently active user's name appears in the menu bar.

To see other user names and to see which ones are logged in, single-click on the current user name in the menu; a menu drops down showing all users. Users in the list that have a checkmark next to them are already logged in. The currently active user is grayed-out.

To enable fast user switching, click the checkbox "Enable fast user switching" in the "Login Options" pane of the Accounts system preferences (see page 242).

To switch to another user, choose one from the user menu, as shown above. If you (the Admin) assigned a password to the chosen user, a login window opens so the user can type a password. Enter the correct password and the user's own personal Desktop environment opens.

If a password was not assigned to a user, that user's Desktop opens immediately, without a password-protected login window. Actually, it doesn't just open

—continued

like some ordinary computer; the entire Desktop rotates like a cube to the new user space.

> **TIP** ▶ If the rotating-cube effect isn't happening for you, the graphics card installed on your Mac might not be able to handle the intense processing that this effect requires. Only the newest and most powerful of the seven Macs in our office can display this fancy effect—the others just change screens without rotating.

To open the main login window, choose "Login Window…" from the user's list in the menu bar, as shown on the previous page. This is a convenient way to leave the screen if you have multiple users. The next user that sits down at the Mac just clicks her name to log in and start work (or play).

Allow Other Users to be Admins

An Admin can select another user and give that user Administrator privileges. In the Accounts preferences, select the user in the left panel, then go to the **Password** pane. Click the button to "Allow user to administer this computer."

A standard user can give himself Admin privileges if he knows the name and password of an Administrator. All he needs to do is click the lock icon and enter the correct information.

Adjust User Settings

You, as Admin, cannot make changes to another user if that user is already logged in (*unless* fast user switching is turned on; see the previous page). So if you try to make changes and it won't let you, log out that user.

Let Users Adjust their own Settings

Once a **standard user** is logged in, she can adjust some of the login settings, even if she's not the Administrator. She can change her password (she has to know the current password before she can assign a new one). She can change the login picture, apply parental controls to herself, and choose which applications open automatically when she logs in.

Below you see the applications that my mother likes to have open automatically when she comes to visit and uses my Mac. See the following page for details about Login Items.

Set Permissions for Shared Files

Every file on your Mac has "permission" settings. Some of these permissions you can change, if you like. For instance, you might want to send a memo to all users of this Mac, but you don't want them to be able to edit it. So select that document and give the others a permission of "Read only." Or perhaps you don't want anyone to access your Sites folder; give it a permission of "No Access." Maybe you want to share your Movies folder so another user can drop movie files into it; select the folder and change its permission to "Read & Write" or "Write only" (which means they can put files *into* your folder but can't take them out.)

To change permissions on a file or folder:

1 Single-click on a file or folder to select it.

2 Press Command I to display the Get Info window, as shown below.

3 Click the disclosure triangle next to "Ownership & Permissions."

4 Click the little menu next to "Others" to change the permissions.

5 When you're finished, just close the Get Info window.

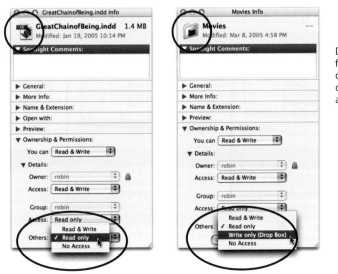

Documents and folders have different sorts of permissions available.

Apply Parental Controls

There are several levels of limited user access you can create. Once you apply any of these parental controls, the user changes from a "standard" user to a "managed" user. Choose the level of access you want to control. Each of these options is explained on the following pages.

Email: Limit a user to exchanging email with only people of your choice.

iChat text, audio, and video messaging: Limit a user to exchanging any kind of chat with only people of your choice.

Safari: Limit web surfing to sites you select.

Dictionary: Limit the sorts of words a user can look up.

Application access: Limit the applications a person can use, plus how much of the Finder she will have control over.

Simple Finder: Simple Finder is the most serious limitation. This is appropriate for very young children who want to use their educational software and games on your Mac and really don't know how to surf or chat anyway. It makes the Mac very easy for them to use.

Set limitations on certain applications

These are the limitations you can put on the applications that allow a user to communicate with anyone in the world. If you have not made a user yet, please see pages 238–243 first.

To limit email, iChat, and Safari web browsing:

1 Make sure that the user is not logged in. If he is, log him out.

2 Go to the Apple menu and choose "System Preferences…."
   Single-click on the "Accounts" icon.

3 If the lock icon in the bottom-left corner is locked, single-click on it
   and enter the Admin name and password. Click OK.

—continued

4 Select the user in the left-hand pane (if you haven't made a user yet, see pages 238–243 to set one up).

5 Single-click the "Parental Controls" tab.

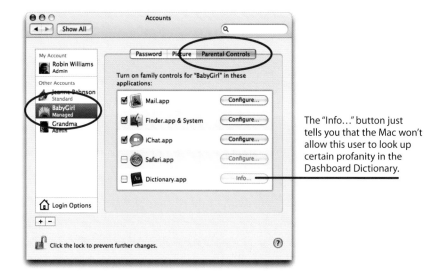

The "Info..." button just tells you that the Mac won't allow this user to look up certain profanity in the Dashboard Dictionary.

6 Put a check next to the application that you want to limit. Then click the "Configure..." button to choose email addresses, iChat buddy names, or add web sites. For details on web sites, please see page 224.

Limit the applications and activities

The next step in parental control is limiting the actual applications a user can have access to. This is one way to make sure another user doesn't open your financial applications or any work projects.

To limit applications and activities:

1 Make sure the user is logged out, then open the "Accounts" preferences.

2 If the lock icon in the bottom-left corner is locked, single-click on it and enter the Admin name and password. Click OK.

3 Select the user in the left-hand pane, then click the "Parental Controls" tab.

4 Put a check in the box next to "Finder.app & System," then click its "Configure…" button. The pane shown below drops down.

5 Check the button, "Some Limits." Now use this pane to limit or provide access to the various parts of the Mac.

Simple Finder

The Simple Finder is the most serious limitation. The illustration below shows what a user logged in using **Simple Finder** might see.

- The Applications and Utilities are limited to what you allow.

- The user has no access to a Desktop, hard disk, or other partitions.

- The user has three folders in her Dock: My Applications, Documents, and Shared. The Shared folder contains items placed in it by other users of the computer, as explained on page 249. Anything anyone puts into the "Shared" folder (shown in the Dock) will be available even to users running Simple Finder.

- The Finder windows have no Sidebars or Toolbars.

In Simple Finder, click an icon just once to open it.

My Applications folder.

Shared folder.

Documents folder; all saved documents will be in this folder.

To set up a user with Simple Finder:

1 Go to the Apple menu and choose "System Preferences…." Single-click the "Accounts" icon.

2 If the lock icon in the bottom-left corner is locked, single-click on it and enter the Admin name and password. Click ok.

3 Select the user in the left-hand pane (if you haven't made a user yet, see pages 238–243 to set one up).

4 Single-click the "Parental Controls" tab.

5 Put a check next to "Finder.app & System." Then single-click its "Configure" button. The pane shown on the following page drops down.

—continued

6 Click the button for "Simple Finder."

7 Click the "Applications" checkbox to select everything in the listed folder. Every checked item will be available to the user in Simple Finder.

To deselect some applications, click the small disclosure triangle next to "Applications" to see a list of the applications, each with its own checkbox. Uncheck a box to deselect an item.

Click OK when you're done.

Override the Simple Finder

While in the Simple Finder, an Admin user (or anyone with an Admin name and password) can go to the Finder menu and select "Run Full Finder." A dialog box opens that requires the Admin name and password, and then the current user has access to a complete menu bar, hard disks, and Finder windows with Sidebars and Toolbars.

Delete a User

Any Admin can delete a user. Tiger gives you two choices about what to do with all the files that belong to a user when you delete her.

When you delete a *user,* her *files* are not really deleted but are compressed into a "disk image" and put into a folder named "Deleted Users," which is inside the Users folder (shown on the following page) This gives you an escape in case you decide it was a drastic mistake to remove a user—at least you have their important files.

If you *know* it's really okay to delete the user **and all their files,** you can choose to delete everything belonging to that user immediately.

To delete a user:

1 From the Apple menu, choose "System Preferences…," then click the "Accounts" icon.

2 If the lock icon in the bottom-left corner is locked, single-click on it and enter the Admin name and password. Click OK.

3 Click once on the name of the user you want to delete. If the user name is gray and you can't select it, that means that user is logged in. She must log out before you can delete the account.

4 After you select the user, click the "minus" button at the bottom of the list of users pane.

—continued

5 A drop-down sheet, shown below, asks if you really want to delete this user account.

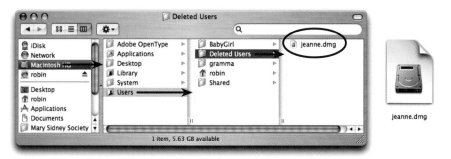

Click "Delete Immediately" if you're certain you don't need anything the deleted user may have in her Home folder. The user account and all files in the user's Home folder will immediately disappear.

Click "Cancel" if you change your mind about deleting this user.

Click "OK" if that's what you really want to do. The contents of the user's Home folder will be compressed as a disk image format (.dmg) and saved into a "Deleted Users" folder located in the Users folder. This is a nice safety net in case you need to access that user's files later.

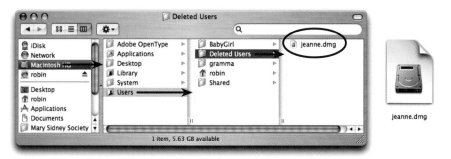

To access those user files later, double-click the .dmg file. It will open to a hard disk icon. Open the hard disk icon and you'll find all the files.

What You've Learned

▼ Why it's so useful to have multiple users for one Mac.

▼ How to create new users.

▼ How to add a photo or an image to a user.

▼ How to log out and log in.

▼ How and why (or why not) to enable fast user switching.

▼ How to allow other users to be Administrators.

▼ How users can adjust some of their own settings.

▼ How to set up items to automatically open when you log in.

▼ How to share files with other users on one Mac.

▼ How to limit the accessibility of files.

▼ How to apply parental controls from mild to serious.

▼ How to set up the Simple Finder for very young users, and how you can override it when necessary.

10

Goals

Provide users with an understanding of how their Macs connect to the Internet.

Teach users how to troubleshoot their Internet and network connections.

Teach users how to share files over a network.

Get Connected—
and Stay Connected

On a Mac, you have various ways to connect to the Internet. You might have a dial-up account that goes through your phone line, a cable modem, a DSL modem, a wireless connection, an ethernet office connection that plugs into a broadband setup, or some other arrangement.

And you have various ways to connect your Macs together in a home or office. Once your computers are on a local network, you can transfer files between them and even access your own Mac from another computer.

How Your Mac Connects to the Internet

When you first turned on your Mac and walked through the setup process, you probably filled in the information for your Internet connection. The Network preferences is where your Mac stored that information and where you can change it, adjust it, or troubleshoot it.

The Network preferences lists all of the ways that your Mac might be connected and displays the current status of each option. You can configure all interfaces for all your possible connections from this one window.

Network

To open the Network preferences, go to the Apple menu and choose "System Preferences...." Single-click the "Network" icon.

When you first open the window, it probably looks something like this, below, showing you the status of any possible connections your Mac might have access to.

Click this button to change settings
for the selected configuration.

Or choose a configuration from the
Show menu to display the settings.

Check the port configurations

You might have several options for connecting. For instance, your Mac recognizes that you have a modem port (whether you use it or not), and it might find a wireless card and an Ethernet port. Every possibility it finds is listed in the "Port Configurations." To see the possibilities, choose "Network Port Configurations" from the Show menu, as shown below.

Your Mac goes down this list in order and chooses the first interface that works. It's a good idea to make sure your preferred connection is at the top of the list—just drag it to the top and drop it. If there is a connection listed that you don't want it to even try, like a dial-up internal modem, uncheck it.

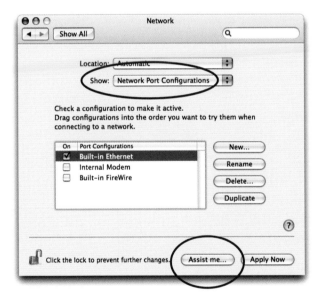

Establish a new connection

If you didn't set up your Internet connection when you first installed Tiger or turned on your brand-new Mac, you can always do it in this Network preferences pane. Just click the button (circled above), "Assist me…." A sheet will drop down from the title bar (as shown on page 265). In that sheet, click the button labeled "Assistant…." It will walk you through the process.

Troubleshoot Your Internet Connection

If your connection doesn't work when you first turn on your Mac, perhaps the information you entered in the setup process wasn't correct. Or if you changed Internet Service Providers or changed your connection process, you'll need to change the information. Use the Network preferences.

Network

1 From the Apple menu, choose "System Preferences…," then click the "Network" icon.

2 In the Show menu in the Network pane, choose the connection that you need to fix or change.

```
●●○                     Network
◀ ▶    Show All                              🔍

                Location:  Automatic              ◆
                   Show:  Built-in Ethernet       ◆

         TCP/IP   PPPoE   AppleTalk   Proxies   Ethernet

   Configure IPv4:  Using DHCP                    ◆

       IP Address:  10.0.1.4                  Renew DHCP Lease

     Subnet Mask:  255.255.255.0   DHCP Client ID:  [            ]
                                              (If required)
          Router:  10.0.1.1

      DNS Servers:  [                              ]   (Optional)

   Search Domains:  [                              ]   (Optional)

    IPv6 Address:  fe80:0000:0000:0000:0208:93fe:fe1a:87da

                 ( Configure IPv6... )              ⑦

🔒  Click the lock to prevent further changes.   ( Assist me... )  ( Apply Now )
```

3 Change the appropriate settings. If you're not sure what the appropriate settings are, you have two choices:

a Call your ISP (Internet Service Provider) and ask them what to enter in which panes. Your ISP is the company to whom you pay the monthly fee for your connection to the Internet. Although these windows look scary, there are only two or three settings you need. If you use cable or DSL with "DHCP," it might set it up for you automatically. To check, open Safari and see if it goes to a web page. If it does, you're done.

b Use the **Network diagnostics tool,** as described in the following steps. This tool will automatically appear when your connection goes down, but you can also call on it here whenever you need it.

4 Click the "Assist me…" button at the bottom of the Network pane.

This drops down a sheet from the title bar, as shown below. For troubleshooting help, click the "Diagnostics…" button.

Click the "Assistant…" button if you want to create a **new** connection.

5 The diagnostics tool will check all the relevant settings on your Mac and ask you simple questions. If it can't fix the problem, it will at least pinpoint it so you can call your ISP with the specific issue.

Talk to your ISP; check your cables

If everything seems okay on your end and you still can't get connected to the Internet, call a friend who uses the same ISP and see if she is connected. If her connection is down as well, then just let go and wait until they fix it. But if her connection is working, call the ISP. They can check your modem and help pinpoint the cause. Also check your cables! They might have wiggled loose or one might have gone bad. They do that sometimes. If you're using an Ethernet cable, make sure it's the right kind; see page 268.

Troubleshoot Your Mail Account

If you have problems getting your email, there are several things you can do. The first, of course, is to check your account information:

The **Description** is anything that will tell you which account this is.

The **Email Address** and **Full Name** describe your mail to those you send it to so they know who it's coming from.

▼ The **Incoming Mail Server** is information that you have to get from whoever hosts that particular email account. I have six or seven email accounts, not one of which is with my ISP. So I need to get the Incoming Mail Server of each of the hosts where I have the email *coming from.*

▼ Keep in mind that some ISPs have a different **User Name** and **Password** *for your account with them* than the user name and password to get your email. If your email account is not with your ISP, then of course the account information in your Mail window is definitely not the same as for your ISP. You might have to call your email host and ask what to enter here.

▼ The **Outgoing Mail Server (SMTP)** is always from your ISP, no matter where your email account is located. Well, there are exceptions, like you can use a mac.com SMTP, but in general, you are always assured of being able to *send mail out* if you use your ISP's SMTP. If you don't know what the SMTP is, call and ask them or check their web site—it should be listed. For all six of the accounts listed above, I use the same SMTP.

To change your SMTP setting, click on the SMTP menu and choose "Add server…," then click OK. Next, choose that server from the menu.

Some cheesy companies will not give you an SMTP address. For instance, if you get a Qwest broadband account here in New Mexico, you'll discover they are in cahoots with Microsoft and provide no SMTP. You cannot use the Mail application—you are forced to go to the MSN web site and do all mail online (where Microsoft can keep track of you). Change companies.

Reminder: where to get the information

Your email provider's web site should include the information for the *incoming* mail server, user name, and password. Your ISP's web site should provide the SMTP (*outgoing* mail server) information.

If you have a **free webmail account** like Yahoo or Hotmail (which is Microsoft), you probably can't set up Mail to check your mail. However, the free services often have a paid option as well, and with the paid service you can usually get the specs to set up your account in the Mail program. But if you have to pay for it, why not get a .Mac account (see Lesson 11)?

Use the Mail Connection Doctor

If your account information is correct but email still isn't working, check this utility: In Mail, go to the Window menu and choose "Connection Doctor." You'll get the window shown below; it will automatically check your accounts. If it finds a problem, the dot is red; depending on the problem, you may be able to click the "Assist me…" button to help pinpoint the issue further.

In this case, I had the wrong information in the Accounts pane.

Share Files on a Network

Sharing

File sharing on a local network is so great—as Apple says, your Mac just "discovers" other Macs. But it can't discover them unless the computers are connected in some way. So first, a bit about networking.

Simple networking

The Macs you want to share files between must be **networked** together—you must have some sort of cable connecting them to each other or both to the same printer, or AirPort cards installed so they can connect to each other wirelessly. Networking a couple of Macs is a simple procedure.

Networking can get very complex and specialized. I am only going to explain the simplest method to get a couple of Macs talking to each other.

Ethernet cables

You will probably have to buy Ethernet cables.

▼ If the cables go directly from computer to computer (or any two Ethernet devices, like a Mac to a printer), you need **crossover cables.**

▼ If the cables are going from the computer into a hub, router, or switcher, or into a cable or DSL modem, you need **straight cables**—not crossover.

To tell if an Ethernet cable is crossover or not, hold both ends up, facing the same direction, with the locking clip facing up. Look at the colored wires coming through the end.

A straight cable has the colored wires in *exactly the same order.*

A crossover cable does *not* have the colored wires in the same order.

What else you need

Two computers can be connected with one crossover Ethernet cable. If you have a number of machines in your office, you will need something called a **switch** or **Ethernet hub** that can connect all of your machines, including your printers. The switch/hub will have a number of Ethernet ports; you connect each Mac and printer *to that box* with straight (not crossover) Ethernet cables.

If you have several computers in your office, a broadband connection, and all your Macs can get on the Internet at the same time, you're probably using a **router**—you're already set up for networking.

If the router doesn't have enough ports for the Macs and printers in your office, you can buy a small **hub** or **switch** and connect the router to the hub or switch with a straight Ethernet cable.

Peer-to-peer network

This simple network in a small office is called a **peer-to-peer network,** where every computer is considered a "server," which is a computer that can "serve" files to others. This is different from a client-server network in a large corporation, where lots of computers connect to one huge, main server and everyone gets files from that main server, rather than from each other's computers.

Turn on Personal File Sharing

Now that your computers are connected, you need to tell them it's okay to share files. On each Mac, go to the Apple menu and choose "System Preferences…." Click "Sharing." Put a checkmark in "Personal File Sharing."

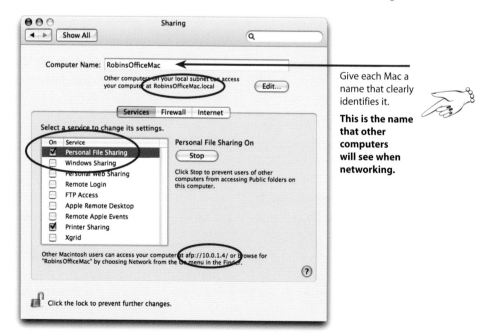

Give each Mac a name that clearly identifies it.

This is the name that other computers will see when networking.

Connect to Another Mac

Once the Macs are connected in some way and you've turned on Personal File Sharing in the Sharing preferences (as explained on the previous pages), you're ready to connect. It's easy.

1 Make sure you are in the Finder (single-click on any blank space on the Desktop). Then follow *either* Steps **a** or **b**:

   a From the Go menu, choose "Connect to Server…."

     The little window shown below appears. Your window might be empty, though—that's okay; in the example below I have added favorites (see page 273).

     If you know the name of the Mac you want to connect to (as shown in the Sharing pane of the *other* Mac; see the previous page), type it in here, with ".local" after its name. Then click the "Connect" button. Skip to Step 3.

     Or click the "Browse" button, which takes you to the window you see in Step **b** at the top of the opposite page. Follow the steps from there.

   b Open any Finder window. Click the Column View icon (shown circled on the next page, top). In the Sidebar, single-click the "Network" icon.

     (If you don't see a Network icon, it's probably turned off in the Finder preferences; see page 141).

     Your window looks like the one shown on the opposite page. This lists the connected computers. Double-click the one you want to connect to.

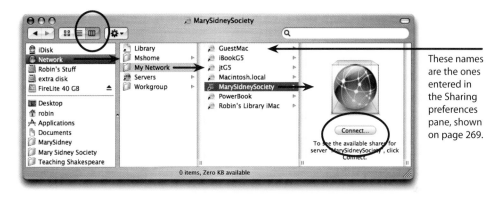

These names are the ones entered in the Sharing preferences pane, shown on page 269.

2 Either double-click a server name, *or* single-click it and then click the "Connect…" button in the preview pane, as shown above.

3 You will get a window in which you need to enter a name and password. **Important!** Even though it has *your* name in the field, it doesn't want *your* name and password! It's asking for the name (long or short) and password of the computer you're trying to connect to! Took me a while to figure *that* one out.

So anyway, if you know the name and password of the other computer, you can connect as a "Registered User" and *you will have access to the entire machine,* all the files, all the folders, all the documents. This is great when you are on someone else's computer and need to access your own.

If you don't have the name and password of the other Mac, you can connect as a "Guest"; see the following page.

4 Enter the name and password, then click "Connect."

—continued

5 The next window that appears lists the hard disk, the Home folder, and any partitions or other hard disks attached to the other Mac. Double-click the name of the one you want to connect to.

To have access to more than one of the partitions, hold down the Command key and click on as many as you want to connect to, then let go of the Command key and click OK. You can also repeat the process if you decide later you need to connect to another volume.

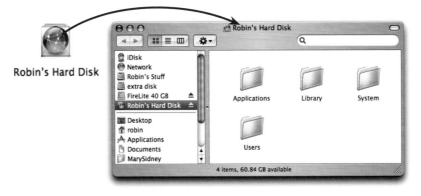

6 On the Desktop of the computer you're working on, you'll see a network icon for each volume you connected to, shown below-left. Double-click that icon to open a window to that drive, shown below-right.

It's not an easy task to keep track of which windows are on which machine since they all have the same names! Don't *open* any applications or documents from the window of the other Mac because you will actually be working on the other machine at that point, which might affect the person using it. It's best to drag the necessary documents to your computer before you open them.

Connect as a Guest

Follow the steps on the previous pages up to Step 3. When you get to the window shown below, click the "Guest" button. Then click "Connect."

You will skip the rest of the steps because the Mac will open the **Public folder** of the computer you are connecting to, shown below. The only things you will have access to on the other computer are the files that user has put in her Public folder for you. The only place you can move documents *to* on the connected Mac is the Drop Box, shown below.

Create Favorite servers

In the "Connect to Server" window (choose it from the Go menu at the Finder), type in the name you want to connect to. Then click the **+** button to add that server to your favorites in the list below. Now you can just double-click on one.

Bonjour—Share Files Locally

Once your Mac is on a network of computers running OS X, version 10.2 or later, you can send files back and forth to everyone through Bonjour, which is part of iChat (in OS X versions earlier than Tiger, 10.4, it's called Rendezvous, not Bonjour). The iChat icon should be in your Dock; if not, it's in your Applications folder.

If you didn't **turn on Bonjour** the first time you opened iChat, you can do it in the iChat preferences, in the Accounts pane:

But you can also turn it on with this shortcut:

1 Open iChat.

2 From the Window menu, choose "Bonjour" (or press Command 2). If you're not already logged in, it will ask if you want to start it up.

3 Click "Login."

And now the Bonjour window is open as well, as shown on the next page.

Send a file to someone on the network

This is so easy it will boggle your mind.

1 First open the Bonjour window: Open iChat, then press Command 2 (or from the Window menu, choose "Bonjour").

2 Now drag a file and drop it on someone's name. That person will get a message that she has an incoming file.

3 She clicks once on that message, then she has a choice to "Decline," in which case the message will disappear, or "Save File," which downloads the file to her Desktop.

Drop a file.

Click the message.

Click "Save File."

Here's another way to send a file (this also works in iChat). Just open a chat with someone in either Bonjour or your Buddy List (double-click a name to open a chat). Drop a file in the text field and hit Return.

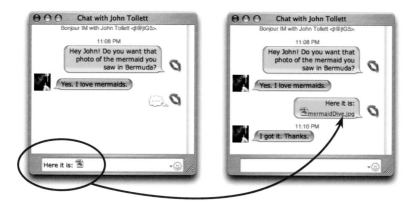

Share Mac OS 9 Files with Mac OS X

If your old Mac is running System 7.1 through 9.2, you can still connect it to your new one and transfer the files. Connect the two Macs per one of the suggestions on pages 268–269. Do the following four steps on the Mac running OS 9 (or earlier), then connect as usual from your OS X machine.

1. Set up File Sharing in Mac OS 9 or earlier:

a From the Apple menu, choose "Control Panels," then "File Sharing."

(In Systems 7 through 8.1, choose the "Sharing Setup" control panel.)

b In the first three fields, enter your name, password, and a computer name so you'll recognize this Mac. If the password is already filled in and you don't know what it is, replace it by typing a new one (very secure, huh?).

c Write down the IP address, as shown below.

d If the "File Sharing" button says "Start," click it. If it says "Stop," leave it alone because that means file sharing is already on.

e Check the box to "Enable File Sharing clients to connect over TCP/IP."

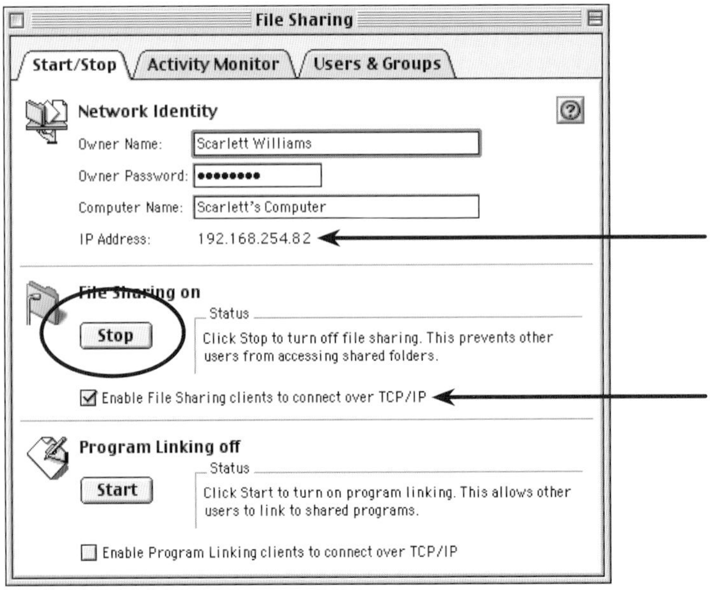

2. Set up a File Sharing User in Mac OS 9 or earlier:

a If the "File Sharing" control panel is not already open, go to the Apple menu, choose "Control Panels," then choose "File Sharing."

If the Mac is older than OS 9, open the "Users & Groups" control panel.

b Click the "Users & Groups" tab.

c Click the button, "New User."

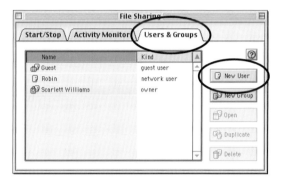

d In the "Identity" pane that appears, shown below, type in a name and password. Write down this name and password on a piece of paper!

e From the "Show" menu, choose "Sharing," and make sure the box is checked to "Allow user to connect to this computer."

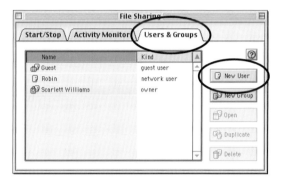

f Click the close box to put this little dialog box away.

g Click the close box to put the "File Sharing" control panel away.

—continued

3. Set up File Sharing Info in Mac OS 9:

a On the Desktop, single-click on the hard disk icon that you need files from.

b Press Command I. **Or** go to the File menu, choose "Get Info," then choose "Sharing."

In systems earlier than OS 9, go to the File menu and choose "Sharing."

c If you do not see "Sharing" in the "Show" pop-up menu in the Get Info box, as shown below, choose "Sharing" from that menu.

d Check the box to "Share this item and its contents."

e In the "User/Group" pop-up menu, choose the name of the user you created in Step 2.

f In the "Privilege" column, choose the "Read & Write" icon (the eyeglasses and pencil) for this user/group.

g Close the Get Info box.

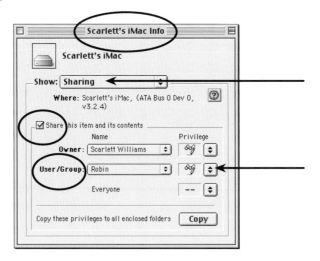

4. Set up AppleTalk Ethernet in Mac OS 9:

a Go to the Apple menu, choose "Control Panels," then choose "AppleTalk."

b In the "Connect via" pop-up menu, choose "Ethernet."

c Close the "AppleTalk" control panel. If you are asked to save changes, click "Yes."

Now when you follow the steps to connect to another server (pages 270–273), this OS 9 machine should be in the list! Remember, enter the name and password of the machine you are trying *to connect to*, not your own name and password.

Disconnect

Disconnect from any connected servers in the same way you disconnect from any other hard disk.

- ▼ **Either** drag the server icon to the Trash basket.

- ▼ **Or** select the server icon. Go to the File menu and choose "Eject."

- ▼ **Or** select the server icon and press Command E for Eject.

- ▼ **Or** Control-click on a server icon to get the contextual menu; choose "Eject."

What You've Learned

▼ How to check the Network preferences for your connection settings.

▼ How to tell your Mac in which order to try the possible connections.

▼ How to create a new connection.

▼ How to use the Network Diagnostics tool for finding the source of a connection problem.

▼ How to set up your email accounts.

▼ How to use the Connection Doctor to troubleshoot your email accounts.

▼ Where to get the information you need for the connection.

▼ How to share files between computers on a network:

- How to connect two or more Macs.

- How to turn on Personal File Sharing and name your Mac.

- How to connect to any other Mac on the network, either as a Registered User with full access to the other computer, or as a Guest with limited access to only the Public folder and the Drop Box.

▼ How to share files on a network with Bonjour.

▼ How to send files to anyone through Bonjour or iChat.

▼ How to set up a Mac running on old operating system so your new Mac can get files from it.

Keyboard Shortcuts

Command K	In the Finder, opens the "Connect to Server" window
Command E	Disconnect from the selected server
Command 2	In iChat, opens the Bonjour window

11

Goals

Learn how easy it is to keep multiple computers synchronized.

Discover how syncing is different in Tiger from earlier versions.

Lesson **11**

Use Your .Mac Account to Stay in Sync

A .Mac (pronounced *dot mac*) account is a wonderful thing. It has so many worthwhile features, plus an email account (and alias accounts, which are really great too) that you can check anywhere in the world. In this lesson I'll provide an overview of a .Mac account and focus on the synchronization feature that is particularly useful if you have more than one Mac: Perhaps you have a desktop machine plus a laptop plus a Mac at work and sometimes you update your Address Book on one Mac and sometimes on another. Sometimes you make Safari bookmarks on one computer and sometimes on another, or you add events and to-do items in iCal on this or that machine. iSync will make them all match. And it will update your iPod, Palm, or digital phone with the latest data from those applications.

The Benefits of a .Mac Account

A .Mac account includes a large number of features, explained in an overview below. For step-by-step details of each one of these features and exactly how to use them, please see *Cool Mac Apps,* by John Tollett and me.

Syncing, the focus of this chapter, is just one of the many features included with .Mac, but it's particularly useful for those of us who use more than one Mac. If you use just one Mac and you never leave home and never need to get to your Mail or Address Book or files from your home machine, then you can skip the rest of this chapter altogether! Well, skip it after you read about the benefits a .Mac account provides.

 iDisk: The iDisk is a central part of your .Mac life. Your .Mac account comes with a total of 250 megabytes of disk space on Apple's servers (and you can always buy more). You can divide up that 250 megabytes however you like between your email storage and your iDisk. You can access anything you put on your iDisk from just about any computer anywhere in the world. Use it to backup files, store files, or transfer files from one place to another. You can put files in your Public folder on your iDisk so you or anyone you like can download the files anywhere in the world. You can access your iDisk from a PC, so it can be a great way to send files back and forth from PC to Mac. There's no FTP address to memorize—just drag and drop. You can password protect your iDisk, and you can allow selected users to put files in your iDisk for you; use the "iDisk" pane of the .Mac preferences, as shown on page 289.

 Mail: Access your email account on the .Mac web site so you can get your mail using any kind of computer anywhere in the world. It's an account **@mac.com.** I've gotten my .Mac mail from Pokhara, Nepal, and Beni Suef, Egypt, among other places. On your desktop Mac, you can put email messages from any account into a .Mac folder that you will later be able to access through the Mac.com web site.

Your mac.com email address is not dependent on your ISP, so if you change Internet providers, you still keep your email address. Under one .Mac account you can buy up to ten email accounts for your family. And you can have aliases—email addresses of different names that all come to your .Mac mail account. With an alias, you can keep track of who is selling your email address, and you can throw away the alias address so that person can never contact you again.

You get 125 megabytes of email storage* and can send attachments up to ten megabytes. And there's no annoying advertisement at the bottom of every message you send.

The web mail includes a spell checker, signatures that can include both text and photos, mail forwarding, and more.

*Actually, you get 250 megabytes of server space to divvy up between your email and your iDisk.

Address Book: With a .Mac account, you can synchronize your Address Book on your desktop Mac with your online Address Book. This means you have full access to everyone you know and love while you are traveling anywhere in the world, with or without your own computer. If you add contacts to the online Address Book while you're visiting Budapest, you can sync it to your desktop Mac when you get home. And you can even add names to a "Quick Address" list for extra-easy access while sending email from the web site or when sending iCards.

Bookmarks: As you're traveling from country to country or just from office to office down the hall, with a .Mac account you can make sure your favorite web page bookmarks are accessible no matter which computer or browser you're using. If you add or delete bookmarks while away from your own Mac, you can synchronize them when you get home so your desktop Mac matches your online collection.

HomePage: Create your own web pages and post them immediately with just a few clicks of a button. It's really amazing—my 75-year-old mother has a dozen web pages online. You can post your iMovies or create a slideshow web site using your iPhoto photos and a button click, or use the HomePage templates to create online newsletters, résumés, baby announcements, school events, invitations, and more. You can also write your own HTML pages and use them on their own or combine them with HomePage templates.

With HomePage, you can also post large files for others to download. And protect any page at all with a password. With your .Mac account you get 250 megabytes of space for your web site, email, and iDisk (you can always buy more space). And no stupid ads! No banners! No pop-ups!

iCards: iCards are elegant online greeting cards that you can send and receive to and from Macs and PCs. You don't need a .Mac membership to send or receive iCards, but with a membership you can create your own cards that use your own images. Also, with a membership you can take advantage of the Quick Address feature that stores your most-often used addresses so you can send cards with a quick click. And as a member, you can submit your own photos for possible inclusion in the Members' Portfolio of digital images.

Backup: Backup is a separate application that makes it easy to save backup files to your iDisk, another drive, a CD, or a DVD. Or if your backup files take up huge amounts of space, Backup can spread the data over several disks. You can schedule it to run regularly and automatically, and even tell it to search for specific kinds of files to back up. And a great part of this process is that if you crash your computer or it gets stolen or you accidentally destroy an important file, Backup makes it easy to restore.

Access Your Data Online

A side benefit of syncing your data to your .Mac account is that then it's all available online. Your .Mac email, including any Smart Mailboxes and signatures you've created, is set up so you can access it online anywhere in the world. You can also get to your Address Book contacts and your Safari bookmarks. You can do this on a Mac or a PC in Internet cafes from Atlanta to Zimbabwe. Or of course on your own traveling laptop.

To access your email online, go to **www.mac.com.** Click the "Mail" tab in the blue bar. It will ask you to log in. Do so, and there's your mail.

To access your Address Book online, do the steps above but click the "Address Book" tab in the blue bar and log in. If you're already logged in to Mail, just click the "Address Book" tab.

Access and use your Safari bookmarks anywhere

To use your bookmarks is a little different since you might not be using Safari at all. But it's very easy and interesting.

1 Go to **www.mac.com;** click the "Bookmarks" tab in the blue bar. You will be asked to log in.

2 Click the "Open Bookmarks" button you see.

— continued

3 A bookmark pane appears on the screen that contains all of the bookmarks you synced to your .Mac account. Amazing. You even have preferences, as shown below, right.

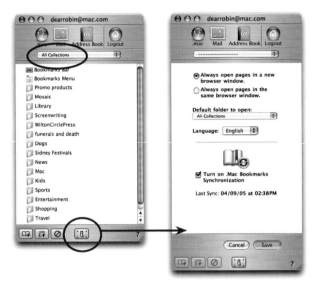

Notice you can also use these buttons in the toolbar to instantly access Mail and Address Book.

4 To go to a bookmarked page, single-click any one of the folders or individual web addresses. When you click on a Collection folder (which is one of your Collections that you made on your own Mac) or on "Bookmarks Bar" or "Bookmarks Menu," that item appears in the tiny menu at the top, along with all of the other bookmarks. Other folders of bookmarks will appear with disclosure triangles. Single-click a bookmark with a globe icon to go straight to that page.

All of your bookmarks are always listed in this menu.

5 To make a new bookmark, click the "Add Bookmark" button at the bottom of the .Mac bookmarks pane. It's the open book with a **+** sign.

Type a name for the bookmark in the field shown below, and type the web address (URL) as well. Choose where to store the bookmark in the "Add Bookmark To" menu. Click "Add."

Notice you can also add a new folder.

6 To delete a bookmark, click the Delete button (the circle with the line through it). An **x** will appear next to every bookmark and folder. Click the **x** next to the one you want to delete. You will be asked to confirm the deletion. You can only delete one at a time.

7 To reorganize, rename, or copy bookmarks or folders—you can't. You'll have to do that on your own Mac in Safari and then sync your bookmarks back to your .Mac account.

All of the changes you make to your bookmarks through this pane will be stored in your .Mac account. The next time you sync, they will be added to all the computers that you sync it with.

Sync with Other Devices

Besides syncing your Mac computers with each other, you can sync your contact information and calendars with a PDA such as a Palm device, your iPod, or a Bluetooth-enabled or USB mobile phone. To sync with these other devices, you do NOT need to have a .Mac account! Instead of using the .Mac preferences, you'll use the **iSync application.**

Sync your iPod

Before syncing any device, you have to first add it to iSync. You only need to do this once. Make sure you have the latest software update on your iPod (check the Software Update preferences, page 60, if you're not sure).

To add an iPod to iSync, first connect the iPod to the Mac as usual. Then open the iSync application (it's in your Applications folder). From the Devices menu, choose "Add Device...." In the little window that appears, double-click "iPod."

Use iTunes to add music to your iPod. Use iSync to add contacts and calendars.

A few tips for other devices

It's best to sync your phone and your Palm OS device with only one computer or you could end up with duplicates or incorrect information. But perhaps you've been syncing your phone with your home computer and now you want to sync it with your office Mac: First *remove* it from your home Mac, erase the data on it, and then add the device to the office Mac and sync it there.

Selectively choose what information you want transferred so you don't waste space and memory on the smaller device. For instance, for your phone, you might want to make a Group of contacts (see page 91) in the Address Book and transfer just that Group. Keep in mind that iSync will only transfer contacts that include telephone numbers to a phone! In iCal, you can choose to sync individual calendars instead of everything that's in there.

If you're syncing to a Palm OS device, it's faster if the HotSync Progress window is in front and active.

To add a Palm or phone to iSync, please see the Help files: Open the iSync application, then go to the Help menu and choose "iSync Help." There are just too many details for the individual items to explain them all here! And the help files will be very up-to-date.

To remove a device, open iSync. Select the device. From the Devices menu, choose "Remove Device." You can then sync it to another Mac as if it's syncing for the first time: Choose "Erase data on device, then sync."

Turn Off All Syncing

To disable syncing altogether for all devices and for your .Mac account, use the iSync application preferences. Open the iSync application (it's in your Applications folder). From the iSync menu, choose "Preferences…." Uncheck the box to "Enable syncing on this computer."

The next time you choose to sync, you can use the .Mac preferences as explained on pages 290–291. As soon as you click "Sync Now" in the .Mac prefences Sync pane, this button in the application preferences pane will automatically check itself on.

What You've Learned

▼ The benefits of the various features of a .Mac account.

▼ The cost of a .Mac membership and where to sign up for one.

▼ The difference between the .Mac preferences and the iSync application.

▼ How to synchronize Address Book, Mail, iCal, and Safari bookmarks between two or more Macs.

▼ How to put the iSync menu in the menu bar.

▼ How to check which computers are registered.

▼ How to register a Mac running a previous version of OS X.

▼ How to "start over" by resetting sync data.

▼ Why conflicts might appear and how to resolve them.

▼ How to access your .Mac data online anywhere, including bookmarks.

▼ How to transfer Address Book and iCal information to your iPod.

▼ The basics of how to sync devices like PDAS or mobile phones.

▼ How to disable all syncing.

12

Goals

Learn how to use Spotlight effectively and efficiently.

Get used to looking for and using Spotlight searching in other applications.

Learn to create and use Smart Folders.

Experienced users, transition to Spotlight searching instead of clicking windows open and closed.

Find What You Want, Fast— with Spotlight

Spotlight is not just a new search feature in Tiger, it's a new way of working with your Mac. Once you get accustomed to its speed, versatility, and usefulness, you'll find yourself using Spotlight regularly instead of opening and closing folders and windows.

If you find you perform a certain search regularly, save it as a Smart Folder. Files that match the search criteria are automatically listed in this folder and the folder updates itself every time a matching file is created or changed.

You'll never be the same.

The Many Faces of Spotlight

Spotlight really has **four** different ways of working. You'll find yourself using one or the other at different times. Experiment with each one so you'll know which is the most appropriate for what you need to do. Details for each option are on the following pages.

1. Spotlight menu

Click the Spotlight icon in the upper-right of the menu bar, **or** use the keyboard shortcut, Command Spacebar.

Type your query into the field that appears and Spotlight instantly starts presenting results. As you type more letters, the search narrows and updates.

Access to the Spotlight menu is available no matter which application you're using—you don't have to go to the Finder to run a search. See pages 310–311 for all the details.

2. Spotlight window

To get this Spotlight window that displays more information: **Either** click the option to "Show All" at the top of the Spotlight menu, as shown above. **Or** use the keyboard shortcut, Command Option Spacebar, to display this window directly. See pages 312–313 for details.

The keyboard shortcut works in most applications so you don't have to go to the Finder first.

3. Spotlight-powered search in the Finder, plus Smart Folders

When you type into the Search field in a Finder window, Spotlight instantly kicks in and show you simple results directly in the window. It automatically looks in the last "location" that was chosen ("Home" in the example below).

If you don't see this "Save" button and the **+** sign, open your window wider.

Click the **+** sign to get the options to narrow your search.

You can save a search as a **Smart Folder** (see pages 316–317) that will automatically update itself.

Choose "Find…" from the File menu (or Press Command F) to get a window similar to the one above, but with two refinements ("Kind" and "Last Opened") already set up. See pages 314–317 for details, including **Smart Folders.**

4. Spotlight-powered search in many applications

Mail and Smart Mailboxes, pages 318–321.

Address Book and Smart Groups, pages 322–325.

System Preferences, page 326.

Automator, page 327.

Spotlight in text-based applications, page 328.

Open and Save As dialog boxes, pages 329–330.

But Before You Begin

There are several things you might want to know before you change your life using Spotlight. In the Spotlight preferences, you can choose which **categories** of items you want Spotlight to search through. You can also choose certain disks and folders that you (or anyone using your machine) *cannot* search through, giving you some extra **privacy.**

And on the following pages are some tips for searching.

Choose the categories for searching

1 From the Apple menu, choose "System Preferences...."

2 Single-click on the "Spotlight" icon.

3 Click the "Search Results" tab if it isn't already highlighted.

4 *Uncheck* boxes for categories you *don't want* Spotlight to search.

Create some privacy

1 If you haven't already, open the Spotlight preferences, as explained on the opposite page.

2 Click the "Privacy" tab.

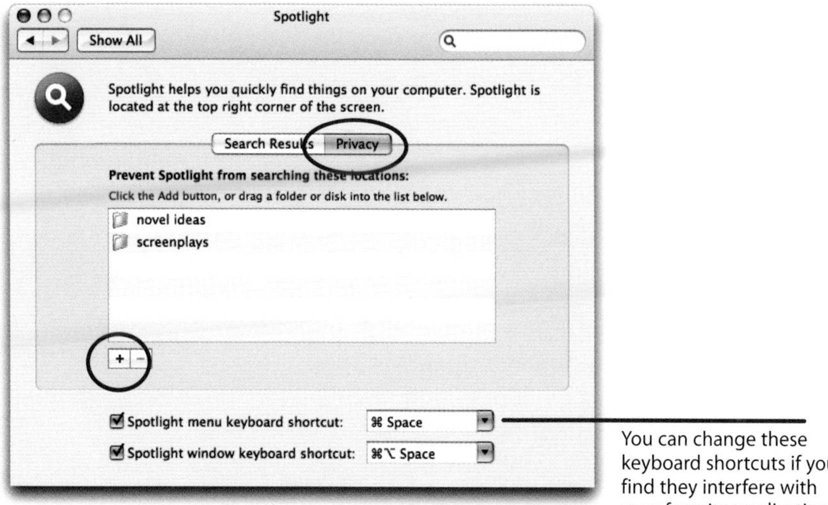

You can change these keyboard shortcuts if you find they interfere with your favorite applications.

3 Click the **+** sign to open a dialog box where you can choose any folder or disk on your Mac that you don't want Spotlight to search.

Or drag any folder or disk icon from the Finder and drop it into this pane.

Note: This isn't a very *safe* privacy feature because anyone using your computer can just open the preferences and remove these items.

Keyboard shortcuts to open Spotlight

Notice in the illustration above that these preferences also include options for you to change the existing keyboard shortcuts or to turn them off altogether (uncheck the boxes).

Don't search just file names

Spotlight doesn't just search file names. It searches the contents of email messages, it knows who sent you email, it can look through the contact information in your Address Book, images and graphics, calendars and events and to-do lists, System Preferences, PDF text, the contents of TextEdit pages (but not text clippings), even iChat logs (if you previously chose to log them).

Expand the search with metadata

Spotlight also looks in the **metadata** that every file contains. Metadata includes information about who created the file, when it was created and modified, the copyright date, the file type, the color space for a photo or image, even what kind of camera a particular photo was taken with. Different kinds of files have different kinds of metadata associated with them.

To make a metadata attribute appear in the parameter menu, select it in the list and then check the box to "Add to Favorites."

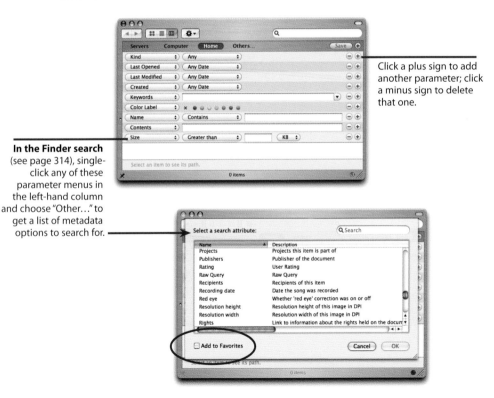

Click a plus sign to add another parameter; click a minus sign to delete that one.

In the Finder search (see page 314), single-click any of these parameter menus in the left-hand column and choose "Other…" to get a list of metadata options to search for.

Expand your repertoire of search terms

You're not limited to searching just for *words* that might be found in a file. In the Finder Spotlight search, you can use the existing parameters to find particular categories of files. For instance, you can look for "music" to find all your music files, or "images today" to find all the images you have opened today.

Leave the search field empty when you use these parameters if you want to find all files of a particular type.

Use keywords when necessary

There are some files that, even with all the options in Spotlight, still won't be found because there is nothing associated with them that Spotlight can decipher. For these files, you can add your own **keywords.** For instance, the example below is a music file of a Gregorian chant written by Hildegard von Bingen in the early 12th century. I can search for "music," "bingen," and other data, but if I search for "gregorian," this piece of music won't be found. So I added "gregorian" and "chant" to the Get Info window for this file and for all the other Gregorian chants I have on my Mac. Now Spotlight can find them.

To add a keyword, select the file. Then press Command I to get the Get Info window. Type your keywords into the "Spotlight Comments" area.

If you have more than one file to which you want to add keywords, select one file, then press Command *Option* I. Now as you select other files, this Get Info window automatically displays the information for the currently selected file.

Spotlight Menu

The Spotlight menu is available no matter which application you are using at the moment (although this is *not* the tool to use to search within your application, such as searching the text on a visible web page or in your word processor).

To open the Spotlight menu:

1 Simply click on the Spotlight icon in the upper-right of the menu bar.

2 A small field appears. Start typing in it.

Results appear instantly in the Spotlight menu, as shown below. The more letters you type, the narrower the search becomes.

To use the Spotlight menu:

Below are callouts of the various parts of the Spotlight menu. Use the Spotlight menu for a quick search for something you think can be easily found.

Single-click the **X** to delete everything in the field.

Single-click "Show All" to display the Spotlight window, as shown on the following page.

Single-click any item to open it.

These are the categories that Spotlight is searching. See page 306 for a list of the categories possible.

This opens the same preferences you see on pages 306–307.

Keyboard shortcuts

Show All	When "Show All" is highlighted, hit Return to open the Spotlight window.
Top Hit	*Hold down* the Command key and tap the Return key to open the Top Hit file.

Spotlight Window

Use the Spotlight window when you would like to be able to sort (organize) the results, see details about individual items, or preview images and movies. **To open the Spotlight window,** press Command Option Spacebar, **or** choose "Show All" from the Spotlight menu, as explained on the previous page.

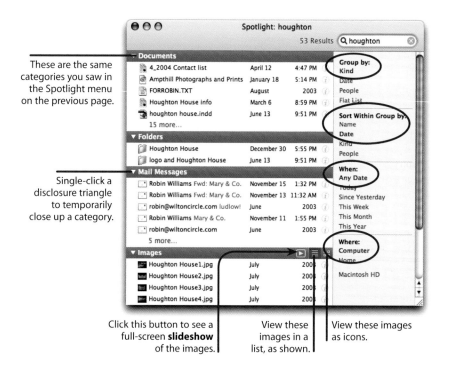

These are the same categories you saw in the Spotlight menu on the previous page.

Single-click a disclosure triangle to temporarily close up a category.

Click this button to see a full-screen **slideshow** of the images.

View these images in a list, as shown.

View these images as icons.

Enter text in the search field (unless you chose "Show All" from the Spotlight menu search, in which case the search field is already filled in).

To organize the results, first choose an option in the right-hand pane under "Group by," then "Sort Within Group by." You can see above by the blue color that these items are grouped by "Kind" and sorted (alphabetized) by "Name."

To filter the results, choose a time frame, if you like. Above, you can see the results are from "Any Date."

To limit the results, choose a location, "Where," for Spotlight to search. Above, you can see that Spotlight has been limited to just the "Home" folder.

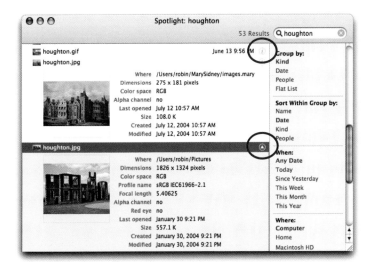

This is an example of grouping the results by "People." Spotlight displays each person who has authored a file that contains the words you searched for.

Within each "People" category, the results above are organized by "Date."

To view a preview of an image **or details** of a file, single-click the "*i*" button, circled below. If the file is a movie, you can click its play button to view the actual footage; if it's music, you can listen to it.

To close these details, single-click the triangle, circled below.

Spotlight in the Finder

There are two ways to use Spotlight in the Finder, both of which use your Finder window. You can do a **quick search** by simply typing in the search field. Or press Command F to get a more **specific search** window with options to narrow your search. Use the Finder Spotlight when you want to limit your search to certain disks, folders, or parameters.

Quick search in a Finder window

Below are the **results** of a quick search for "iambic penta." As soon as you start typing in the search field, results appear. Also, a bar appears that tells you exactly where Spotlight looked (in the example below, it searched the "Home" folder).

In this window, you can easily choose another location for Spotlight to search—just single-click one of the locations in the bar, shown below.

You can also click the **+** button that now appears (circled, below) to add more parameters for narrowing your search, as shown on the opposite page.

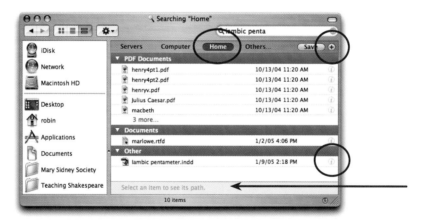

To see where a file is located, single-click any result; the path to that file (the folders within folders) will appear at the bottom of the list.

To open the folder that holds the selected file, press Command R (or Control-click, right-click, or use the Action menu to choose, "Open Enclosing Folder").

To see more information about a file, click the "*i*" on the right side.

To open that file, double-click it.

Specific search in a Finder window

On the Desktop, press Command F and the active window will switch to what you see below. If no window is active, this new one will open. This window includes the search field, and the location bar is already visible.

Choose a location to search.

This Find window also provides two parameters ready for you to work with. To add more, click the plus sign; to delete any, click its minus sign.

To change the options, single-click on a parameter menu to choose a different option. Start with the menu on the left, as shown above, which will change the specifics in the next menu to the right, which might then create a new field for you to enter a new parameter, also shown above.

The "Save" button is to create Smart Folders, which are explained on the following pages.

Finder and Smart Folders

Once you do a great search in the Finder via Spotlight, you might like to create a **Smart Folder** that automatically keeps track of every file that fits that search. This folder doesn't store the original files—the originals stay in their original folders, and the Smart Folder just keeps a list of everything.

For instance, you might want a Smart Folder that contains all the various presentations you've made so you don't have to go looking through numerous folders to find a particular one. If so, make a Smart Folder that just stores presentation files.

Or you might have used the Labels feature on your Mac (see page 140) to color-code all the files that belong to a certain project. For instance, your newsletter might include a **document** in the application Pages, **images** from the last event, **word processing files** your authors have sent you, and a **spread-sheet chart** from AppleWorks. And you used the Labels to give them all a label color of green. Your Smart Folder can keep track of all the green-labeled files in one place for you, even though the files themselves are organized into their own particular folders. The Smart Folder updates automatically as new files are labeled or old files are trashed.

To create a Smart Folder:

1 At the Finder, press Command F to open Spotlight in a Finder window.

2 Define your parameters. Below is a simple search of all files in my Home folder that are presentations. Notice there is *nothing* typed into the search field at the top of the window because I want to find *all* presentations regardless of their names.

3 Click the "Save" button, which is just below the search field. You will be asked to name this Smart Folder and where to save it. In the example below, I saved this into my Home folder, "robin."

If you want this folder to be visible in your Sidebar, check the box to "Add To Sidebar." Click "Save."

4 Now that the Smart Folder is saved, all you need to do is double-click on it and your Mac will display all the files that match the criteria you originally set. (If the Smart Folder is in the Sidebar, just single-click on it.)

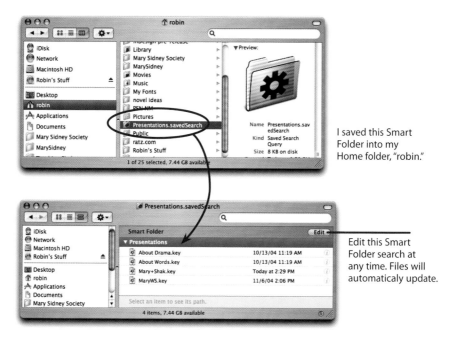

I saved this Smart Folder into my Home folder, "robin."

Edit this Smart Folder search at any time. Files will automaticaly update.

Spotlight in Other Applications

You can find Spotlight-enabled searches in many other applications. Some of them also let you create other forms of Smart Folders (as explained on the previous pages).

Mail search

In Mail, Spotlight searches very thoroughly. It's very simple.

1 Choose an account in the Mailboxes drawer (shown below, left).

2 Enter a word or phrase in the search field; results immediately appear.

3 A new bar also appears, as shown below. In this bar you can choose which account to search, and which part of the email to search.

Choose "All Mailboxes" or just the one account that is showing.

"Entire Message" includes not only the message, but the From, To, and Subject lines as well.

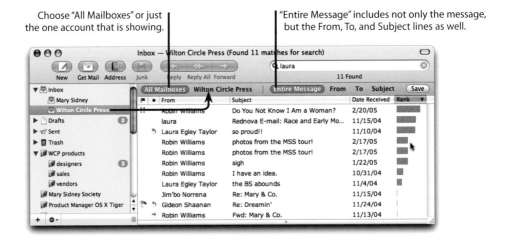

Smart Mailboxes in Mail

You can also create **Smart Mailboxes** that will hold all the email messages that meet certain search criteria. If you are familiar with the Rules (filters) you can create in Mail, as explained on page 87, you'll notice there are a couple of differences between Rules and Smart Mailboxes.

- A Rule is an *action* that is applied to a message, such as filtering certain email into a certain folder. The *original* email is sorted into the folder.

- A Smart Mailbox contains messages that match search criteria. No action is taken on the messages.

- A Smart Mailbox does not contain the *original* message, thus the same message can be "stored" in a number of Smart Mailboxes.

- A Smart Mailbox automatically updates itself as messages come in or are deleted.

- A Smart Mailbox applies the search rules to mail that is already in your box, not just on future incoming mail.

Below you see an example of several Smart Mailboxes in the drawer. The one named "WCP Products" is actually a Smart **Folder** that contains three other Smart **Mailboxes.** The folder is just for organizational purposes. Both are explained on the following page.

A **Smart Folder** has a disclosure triangle to its left, indicating it holds other mailboxes.

These other five folders shown here are **Smart Mailboxes.**

There are several ways to **create a Smart Mailbox.** One is from the Mailbox menu (below) and another is the Save button, as shown on the opposite page.

To create a Smart Mailbox from the Mailbox menu:

1 If you go to the Mailbox menu, you'll see there are two similar options, "New Smart Mailbox Folder…" and "New Smart Mailbox…."

The **Smart Mailbox Folder** creates a folder with no search parameters; it is simply for organizing other **Smart Mailboxes** inside (as shown on the previous page). If you choose this, simply name the folder and click OK.

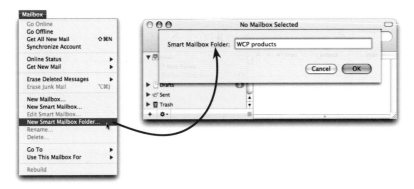

If you want your Smart Mailbox to be *inside* of an existing Smart Folder, first select that folder in the Mailboxes drawer; if not, make sure that folder is *not* selected. When you choose "New Smart Mailbox…," the search box shown below appears. Choose your parameters and click OK.

2 If you need to edit the parameters of your new Smart Mailbox, select it, then either Control-click, right-click, or go to the Mailbox menu and choose "Edit Smart Mailbox…."

To create a Smart Mailbox from the Save button:

1 Do a search as usual, as explained on the previous pages.

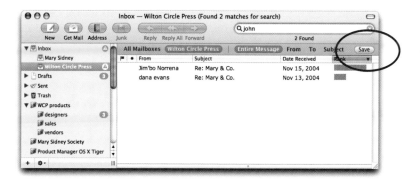

2 If the search gives you what you need and you think you'll want to use the same search again, click the "Save" button.

3 The saved search is automatically named with the search phrase you just used. You can refine your search here, if you like. When ready, click OK.

4 If you need to edit the parameters of your new Smart Mailbox, select it, then either Control-click, right-click, or go to the Mailbox menu and choose "Edit Smart Mailbox…."

Address Book

You can do a standard, simple search for anyone or any information in your collection of contacts. And you can also do a Spotlight search of anyone in your Address Book that searches your entire hard disk for everything related to that person.

To search your Address Book for a contact:

1 **To search for a contact within a Group,** single-click the Group name you want to search.

   To search your entire database of contacts, click the "All" group, as shown below.

2 Single-click in the search field.

3 Type the first couple of letters of the name of the person you want to find, either first or last name or the business name. As you type, results will appear in the center "Name" pane.

4 Type more letters to narrow your search, or single-click one of the contacts in the "Name" pane.

Click this **X** to delete everything in the search field.

If there is even one character in this field, you won't see all of your contacts.

5 **To display all of your contacts again,** click the **X** in the search field, and single-click on the "All" group.

To search for a person or business in Spotlight:

1 Find the person you want to Spotlight, as explained on the previous page.

2 From the Action menu (the gearwheel, circled below), choose "Spotlight 'This Person'" (where 'This Person' is the name of the contact you just searched for; that name automatically appears in the menu). See the illustration below.

3 You will get the Spotlight window, as explained on page 312. It will show you every file on your computer that is connected with this person, such as email she's sent, files she's mentioned within, documents she has created and sent to you, images of her, and more.

Smart Groups in Address Book

A Smart Group is a list of contacts that automatically updates itself as contacts meet its criteria. For instance, you might want a Smart Group that automatically adds people who work for a certain company or who are part of your salon. You can create a Smart Group that tells you when someone's birthday or anniversary is approaching. Or you might want to gather a list of everyone in a particular city without having to find them all in your Address Book—a Smart Group will find existing contacts and automatically collect them.

Some of these searches require, of course, that you have a particular field on your card and that it has data in it. For instance, you can't have a Smart Group that tells you when a birthday is coming up if you don't have the Birthday field on your cards. For directions on how to **add new fields** to individual cards or to all cards, please see page 91.

To create a Smart Group:

1 Either from the File menu across the top of the screen or from the Action menu in the Address Book, choose "New Smart Group…."

2 In the sheet that drops down, as shown below, choose your parameters.

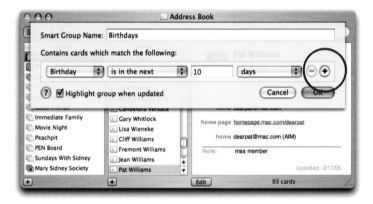

3 Click the **+** sign several more times to add several more parameters, if you need them.

4 If you want to see a visual clue that a new item has been added to the Smart Group, be sure to check the box to "Highlight group when updated." Then when a new item is automatically added, the Smart Group will change color, as shown below.

Here you see three Smart Groups. This one is in a different color because it added a new contact to itself.

5 As mentioned on the opposite page, some of the parameters require that you add that field to the template, as explained on page 91.

System Preferences

As explained in Lesson 6, Spotlight also works in System Preferences. This is great when you want to open a System Preference to do something in particular, but you're not sure which one is the one you need.

To search in System Preferences, simply type into the search field. As you type, Spotlight highlights all the possible preferences that might help you.

When you click on one of the options in the menu that appears, Spotlight highlights the best preference for that option in a bright white spotlight, as shown below, then opens it for you automatically.

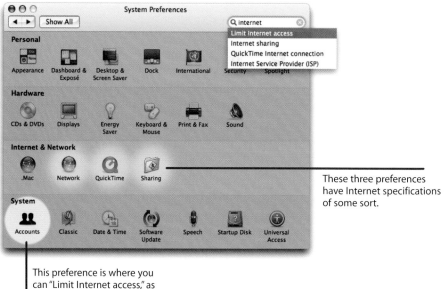

These three preferences have Internet specifications of some sort.

This preference is where you can "Limit Internet access," as selected in the menu above.

Automator

Automator, as I explain in detail in Lesson 16, lets you automate repetitive tasks with the click of a few buttons. Spotlight is great in Automator because sometimes you know what you want to do, but you don't know which action will do it. Just use the search field, as shown below.

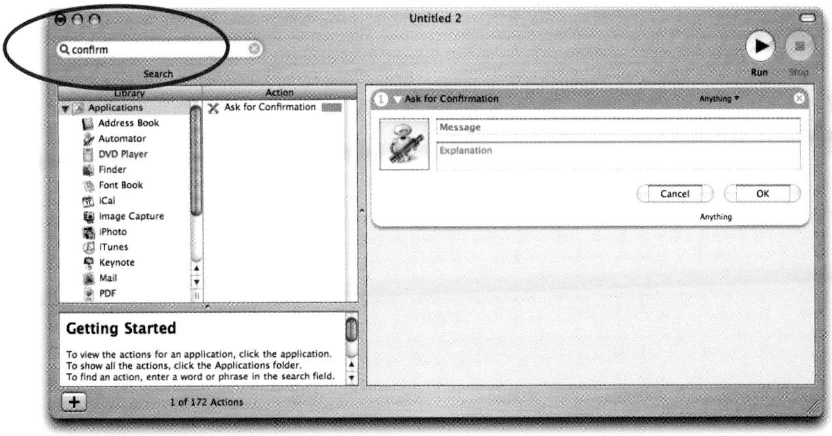

Spotlight in text-based applications

In some applications on your Mac, you can select a word or phrase and let Spotlight find other occurrences of that word or phrase on your Mac. This might be useful when you're browsing the web and find the name of someone in the news and it makes you say, "Hmm, didn't she send me an email last month?" Or if you're in your word processor and you're writing an essay and you want to find the article you saved earlier on a topic that's mentioned.

For instance, try this in Safari or TextEdit:

1 On a web page, press-and-drag to select a word or phrase.

2 Control-click (or right-click) on that selected word or phrase.

3 From the contextual menu that appears, choose "Search in Spotlight." Remember, Spotlight searches your Mac, not the Internet!

Open dialog box

In any Open dialog box, as shown below, you can search for a **file name.** Spotlight will locate all files that your open application thinks it can open and display, plus all folders with that search phrase in the name (it does *not* search contents or to-do list items, etc., in this dialog). Any Smart Folders you have placed in the Sidebar will also appear here.

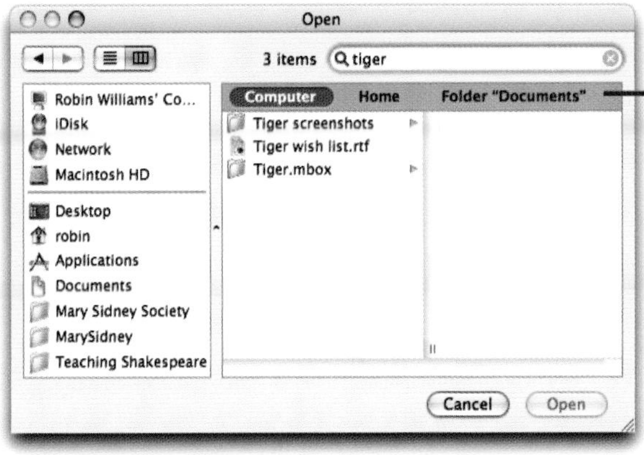

After you start typing a search entry, this bar appears.

Narrow or expand your search by clicking on one of these locations.

Save As dialog box

You can do a search in the Save As dialog box and Spotlight will find **folders** for you to save into. Any Smart Folders in the Sidebar will also appear here.

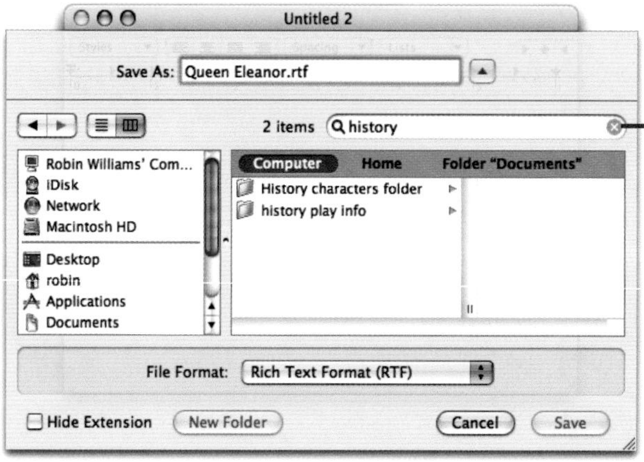

Click the X to delete the entire search string.

What You've Learned

▼ The different ways to access Spotlight.

▼ How to choose or change the categories for searching.

▼ How to prevent selected folders from being searched.

▼ How to expand the search with metadata and add a metadata parameter to your list.

• How to add searchable keywords to files.

• How to use Spotlight in the menu bar.

• How to use the Spotlight window.

• How to use Spotlight in a Finder window.

• How to create Smart Folders.

• How to take advantage of Spotlight in other applications.

• How to create Smart Mailboxes in Mail.

• How to create Smart Groups in Address Book.

• How to use Spotlight in Open and Save As dialog boxes.

Keyboard Shortcuts

Command F	Search in Finder window with search parameters and metadata
Command Spacebar	Search via the menu bar
Option Command Spacebar	Search window with sort categories

13

Goals   To help you think of Dashboard and widgets as your primary
sources for accessing information without interfering with
your current workspaces

To show you how to add, delete, and customize widgets,
as well as how to download additional widgets from the
Internet

Dashboard—Important Information at your Fingertips

Ever want to know what time it is right now in London? Or what the weather is like where you mother lives? Do you need to track the plane your daughter is taking to Istanbul—including whether it's going to leave on time and from what terminal—and then follow the flight path across the world in real time?

These are just a few of the many things you can do with literally the click of one button, using Dashboard. The information appears to you in the form of widgets. Some widgets are already on your Mac, but many others are being created by people and developers. Oh, the things we will see!

Take a Look at Dashboard

Dashboard provides quick access to information customized just for you, displayed in the form of **widgets.** Dashboard pops up in a split second only when you want it. With the click of a button, it goes away just as quickly. Below is an example of my **Dashboard,** with the **Widgets Bar** showing (the Widgets Bar doesn't appear until you ask for it; see page 336).

When you activate Dashboard, the widgets instantly appear on top of a greyed-out Desktop, on top of any windows or applications you have open. Do what you need, then click in any blank area to send them all away. Use the Widgets Bar to add and delete items, as explained on page 336.

Each of these items is a widget.

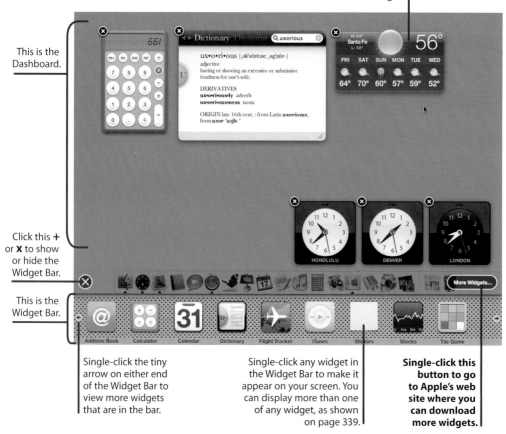

This is the Dashboard.

Click this **+** or **X** to show or hide the Widget Bar.

This is the Widget Bar.

Single-click the tiny arrow on either end of the Widget Bar to view more widgets that are in the bar.

Single-click any widget in the Widget Bar to make it appear on your screen. You can display more than one of any widget, as shown on page 339.

Single-click this button to go to Apple's web site where you can download more widgets.

Discover Different Kinds of Widgets

There are three different kinds of widgets, although they are all so interesting and easy to work with, you won't really care which is which!

▼ **Information widgets** work with data from the Internet. You can check external events such as the weather anywhere in the world, the flight status of any plane, or current prices of your favorite stocks. You must be connected to the Internet to get the information for these widgets.

▼ **Application widgets** work with applications on your Mac. They typically provide a small and easy way of displaying the critical features of the main application. For instance, the iTunes widget is a small controller that gives you buttons—start, stop, play songs, and more—to listen to your Playlists or Internet radio without having the iTunes interface take up your whole screen. If the main application requires the Internet to function, so will the application widget.

▼ **Accessory widgets** are self-contained little utilities that provide a variety of features. Widgets such as clocks, calculators, notes, or timers are accessories. You do not have to have Internet access to use these, nor are they dependent on an application.

Activate Dashboard and the Widgets

Dashboard is built into your Mac—just single-click the Dashboard icon in your Dock to **make it appear,** or press the F12 key.

If you're using a **laptop,** you might not have an F12 key, or it might be used for something else. You can change the keyboard shortcut; see page 340.

Add Widgets to Your Dashboard

To add widgets to your onscreen Dashboard, first bring up the **Widget Bar:** Single-click on the plus sign you see in the bottom-left of your screen. (The plus sign then turns into an **X** to **close** the Widgets Bar; see page 334.)

Address Book   Calculator   Calendar   Dictionary   Flight Tracker   iTunes   Stickies   Stocks   Tile Game

> **To add a widget,** single-click on it.

> **To see other widgets** that are already installed, single-click on one of the tiny arrows that appear at either end of the Widgets Bar.

Organize widgets on the screen in any arrangement you like—simply press anywhere in a widget and drag it around. They will stay where you put them, even after you put away Dashboard.

Remove Widgets from Your Dashboard

You can only remove widgets from the Dashboard when the Widget Bar is visible. So first display the Widget Bar: Single-click the plus sign shown above.

Now you will see an **X** in the upper-left corner of each widget. **To remove a widget,** click that **X**. It will stay in your Widget Bar until you want it again.

Put Dashboard Away

To put Dashboard away, single-click outside of any widget, *or* press your keyboard shortcut again. When you reopen Dashboard, your widgets are right where you left them.

Work with Widgets

Different sorts of widgets have different sorts of features. Experiment with them all! For instance, open the Unit Converter and check all the different sorts of conversions you can make.

Many widgets (not all) have a tiny *i* in a corner, the **info button.** It's not in the same corner for all widgets, and it won't even appear until your pointer gets close to it. So hover over the corners of a widget to see if an *i* appears, then click on it—the widget turns over so you can change preferences.

Single-click the *info* button
to flip the widget.

On the back side of many widgets are preferences for that particular item. For example, this information tells the Phone Book widget where to look.

Enter information into a field, then be sure to hit the Enter key to enter that data.

Experiment with Your Widgets!

Lots of different people create widgets and I can't explain here all the different things they will do. So be sure to pay attention to the sometimes-subtle visual clues that are built into widgets.

In the iTunes widget shown below, notice the tiny dot in the outer circle. That's a clue! Drag that tiny dot around to change the volume.

Notice the info button that appears (the *i*)—click on it to flip the widget and see what options are available on the other side. In this case, you can choose which iTunes Playlist to listen to.

In the Dictionary widget below, there are several visual clues, as shown.

The word "Thesaurus" is barely visible here. But it means there is a thesaurus entry for the word you looked up in the Dictionary. Single-click on "Thesaurus."

Back and forward arrows indicate you can return to words you previously looked up.

Now "Thesaurus" is highlighted, indicating you are looking at the thesaurus entry.

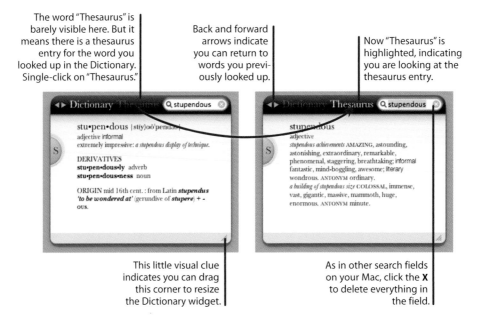

This little visual clue indicates you can drag this corner to resize the Dictionary widget.

As in other search fields on your Mac, click the **X** to delete everything in the field.

Display More than One of a Widget

You can display multiple copies of any kind of widget. For instance, you might like to know the weather in several different places, view the flight paths of a number of different flights, open several different dictionary widgets to compare words, or view a number of different conversions at the same time.

To display more than one of any kind of widget, open the Widget Bar (when Dashboard is showing, click the **+** sign in the bottom-left corner of your screen). Then just single-click the widget as many times as you want, one for each display on your screen. Each new widget shows up in the center of the screen. Just drag it to any position and it will stay there.

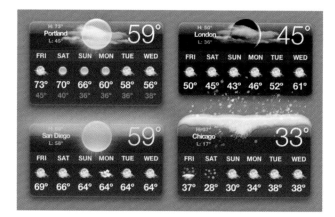

Here I can see at a glance what the weather is like (and whether it's day or night) in the different cities where my kids live.

TIP To change the picture in the tile puzzle, do this: When Dashboard is open, put the tile puzzle on your screen. Close Dashboard.

In the Finder, find the picture you want to use in the tile puzzle. Start dragging it to nowhere in particular. While you are dragging (don't let go of the mouse), press F12 (or whatever your shortcut is, if you've changed it) to open Dashboard. Drop the picture you're dragging onto the tile puzzle.

Change the Keyboard Shortcut to Open Dashboard

If you don't like the default shortcut that opens Dashboard, you can change it.

1 At the Finder, when Dashboard is *not* active, go to the Apple menu and choose "System Preferences…."

2 Single-click "Dashboard & Exposé."

3 In the preferences pane, as shown below, choose an Fkey from the menu (circled) to use as your shortcut.

To add one or more of the modifier keys to your shortcut, just press that key(s) while the little menu is open. The menu will change to reflect the key combination you are pressing. For instance, you might want to use Control F1 to activate Dashboard. So hold down the Control key and click the Dashboard menu, then choose ^F1 (^ indicates the Control key).

Modifier keys.

Options for a two-button mouse.

If you have a **two-button mouse** attached to your Mac, you will see the second column of menus, as shown above, where you can choose to use the middle or right mouse button to activate Dashboard. This is great for a laptop—I can't use a shortcut like F7 without holding down the fn key also. This means it takes two hands to open Dashboard. But with the middle mouse button assigned to Dashboard, I can click the button once and Dashboard instantly appears. It's great.

What You've Learned

▼ The different kinds of widgets available.

▼ How to show and hide the widgets.

▼ How to display the widgets you want to have available.

▼ How to flip widgets over and customize them.

▼ How to display more than one of any widget.

▼ How to remove a widget from your display.

▼ How to change the keyboard shortcut that displays your widgets.

▼ Where to go to get more widgets.

Keyboard Shortcuts

F12	Activate Dashboard (unless you changed it)
F12	Close Dashboard (or click anywhere except on Dashboard)

14

Goals   Provide an overview of iChat for video and audio messaging.

Accustom users to consider iChat for group chats and video conferences.

Lesson **14**

Multiple Audio and Video Messaging with iChat AV

In Lesson 4, on pages 102 through 105, I explained how to set up iChat, create your Buddy List, add or change a Buddy's photo, text-chat with one other person or with a group of people, exchange files, limit your availability, and save a printable copy of your chat. I also discussed how to audio chat with one other person, even if that person can't audio chat back to you, and how to do a video chat between two people. And even have a one-way video chat where she can see you but you can't see her (or vice versa).

So in this lesson I focus just on multiple audio and video chats. With Tiger, a very fast Mac, and iChat AV, you can have audio chats with up to ten people at a time. You can have a video conference with up to four people (including yourself). Amazing.

Video Chat with up to Three Other People

To video chat, of course you must have a video camera attached to your Mac. You can use Apple's cute little iSight camera, which costs about $150, or you can attach any FireWire video camera to your Mac.

With whom can you video conference?

A video conference with more than one person takes a powerful Mac and a good broadband connection; please see the specs on page 348. If you are able to *participate* in a video conference with more than one person, the camera icon in your Buddy name shows multiple cameras. If someone in your Buddy List is able to participate, she shows multiple cameras, as well. And it takes the most powerful Mac to *initiate* a video conference with up to four people.

In my home office we've got three desktop Macs and two laptops; in the Mary Sidney Society office across the hall is another tower; and upstairs in my library is a lovely iMac. Of these seven Macs, only two of them (the G5 desktop and the G4 PowerBook) are capable of video-conferencing with more than two people, and only the G5 can initiate it. Sigh.

This is the machine I work on. It can't do anything.

Open a video chat and invite others to join you

To *initiate* a video conference with more than one other person, you need a more powerful machine than you do to *join* a video conference. See the specifications on page 348.

1 Single-click on a Buddy name that shows multiple video camera icons. That person will get a message on her screen inviting her to a video chat. When she clicks the "Accept" button, she will appear in your video window, as shown below.

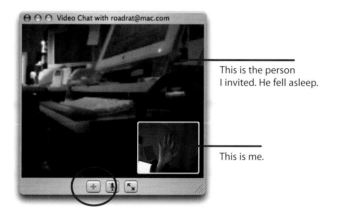

This is the person I invited. He fell asleep.

This is me.

2 To add two more people to your video conference, click the **+** sign; a menu drops down with the names of the people in your Buddy List *who are capable of joining you.* Too bad I can't show you what it looks like— it's really beautiful.

iChat AV preferences

You can make some minor adjustments in the video pane of the iChat preferences. You might try changing the "Bandwidth Limit" to see if it affects your video chat one way or another. Depending on your Internet connection and how many other people use it, a different setting can work better (or worse).

Requirements for 1-to-1 video chat

Minimum: 600 MHz G3, any G4, any G5 running OS X
100 Kbps Internet connection, both ways

Minimum requirements for 4-way video conference

To initiate a 4-way video chat, this is what you need:

Minimum: Dual 1 GHz G4 or any G5 running Tiger
384 Kbps Internet connection, both ways

Better: Dual 1 GHz G4, 1.8 GHz G5 running Tiger
600 Kbps Internet connection, both ways

Best: Dual 2 GHz G5 running Tiger
1500 Kbps Internet connection, both ways

To participate in a 4-way video chat, this is what you need:

Minimum: 1 GHz G4, or a dual 800 MHz G4, or any G5 running Tiger
100 Kbps Internet connection, both ways

Better: 1 GHz G4, or a dual 800 MHz G4, or any G5 running Tiger
200 Kbps Internet connection, both ways

Best: Any G5 running Tiger
500 Kbps Internet connection, both ways

What You've Learned

▼ How to initiate an audio chat and invite others to it.

▼ How to initiate a video chat and invite others to it.

▼ What the limitations are for conferencing.

▼ That you probably need to buy a bigger Mac for yourself and your entire family if you want to video conference with everyone.

15

Goals

Learn about Safari's convenient RSS feeds so you can transition to it for all your news and information

Learn how to organize your RSS feeds for maximum effectiveness.

Keep Up on the Latest News with Safari RSS Feeds

RSS stands for Really Simple Syndication. It is an Internet technology that "feeds" you news and information from a huge variety of sources. Until Apple's latest version of the Safari web browser, you needed a separate application to view these feeds. Now with Safari you can gather the RSS feeds you are interested in and display the headlines from many sources in one place—a web page. And you'll have access to them with one click of a button.

Not only can you gather news articles directly into the application that you probably already have open all day, but you can organize the information, filter the feeds, automatically update them, and more.

So What is RSS?

All major news organizations, as well as thousands of personal web logs and individual web sites, offer article summaries and headlines in the form of RSS feeds. Below is a sample of what an RSS feed from one section of the *New York Times* looks like in Safari.

You can drag the "Article Length" slider (shown below, on the right) to display more or less of an article, and use the categories to organize the information.

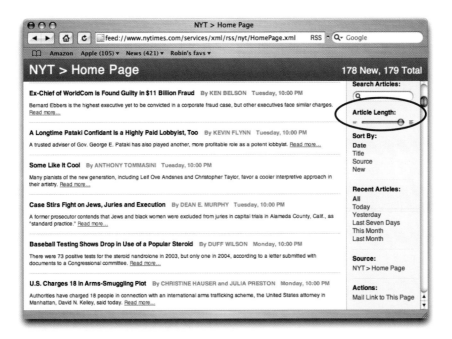

At any time you can add more feeds to Safari, delete ones you don't want to view, search through feeds for particular information, and even bookmark searches to which you want to return.

You can separate the various feeds into your own folders so with the click of a button you can view all the headlines from each particular area of your life. For instance, you might want to see just the technology headlines, or just the screenwriting headlines, or just the personal web log headlines.

View the Existing Feeds in Safari

Apple has provided a number of RSS feeds to get you started. Experiment with these for a while and then start building your own collection of RSS bookmarks, as described on the following pages.

To see the entire list of RSS feeds provided by Apple:

1 Open Safari, your web browser.

2 If the Bookmarks Bar is not showing, press Command Shift B, *or* go to the View menu and choose "Show Bookmarks Bar."

3 Open the Bookmarks Library: Single-click on the little book icon at the far-left end of the Bookmarks Bar (circled, below).

4 In the Collections pane, which appears on the left side of the Bookmarks Library, single-click on "All RSS Feeds." The list will appear on the right. You'll see the blue **RSS** icon for each web site that has a feed.

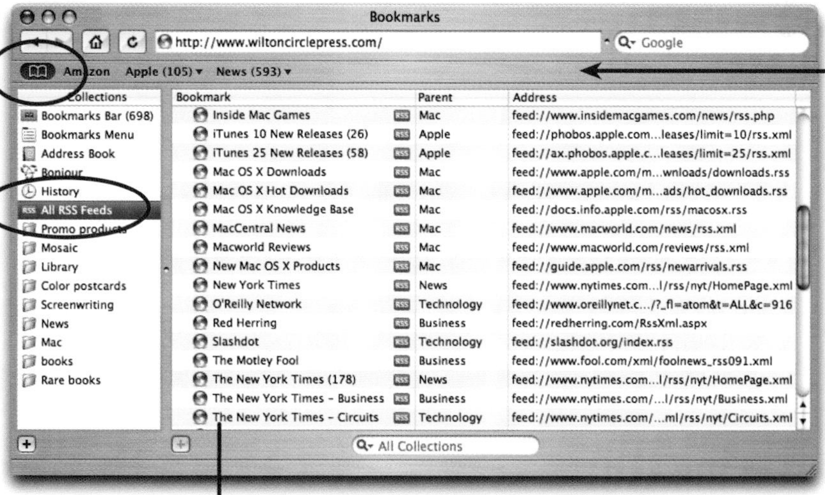

This is the Bookmarks Bar.

This entire window is the Bookmarks Library.

Notice that a large news site might have separate RSS feeds for different sections of the news.

5 Double-click any link to open its feed page.

View the Collections Apple made for you

Apple has placed two folders, or Collections, of bookmarks in the Bookmarks Bar for you, as shown below: "Apple" and "News." These folders hold small selections from the main list. (I suggest you **change this "News" folder** to "News RSS" so you can distinguish it from the "News" folder that is in the Collections pane for web sites, not feeds.)

The folders you drag to the pane of the Bookmarks Bar will appear in the Bar, as shown.

If you click on a folder in the Bookmarks Bar and choose **View All RSS Articles,** as shown below, every headline from every feed in this folder appears on the page. You can organize the information as explained on the opposite page.

If you choose **Open in Tabs,** each bookmark in the list will open as a separate tab (see page 358) and each page will display just the headlines for that source.

The number tells you the total number of new headlines in this Collection.

Customize the Information Display

Once you display an RSS feed page, you can adjust how information is shown. Use the options on the right side of the window to sort the headlines by date or by title, by the source of the headline, or whether it's unread yet. You can view headlines by relative time; for instance, you can view all articles from yesterday or from last month.

In the illustration below, notice that the "Article Length" slider is all the way to the left so only the main headline for each article is shown.

To display an entire article, single-click on any headline.

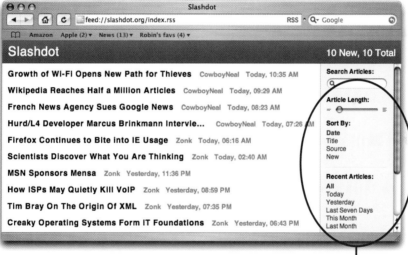

Click these links to sort the headlines.

Find Other Feeds

When you come across a web site that has an RSS feed, Safari will display an RSS icon in the address field, as shown below.

To view the actual RSS feed, click the icon in the address field.

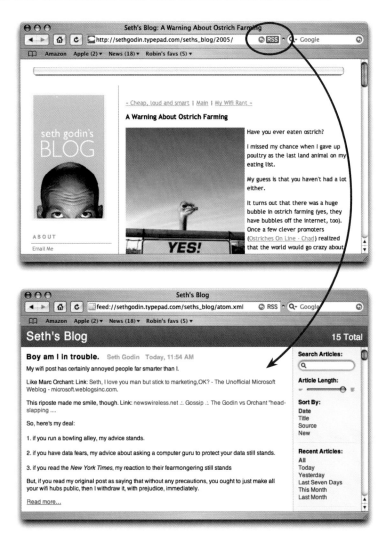

To find a directory of RSS feeds, go to your favorite search tool, such as Google.com. Search for **directory RSS feeds** or **directory XML feeds.**

Bookmark Your Favorite Feeds

There are at least four ways to bookmark a feed you want to keep track of. Before you bookmark, though, you might plan how to organize your feeds into categories, each category in a separate folder, or Collection, in the Bookmarks Library (see page 353). This makes it easy to view just the feeds for a certain interest. Or create a folder for an eclectic collection of headlines in a number of your favorite interests so you will have your own customized "newspaper."

If you plan to categorize your bookmarks, first make folders in the Collections pane in the Bookmarks Library (click the plus sign at the bottom of the pane, then rename the folder).

To bookmark a feed, do one of the following:

▼ Click the RSS icon in the address field, as shown on the opposite page. This takes you to the news feed page. Bookmark that page; in the little sheet that drops down, choose the folder in which to save the bookmark.

▼ Look on the web site for a little **RSS** or **XML** logo, icon, or note (or also check for "Atom"). Single-click it, which takes you to the news feed page. Bookmark that page and choose the folder in which to save the bookmark.

▼ If you find a link to **RSS** or **XML** on a web page, Control-click on it (or right-click). From the menu that appears, choose "Add Link to Bookmarks…." Be sure to give it a name that will describe what it is.

Auto-Click to View Feeds in Tabs

Safari has a nifty little feature called "Auto-Click" that lets you load all of your news feeds into different tabbed pages with the click of a button. Instead of going to each individual page one at a time and then losing the previous page, you can peruse them all while they are all open.

To view all feeds in tabbed pages automatically:

1 In the Bookmarks Library, single-click on "Bookmarks Bar" in the Collections pane, as circled below.

2 Put a check in one of the "Auto-Click" checkboxes that you see next to each folder. (Of course, if there are no folders, you won't see any checkboxes!)

3 As soon as you check the "Auto-Click" box, you'll notice that the tiny triangle in the Bookmarks Bar has changed to a tiny square.

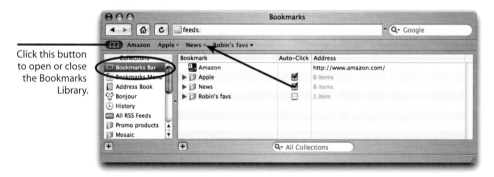

Click this button to open or close the Bookmarks Library.

4 When you click on a folder in the Bookmarks Bar that has the tiny square, every page in that folder opens, each with a different tab (which indicates a different page), as shown below. Single-click a tab to go to that page.

Tabs.

Change the RSS Preferences

It is in the Safari preferences where you can tell Safari RSS how often to check for updates, what color to highlight new articles, when to get rid of old articles, and more.

To open the RSS preferences, go to the Safari menu and choose "Preferences…." Then click the "RSS" tab to get the pane shown below.

If you choose to "Automatically update articles," Safari will put a number after the feed or folder of feeds to tell you how many new and unread articles there are. You can see that number in the Safari illustrations on the previous pages.

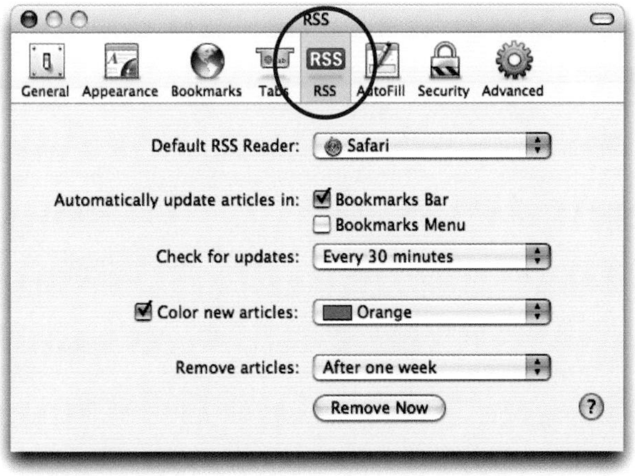

Search RSS Feeds

You can search bookmarks or RSS articles in Safari. Make sure you choose the correct search field for what you want to find.

Search the RSS bookmarks

There is a search field at the bottom of the Bookmarks Library, as shown below. This search will find words that are in the name of the bookmark, the "Parent" (which is the name of the actual folder in which the bookmark is stored), or the web address. This search field does *not* search content!

1 Open the Bookmarks Library (click the tiny book icon on the left end of the Bookmarks Bar, circled below).

2 In the Collections pane, single-click on "All RSS Feeds."

3 In the search field at the bottom of the window, click on the tiny triangle, as shown below. Select "In 'All RSS Feeds.'"

4 Enter characters in the search field. As you enter, the list of results that match those characters appears in the window.

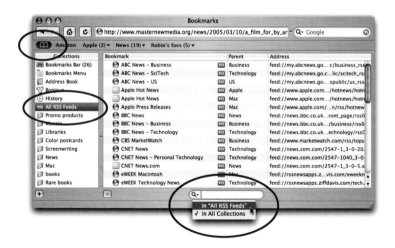

5 To show all bookmarks again, delete all characters in the search field.

Search the RSS articles and headlines

You can also search the headlines of RSS feeds, as well as the article summaries and the sources. Not only can you search the articles this way, you can save this search as a bookmark that will update itself whenever articles appear that match your search.

1 First display on one page the articles you want to search (this is another time when it comes in handy to have your RSS feeds organized into Collections): Click on one of the folders in the Bookmarks Bar and choose "View All RSS Articles."

2 In the right-hand pane, enter your search string (word or phrase) in the search field. The page will instantly limit itself to just articles that match.

3 **To save that search as a bookmark,** press Command D. Name the bookmark, as shown below. Choose the folder in which you want it saved.

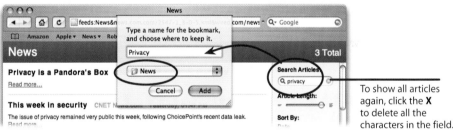

To show all articles again, click the **X** to delete all the characters in the field.

To view the latest articles under that search, choose the bookmark.

Send an RSS Feed to a Friend

If you want to share a feed with someone, simply open that RSS feed page in Safari. On the right-hand side of the Safari window, at the bottom of the pane, is a link called "Mail Link to This Page." Click on it, and your Mail program will open with the link to the page already in the message area and a subject line already written. Just add an address and send.

Use RSS Feeds as a Screen Saver

Ha! This is very clever. You can let the current headlines from your favorite RSS feed become your screen saver. It's sexier than it sounds.

1 From the Apple menu, choose "System Preferences…."

2 Click on "Desktop & Screen Saver," then click the "Screen Saver" tab.

3 In the left-hand pane, choose "RSS Visualizer."

4 Click the "Options…" button to choose your favorite feed. After you have made all the setting changes, close the pane.

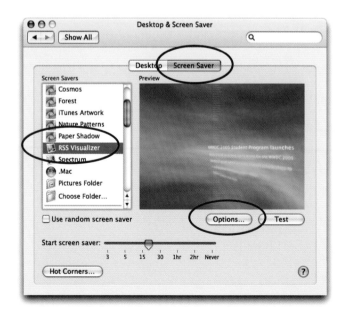

What You've Learned

▼ What an RSS feed is and where it comes from.

▼ How to view the RSS feeds and the Collections that Apple has provided for you in Safari.

▼ How to customize the display of information.

▼ How to find other feeds.

▼ How to bookmark RSS feeds you find.

▼ How to load all your feeds into tabbed web pages, ready when you need them.

▼ How to use the preferences to color-code new articles, automatically check for updates, remove articles automatically, and more.

▼ How to search your bookmarks.

▼ How to search the articles.

▼ How to send a feed to a friend.

▼ How to make your RSS feeds act as a screensaver.

16

Goals

Understand the concept of automated tasks.

Learn how to create simple workflows in Automator.

The more experienced user can learn how to create more complex workflows that cross multiple applications.

Experiment with examples of the different things that can be done in Automator.

Lesson **16**

Automate Repetitive Tasks with Automator

The application called Automator lets you build workflows that accomplish series of individual actions. This means you can automate your repetitive, time-consuming tasks with the click of a button or two. Because you can save workflows as documents or stand-alone applications, you can even share them with friends. These are just a few of the things you can do:

▾ Resize dozens of images to fit a presentation or a web page.

▾ Sequentially rename large groups of files.

▾ Send out automatic birthday greetings or other messages to your friends or business associates using Address Book and Mail.

▾ Send yourself an email message when someone places a new file in a shared folder on your Mac.

▾ Watermark your documents—any PDF document.

▾ Change image files from one format to another, rename them, and move them to a web site folder.

▾ Use a Spotlight search to find and import photos or other images into iPhoto.

I call this useful little guy Young Rossum.

Overview of Automator

There are some things we do on our Macs that are, frankly, tedious. For years the Mac has had AppleScripts, but most of us don't take advantage of them because they require programming. Well, Automator takes care of all the programming for you and lets you set up a series of **actions** to be accomplished automatically. You can save the series of actions as a **workflow** and use it over and over again.

For instance, for this book I have taken many hundreds of screen shots (pictures of what's on the screen). But the software I use, Snapz Pro X, creates each screen shot with the extension of .tiff. When I open these images in Photoshop, Photoshop saves the same files with the extension of .tif so then I end up with two of everything. So I always have to change the extension before I open the files.

Well, using Automator, I can double-click an icon and all the .tiff files instantly become .tif files. And it only took a minute to set up the original workflow.

Below is an example of what an Automator workflow looks like. This one finds people in my Address Book who have birthdays this week and emails them each a birthday card with my message. (This action assumes you have added the birthday field to your Address Book, as explained on page 91.)

Choose an application, then drag one of its actions to the workflow pane.

Quick Start (for those who don't like to read all the directions)

If you just can't wait and want to jump right in, here are the short directions. Everything is explained in detail on the following pages.

1 Open Automator (it's in the Applications window).

2 In the Library pane on the left side, choose an application.

3 In the Action pane in the middle, find the action you want to use.

4 Drag the action from the middle pane and drop it into the large, right-hand, workflow pane.

5 Repeat steps 2–5 to add actions to your workflow.

6 Click the "Run" button at the top-right of the Automator window.

7 If you want to use the workflow again, save it as you would any other document.

You can see in the example on the opposite page how easy this can be. I chose Address Book and an action. Then I chose Mail and an action. I typed in my message and hit "Run."

I *could* choose to find people with birthdays "Today" and include other actions in this workflow so it would automatically send out relevant birthday greetings every morning at 8 A.M.

Actions are the Building Blocks

You create a "workflow" using individual "actions." Each action performs one specific task. These tasks link to each other and are dependent upon each other.

An action might:

- ▼ **Require additional information.** These actions have pop-up menus, fields, and checkboxes where you can specify the information. The action will clearly tell you what it needs.

- ▼ **Require no additional information.** These actions just do what they're told, like "Eject the CD" or "Quit Mail."

- ▼ **Pass information on to the next action.** In a complex workflow, one action often passes information to the next action. The Description field, shown below, tells you whether an action requires input or provides output.

- ▼ **Receive information from the previous action.** Obviously, if one action passes information, the next action receives it. The Description field, shown below, tells you whether an action requires input or provides output and what kind of data it expects.

- ▼ **Change the format of the information.** For instance, one action might find a text file and the following action might turn that into a sound file.

- ▼ **Use information from the System or from another application.** An action might gather input from, say, Spotlight or the Address Book or iCal.

Look at the types of actions available

Below are examples of some of the actions you'll find in Automator. Spend a few minutes to familiarize yourself with them: Choose an application in the Library pane, then single-click on one of the actions. The Description pane at the bottom tells you what that action does and describes any specific requirements it needs.

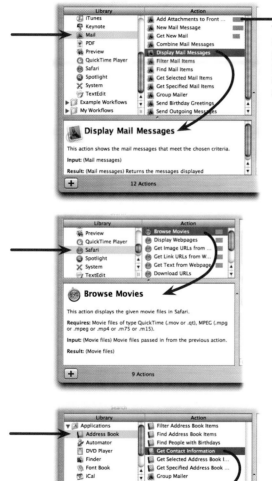

The relevancy rating applies to one of two things: either a search you did to find a particular action (see page 384), or how well the action works with the action already in the workflow pane.

Workflows are the Finished Products

A "workflow" consists of a series of "actions" (actions are explained on the previous pages). When you put a number of actions together, you have a workflow that performs a complex task.

Each Automator window is a separate workflow. You'll drag the actions from the Action pane into the large workflow pane on the right, as described on the previous and following pages. You can copy, paste, or delete actions in the workflow, and you can change the order of the actions.

Once you create a workflow that successfully does what it's supposed to do, you can **save** it in two different ways: As a workflow file, which is a document, or as a stand-alone application.

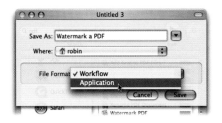

WFLOW

tiff to tif.workflow

▼ When you save a workflow as a **workflow file,** you can store it wherever you like. When you want to use it again, double-click the file, which opens it in Automator. Click the "Run" button to activate the workflow, or press Command R.

Watermark a PDF.app

▼ When you save a workflow as a **stand-alone application,** you can save it wherever you like. When you want to use it, double-click its icon. It will *not* open Automator; it will just execute.

As an application, you can make a workflow automatically execute as a login item (see page 248), add it to a script menu if you use scripts, or link it to a folder action if you use those. **To edit a workflow app,** drop the icon onto the Automator icon.

All the workflows you create, no matter where you save them, appear in the "My Workflows" folder at the bottom of the Library pane in Automator. You can always access them from there (or from anywhere on your Mac). And you can share them with friends and co-workers.

Tips for Building Workflows

On the following pages are sample workflows for you to build and experiment with. Keep these things in mind as you build your own.

Not all actions work together

If an action *needs* a certain kind of input, then of course the previous action must *provide* that kind of output.

Each action's Description field (see page 369) tells you what it will input and output. And when you place an action in a workflow, the input it requires from the previous action is displayed in the upper-right, as shown below. When two actions can work together, they connect in the upper/lower right.

You might, however, build actions that do *not* show a connection, and the text in red, as circled below, sometimes indicates it won't work. But this doesn't really mean it won't work—it just means it *might* not! The only thing you can do is run it and see.

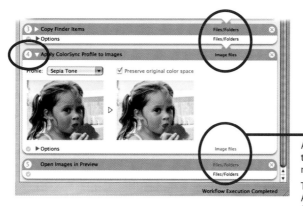

Although the lack of connection and the red text indicates these actions might not work, they really do.

This workflow is one provided by Apple; it's in your "Example Workflows" folder in the Library pane.

Change the order of actions

Drag an action to a different location.

Or single-click the "action number" that you see in the upper-left corner of each action. From the pop-up menu that appears, choose a different order.

—continued

Copy and paste an action in a workflow

To copy an action, click once on any action *in the workflow pane* that you want to copy. Press Command C to copy it (or from the Edit menu, choose "Copy").

To paste an action into the same workflow or a completely different one, click anywhere in a workflow pane. Then paste (Command V, or from the Edit menu, choose "Paste"). The action will always paste in *at the end* of the existing workflow. Then drag it into the position you need it.

Delete an action from a workflow

Click the **X** on the right end of an action. *Or* select the action and hit Delete.

Collapse an action

If you collapse the action boxes, you can see more of your workflow. If an action has a disclosure triangle next to its name, it's collapsible.

To collapse or expand an action, click its disclosure triangle.

To collapse or expand all actions, Option-click any disclosure triangle.

Disable (but not delete) an action

You can disable an action, which means it remains in the workflow but doesn't execute. If information is given to it by the previous action, the disabled action will pass it along to the next one.

To disable an action, click on its number in the upper-left corner. From the menu that appears, choose "Disable." The action will collapse and turn gray. **To enable it again,** use the same menu and choose "Enable."

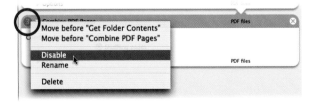

Create a Simple Workflow in the Finder

Here are the steps to create a simple workflow. This example is to rename a large group of files. Let's say you have a bunch of photos that you imported from your camera and they have all those awful names like DGP78XX3.JPG. All these photos are from your trip to Egypt. In this workflow, each photo will be labeled Egypt-01.jpg, each with a different and ascending number.

If you don't have photos like this that you want to rename, you can create a bunch really quickly so you can follow along in these steps: Find one photo. Select it (click once on it), then press Command D; hold the Command key down and tap the D key as many times as you want copies of photos. For instance, if you want five copies, press Command D D D D D.

1 Select the photos whose names you want to change. If all the photos are in one folder, open the folder and press Command A to select all.

2 Do either one of these things:

   • Control-click (or right-click) on one of the selected files. From the menu that pops up, choose "Automator," then "Create Workflow…."

—continued

▼ **Or** drag those files and drop them directly into the workflow pane on the right side of the Automator window.

Either of the above techniques will automatically create the appropriate action in the workflow pane, as shown below.

This is the workflow pane.

3 Now you want to **add an action** that will rename the items. In the Library pane, on the left, choose "Finder." In the Actions pane on the right, find "Rename Finder Items." Drag that action and drop it into the workflow pane, beneath the list of files.

Automator knows that this might cause a situation that may surprise you, so it brings up a warning, shown below.

Decide whether you want to have copies made before you change the names (click "Add") or if you want to go ahead and change the names of the originals (click "Don't Add").

4 In the menu that probably says "Add Date and Time," choose "Make Sequential" (circled, below). Then change the other specifications to suit your purpose. The "Example" in the action box shows you what to expect.

According to the specifications chosen below, this action will name each photo with "Egypt-" and then a sequential number, starting with number 1. Every number will be two digits; if you have a collection of 100 or more photos, make them three-digit numbers.

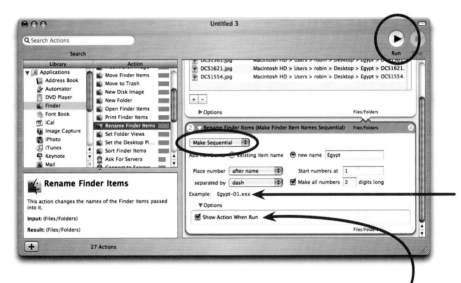

5 If you want an action to stop and show you what it's doing, click the "Options" triangle and check the box to "Show Action When Run." If you just want it to run and do its thing, don't check this box.

6 Your workflow is ready to execute. Single-click the "Run" button in the upper-right of the Automator window. Your file names will change, as shown below. That was easy!

Create a Workflow that Uses Multiple Apps

You can create a workflow that gathers information from one application and passes it to another. You saw an example of this in the very beginning of this chapter, on page 366, where Automator (Young Rossum, as I call him) found all the birthdays in my Address Book for the week and sent them each a birthday greeting from Mail.

The following simple example shows you how to play a particular song to wake you up in the morning on a particular day using iTunes and iCal. This assumes, of course, that you sleep in the same room as your Mac. This can be particularly handy in hotel rooms when you're traveling!

1 Open a new window/workflow in Automator.

2 In the Library pane, select iCal.

3 In the Action pane, find the action titled "New iCal Events" and drag it into the workflow pane, as shown below.

4 This makes a new event in iCal on the day and at the time you specify. So go through each parameter in the action and make your choices.

5 Click the "Alarm" menu to choose "Play Song…." This opens a small window where you can choose any song in your iTunes collection.

This would actually be a lot easier if Apple would just let you add a song to the alarm directly in iCal.

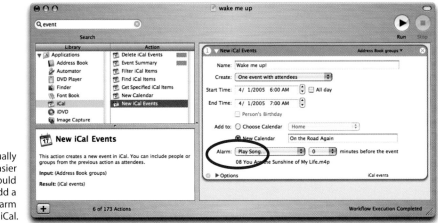

6 Click the "Run" button at the top of the window to run this workflow. iCal opens and displays the event.

If you want this event to repeat, in iCal click the tiny menu next to "repeat" and make your choice. Below you can see that this song will wake me up for four days in a row.

7 You can close iCal and go back to your Automator workflow. You might want to save the workflow so you can run it again.

TIP You can use this in combination with the Energy Saver schedule to make your Mac start up or wake up at a particular time each morning. Your Mac might be completely Shut Down, but this will turn it on for you: In the System Preferences, use the "Energy Saver" pane. Click the "Schedule…" button and set your times.

Create a Workflow that Uses the Internet

This workflow is already created for you. You can find it in the Library pane in the folder called "Example Workflows." It's called "Import .Mac Photo Album into iPhoto." This is great. Let's say your kids sent you a .Mac web page they made with lots of photos on it. You would like to have those photos yourself so you can do things like make a book using the photos or email one or two to friends. That's when you can use this workflow—it makes copies of the photos on the web page (not the tiny thumbnails, but the linked, larger images) and puts them directly into your own iPhoto.

1 In Safari, open the web page whose photos you want copies of. It must be a .Mac homepage. (The first action of this workflow tells you to do this.)

2 Open Automator, if it isn't already.

3 In the Library pane, scroll down to the bottom and single-click the tiny triangle next to the folder called "Example Workflows" to open it.

4 In that folder, double-click the file "Import .Mac Photo Album into iPhoto." This makes it open in the workflow pane (or in another window altogether if something is already in the pane). This is the workflow:

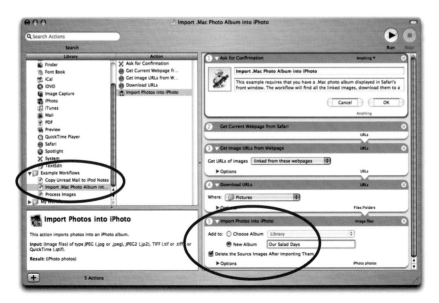

5 iPhoto will probably automatically open when you open the workflow. That's okay.

6 In Action #5 in the workflow, either choose the name of an existing album where you want the photos stored, *or* check the button for a "New Album" and give it a name. Automator will make the new album for you and put the photos in it.

Also in that action, you'll notice the box is checked to "Delete the Source Images After Importing Them." This doesn't do anything to the images on the web page you are getting them from—it deletes the images it downloaded into your Pictures folder in Action #4. (If you want to keep the photos in that folder *instead* of putting them in iPhoto, just disable Action #5; see page 372.)

7 Click the "Run" button in the upper-right of the window. Voilà!

This workflow took copies of the photos from this page and put them into an iPhoto album for me.

Modify an Existing Workflow

In the example below, I modified the Apple-provided workflow that copies unread email and transfers it to an iPod as notes. I modified it to open my unread mail in TextEdit and have it read out loud to me by Fred. That way I can get the ironing done while listening to my email. (Ha!) It takes some trial and error at first to figure out what needs to be input and output, but if it's something you can use again and again, it's worth the time.

I wish I could make Fred do the ironing.

Troubleshoot a Workflow

There are several things you can do while building a workflow to find out where something might be going wrong.

▼ Click the "Options" triangle in an action and check your options. At the very least you will usually have the choice to "Show Action When Run." This stops the action and shows you what it's doing. You might learn something by seeing each step as it goes through its process.

▼ After you run a workflow, you will see a mark next to the Options triangle. It's either a green checkmark, indicating that particular action executed properly, or a red **x**, which means it didn't.

▼ Check the bottom-right corner of the Automator window. Status messages appear here to tell you what's happening.

▼ Display the log so you can record exactly what the workflow does. From the View menu, choose "Show Log." A drawer appears off the bottom.

▼ Place the action called "View Results" (it's an "Automator" action) between two other actions in the workflow. This lets you see the data that is flowing through the workflow at that point.

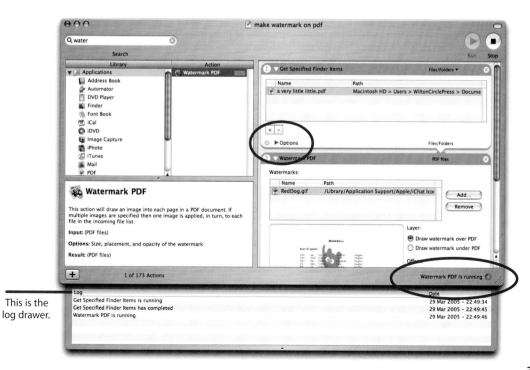

This is the log drawer.

A Few Advanced Automator Techniques

Below are brief descriptions of several advanced techniques.

Run AppleScripts in your workflow

Select the "Automator" action called "Run AppleScript." Drag it into the workflow pane. You can type, paste, edit, and test your scripts right here.

To display the pane where you can view the results of your script, drag the tiny dot in the bar upward, as shown below.

Add a workflow to the Script menu

If you use the Script menu, you might find it handy to add workflows to it. Just drag a copy of the workflow into the Scripts folder that's in the Library folder that's on your hard disk (not the user Library folder).

To make the Script menu appear in your menu bar, open the Applications window. Open the AppleScript folder. Open the AppleScript Utility. Check the box to "Show Script menu in menu bar."

For more about AppleScripts, visit www.apple.com/applescript**.**

Run shell scripts in your workflow

Select the "Automator" action called "Run Shell Script." Drag it into the workflow pane. As you see below, you can choose a script file to execute or write your UNIX commands directly into the action.

Add a workflow as a folder action

If you know how and like to use folder actions, you can attach a workflow as a folder action. A folder that has an action enabled will do "something" when the folder is opened, closed, or when you put something inside of it or take it out. To learn more about folder actions, please see Apple's web site at **www.apple.com/applescript/folderactions.**

Combine workflows

You can string workflows together. In the Library pane of Automator, single-click on "Automator" to see its actions. Use the action called "Run Workflow." In this action you can choose a previously saved workflow. Before you add the next one, you might need to add a transition action, depending on what you are putting together.

Search for an Action

If you don't know where a particular action is, or even if one exists, use the search field.

1 In the Library pane, first select the application you want to search.

To search more than one application, Command-click on their names.

If you want to search *every* application, make sure you select the "Applications" item, as shown below. When the Library pane is active, press Option UpArrow to select "Applications."

To select the search field and make it ready for you to type, press Command Option F.

2 Type a word or part of a word in the search field. Matching actions will appear in the Action list as you type. The more letters you type, the narrower your search.

3 To delete the search so all actions appear in the list, click the **X**.

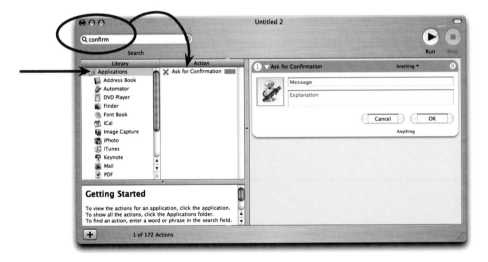

What You've Learned

▼ The difference between actions and workflows.

▼ How to create and run a workflow.

▼ How to save a workflow as a document or a stand-alone application.

▼ How to modify an existing workflow to suit your needs.

▼ Tips on how to run AppleScript or UNIX commands in a workflow.

▼ How to search for a particular action.

▼ How to make your Mac start up or shut down automatically.

Keyboard Shortcuts

Command R	Run a workflow
Option UpArrow	Select the Applications item in the Library pane
Command Option F	Select the search field

17

Goals

Provide an overview of the VoiceOver process for people who might need to help users with visual impairments.

Teach all users how to take advantage of the myriad of features designed to make things easier for people with visual, audio, or mobile challenges.

Lesson **17**

VoiceOver (and more) for Users with Challenges

Apple calls VoiceOver a "spoken user interface." But the "spoken" interface in this case is not the *user* who is speaking—a voice inside the *computer* tells the user exactly what is displayed on the screen, which menus are available, where the cursor is and what it's pointing to, etc. A user with visual impairment can do just about anything on the Mac using VoiceOver—write, send, and read email; surf the web, use TextEdit for word processing, and more. And it's built-in to Tiger. By comparison, the most popular "screen reader" on a Windows machine costs about $1,000!

Speech recognition software is also built into your Mac and has been for years. You can tell the computer to do a huge number of tasks just by talking to it. Your Mac will even tell you jokes. And there are a number of accommodating features for all sorts of challenges, from minor things like slowing down the mouse or the keyboard to zooming in close on your screen. They are all given an overview in this chapter.

I realize that people with vision impairments are probably not reading this book, but most of us know someone who could take advantage of this amazing capability.

Overview of VoiceOver

VoiceOver describes aloud what is on the screen. It reads text in documents, windows, and on web pages. The user controls everything with the keyboard. You can activate buttons, open menus, choose items in menus, open and use applications, read text, edit text, and more. Mail, Safari, TextEdit and Preview are highly accessible; other applications and utilities also provide some (but lesser) accessibility. VoiceOver can be useful for people with broad ranges of visual impairments.

When installing Tiger, take the VoiceOver tour

On installation of Tiger, you'll find a message on the "Welcome" screen to learn to use VoiceOver. If you want to do so at that point, follow the directions and press the Escape key (esc). Your Mac will walk you through a great little tutorial. At the end of the tutorial, you will continue the setup process with VoiceOver turned on. (To turn it off, press Command F5.)

Turn VoiceOver on or off

I wish I could say this chapter is a complete study in VoiceOver, but the software is so amazing and rich and deep that all I can do here is get you started. The Help files are quite extensive and I encourage you to explore further with those (see the opposite page). Someone needs to write a book about VoiceOver.

▼ **To turn on VoiceOver,** press Command F5
(the Fkey, not the characters F and 5).

▼ **To turn off VoiceOver,** press Command F5.

Or from the Apple menu, choose "System Preferences...," and then choose "Universal Access." Click the button to turn VoiceOver on (or off). You'll also see a button that opens the VoiceOver Utility, described on pages 394–395.

Make a laptop easier to use

If you're using a laptop or helping someone else use one, keep in mind that on most laptops the user will have to hold down the **fn key** (bottom-left corner of the keyboard) as well as all the other keys necessary to use VoiceOver. This can be a limiting factor for some people. But you can change that behavior:

▼ Open the "Keyboard & Mouse" system preferences. Click the "Keyboard" tab and put a check in the box to "Use the F1–F12 keys to control software features." See page 403 for an illustration.

VoiceOver Commands

All of the VoiceOver keyboard commands start with Control Option (not the Command key, but the *Control* key). Although the lists of commands are lengthy and can look complex, once you notice that every VoiceOver key combination starts with *Control Option,* it's not quite so intimidating.

You'll finds the lists of commands in the Help files: Open the **VoiceOver Utility** (it's in the Utilities folder, which is in the Applications folder). Then from the Help menu, choose "VoiceOver Commands."

Learn the Keys on the Keyboard

Since VoiceOver is totally dependent on the keyboard, make sure you know where all the keys are and what they're called. Once VoiceOver is turned on, you can practice: Press *Control Option* K to turn on keyboard practice ("K" for keyboard). Each time you press a key, the voice tells you the name of the key.

If you have the Caption Panel turned on (see pages 392 and 395), you will also see the symbol for that key. This, of course, isn't useful for someone who is blind, but may be useful for an assistant.

If you (or someone you are helping) has trouble pressing more than one key at a time, turn on Sticky Keys in the Universal Access preferences (see page 400). This feature lets you press the keys in individual sequence instead of having to hold all of them down at the same time.

Pause and Resume Speaking

Sometimes the speaking voice can make you nuts, or you want it to stop for a moment while you do something. You can pause the voice.

▼ **To pause VoiceOver** in the middle of speaking something, tap Control.

　　If you move the VoiceOver cursor (explained on the following page) after you pause, it will automatically begin speaking again.

▼ **To continue VoiceOver** after you have paused, tap Control again.

▼ **To repeat the last spoken phrase,** press *Control Option* Z.

VoiceOver Cursor

As you navigate around the screen, the VoiceOver cursor highlights and enlarges the items as they are selected. You can turn this feature on or off in the Display pane of the VoiceOver Utility (see page 395), and you can adjust its size. At the smallest size, the VoiceOver cursor is a thin black border that highlights the button or field; at the largest size, the selected item fills the center of the screen. The VoiceOver cursor is useful if you can't see very well (and useless, of course, if you are blind).

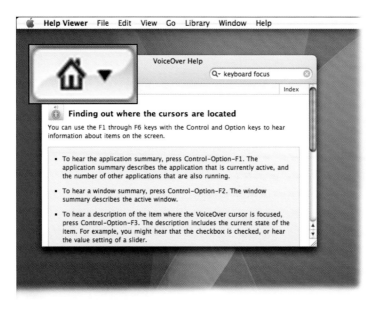

Keyboard Focus

The keyboard focus refers to the area of the screen that will be affected if you press a key. The default (as defined in the VoiceOver Utility; see page 394) is that the keyboard focus and the VoiceOver cursor (opposite) match each other (track each other). That is, when the keyboard focus is on a particular item, that's where the cursor will be as well.

You might, instead, want the VoiceOver cursor to follow your mouse movements instead of the keyboard focus. You can move your mouse around and the VoiceOver cursor follows it, enlarging items as shown above. When you want to activate that item, press the appropriate key.

Navigating in VoiceOver

To use VoiceOver, first turn it on (Command F5). Then use the keyboard to navigate, open applications, choose menu items, and do stuff. In general:

▼ To select items sequentially on the screen, press *Control Option* and the arrow keys.

▼ To activate selected items, press *Control Option* Spacebar.

▼ To leave an open menu without activating anything, press Escape.

Use the Dock

Go to the Dock, choose an application to use, and start working.

▼ **To focus on the Dock,** press D (that is, *Control Option* D).

▼ **To select items in the Dock,** use the arrow keys
(that is, *Control Option* LeftArrow and RightArrow).

▼ **To open a selected item in the Dock,** press the Spacebar
(that is, *Control Option* Spacebar).

▼ **To leave the Dock,** press Escape
(you can skip *Control Option* whenever you use the Escape key).

VoiceOver menu

The VoiceOver menu shows you all of the commands that can be used with the item that is currently highlighted on the screen. This is useful when you're not sure which keys to press to make something happen.

▼ **To open the VoiceOver menu,** press F7
(that is, *Control Option* F7).

▼ **To highlight an option in the menu and hear its key combination,** use the up and down arrows (*Control Option* UpArrow or DownArrow).

▼ **To select a highlighted item and perform the command,** press Spacebar
(that is, *Control Option* Spacebar).

▼ **To close the menu without choosing anything,** press Escape
(you can skip *Control Option*).

Caption Panel

The Caption Panel is a rectangular box that appears on your screen. It contains the text of the spoken words. If you're blind, this is useless. But if you just need help, it can be nice to have a visual reinforcement. Or it might be useful if you're helping someone who is blind.

You can control the size of the Caption Panel, how many rows of text it displays, and how transparent the box is. Use the VoiceOver Utility; see page 395.

Link List menu

When a Safari web page is active (open and in front), you can create a Link List that displays a menu listing every link on the page.

1 Open a Safari web page.

2 **To open the Link List menu,** first use the keyboard shortcuts to select the HTML page (*Control Option* RightArrow until you hear "HTML content"). Then press U (that is, *Control Option* U).

3 **To highlight links in the menu,** use the up and down arrows (*Control Option* UpArrow or DownArrow).

You can type the first letter or two of a link name, if you know it, to highlight a particular link.

4 To select that highlighted link on the web page, press Return (*without* the Control Option keys).

5 To go to that linked page now that the link is selected on the web page, press Spacebar (*Control Option* Spacebar).

To close the menu without selecting anything, hit the Escape key.

Item Chooser menu

The Item Chooser menu lists everything that is in the open, *active* window on the screen (not everything that is open on your Desktop, but just what is in front). If the active window is, say, a web page, the Item Chooser will list every button, field, control, link, graphic, and the HTML page itself.

Slide up and down the Item Chooser menu with the arrow keys (that is, *Control Option* UpArrow or Down Arrow) to highlight items. They will be read aloud to you as you highlight them. Press Spacebar (*Control Option* Spacebar) to choose the highlighted item to appear in front of you.

Use the standard Mac keyboard shortcuts

You can use the regular Mac keyboard shortcuts in addition to the VoiceOver shortcuts. For instance, in the Finder it is faster to open the Applications window using Command Shift A than it is to cycle through the VoiceOver commands. It's faster to press Command S to save a document than it is to find the menu and choose the option to "Save." Use the shortcuts explained on pages 118–119 to switch applications.

Turn on VoiceOver at login

To make sure VoiceOver is on at the login window, go to the Accounts system preferences. Unlock the locked icon, click the "Login Options" button, and put a checkmark in "Use VoiceOver at login window." This does *not* automatically turn on VoiceOver.

Customize Your Access with the VoiceOver Utility

VoiceOver Utility

Although you turn on VoiceOver in the Universal Access preferences, you also have a utility where you can customize so many aspects of this software. The VoiceOver Utility is in the Utilities folder, which is in the Applications folder. These options are fairly self-explanatory.

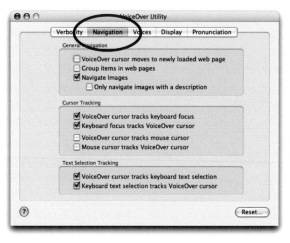

In the **Verbosity** pane, you can control *how much* your Mac talks to you. As you work with the program, you'll figure out how much you want it to tell you. For instance, you might decide you don't need to know if a word is in bold or italic (the text attributes).

Use this to reset all options back to the application defaults.

In the **Navigation** pane, you can control what gets highlighted and talked about and where VoiceOver focuses.

Please see pages 390–391 for an explanation of the difference between the "VoiceOver cursor" and the "Keyboard focus," which will help you decide how you want them to track (follow each other).

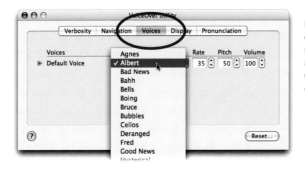

In the **Voices** pane, change the voice that speaks to you. You can also change how fast she or he speaks, the pitch, and the volume.

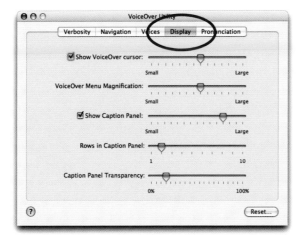

In the **Display** pane, you can choose whether or not to display the VoiceOver cursor or the Caption Panel.

As you can see, you can also determine how large the VoiceOver cursor appears, and you have some control over various aspects of the Caption Panel.

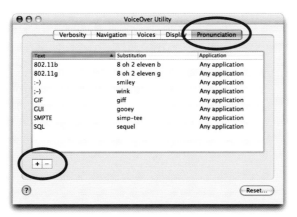

In the **Pronunciation** pane, tell VoiceOver how you want different items to be pronounced.

To change any of the existing pronunciations, double-click the word.

To add more pronunciations, click the **+** sign and enter the words you need.

And That's Not All . . .

VoiceOver works with or without other built-in features of the Mac that are designed for users who need a little extra help. These other features, explained on the following pages, have been built into the Mac for many years.

Take advantage of the View Options

In the View Options palette, you can change the size of the icons and the text labels with a couple of clicks, as shown below. This can apply to just the icons in the open, active window or to all windows on the Mac.

To get the View Options palette, make sure you are in the Finder and you have a window open in front of you. From the View menu, choose "Show View Options." **Or** Control-click (or right-click) on an open window and choose "Show View Options" from the pop-up menu that appears.

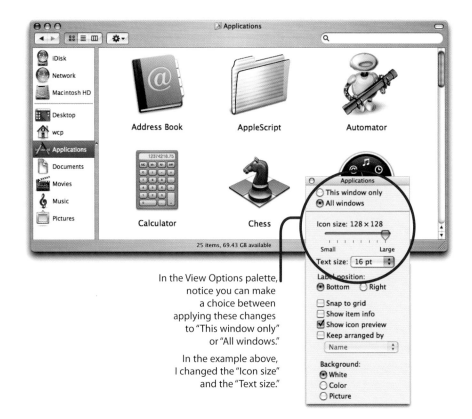

In the View Options palette, notice you can make a choice between applying these changes to "This window only" or "All windows."

In the example above, I changed the "Icon size" and the "Text size."

Universal Access preferences: Enhance the display contrast

Universal Access

In the Universal Access system preferences, be sure to explore how you can make the screen easier to see and read, change the audio alert to a visual one, adjust the keyboard for someone who needs a little extra help with it, or make the Mac respond to the numeric keypad instead of moving the mouse.

If you use special equipment to control your Mac, this is also where you would enable it: Check the box to "Enable access for assistive devices."

To open Universal Access, go to the Apple menu and choose "System Preferences…." Single-click the "Universal Access" icon.

The "Zoom" feature is explained on the following pages.

Easily adjust the contrast on the screen to perhaps make things easier to see. Notice you can change it to grayscale as well.

Universal Access preferences: Zoom in on the screen

You can turn on the Zoom feature and then ignore it until you need it. When necessary, repeat the keyboard shortcut Command Option = (equal sign, which is also the + key) to zoom in and enlarge the screen. To zoom out, use Command Option – (hyphen). Try it. The opposite page shows you what it can look like.

Hold down the Command and Option keys, then tap the = as many times as necessary to enlarge the object to the size you need.

If you like the Zoom feature, experiment with these options so you have total control over it.

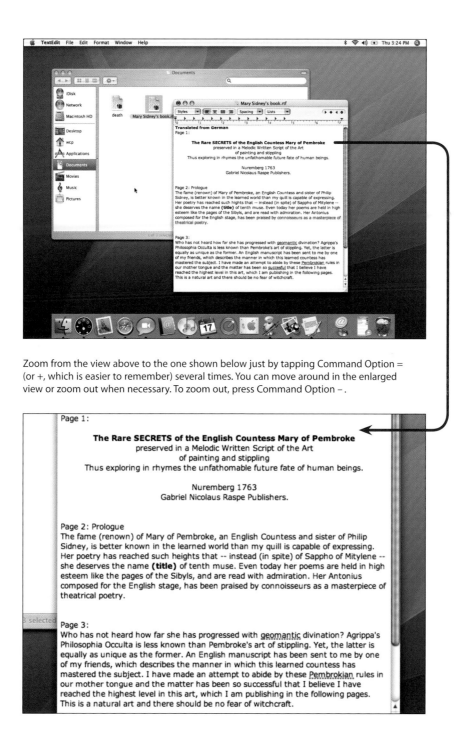

Zoom from the view above to the one shown below just by tapping Command Option = (or +, which is easier to remember) several times. You can move around in the enlarged view or zoom out when necessary. To zoom out, press Command Option − .

Page 1:

The Rare SECRETS of the English Countess Mary of Pembroke
preserved in a Melodic Written Script of the Art
of painting and stippling
Thus exploring in rhymes the unfathomable future fate of human beings.

Nuremberg 1763
Gabriel Nicolaus Raspe Publishers.

Page 2: Prologue
The fame (renown) of Mary of Pembroke, an English Countess and sister of Philip Sidney, is better known in the learned world than my quill is capable of expressing. Her poetry has reached such heights that -- instead (in spite) of Sappho of Mitylene -- she deserves the name **(title)** of tenth muse. Even today her poems are held in high esteem like the pages of the Sibyls, and are read with admiration. Her Antonius composed for the English stage, has been praised by connoisseurs as a masterpiece of theatrical poetry.

Page 3:
Who has not heard how far she has progressed with geomantic divination? Agrippa's Philosophia Occulta is less known than Pembroke's art of stippling. Yet, the latter is equally as unique as the former. An English manuscript has been sent to me by one of my friends, which describes the manner in which this learned countess has mastered the subject. I have made an attempt to abide by these Pembrokian rules in our mother tongue and the matter has been so successful that I believe I have reached the highest level in this art, which I am publishing in the following pages. This is a natural art and there should be no fear of witchcraft.

Universal Access preferences: Make hearing adjustments

If you can't hear the alerts, tell your Mac to flash the screen instead.

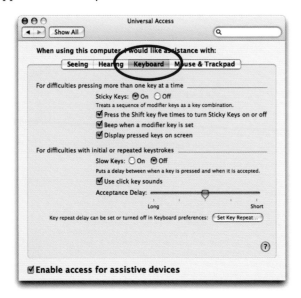

Universal Access preferences: Adjust the keyboard

If it's difficult to hold down more than one key at a time for keyboard shortcuts, turn on "Sticky Keys." This lets you type the keys in a shortcut, such as Command Shift 3, in *sequence* instead of all at once.

The feature called "Slow Keys" creates a pause between when you hit a key and when the action for that key takes place. It's helpful if you find things happen too fast for you.

Universal Access preferences: Skip the mouse

To use the numeric keypad to move the pointer instead of using the mouse, turn on "Mouse Keys" in the "Mouse & Trackpad" pane.

It's very logical which number sends the mouse in which direction, as shown below. The 5 key will activate whatever is under the mouse; that is, if the cursor is on a menu name, hit the 5 key. If the cursor is on a sliding bar, hit the 5 key and the slider will move to that point.

You can also **enlarge the size of the pointer,** as shown below, so it's easier to track as it moves around the screen. Even when it's large, only the very tip of the pointer is the "hot spot" that activates items.

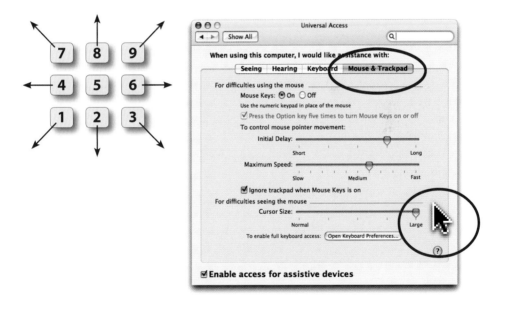

Speech

Speech preferences: *Tell* your Mac what to do

For years your Mac has had the capability to do what you *tell* it to do. You can even play your Chess game (found in the Applications folder) by speaking the playing board spaces out loud (see the Chess help files).

Use the Speech system preferences. When you turn on "Speakable Items," a round microphone window appears, as shown below. You can choose to make it listen only when you have the Escape key pressed (or any other key), or make it listen only when you first say a keyword (the default, as shown below, is "Computer"). Turn on "Speakable Items," hold down the Escape key, and say, "What time is it?" or "Tell me a joke."

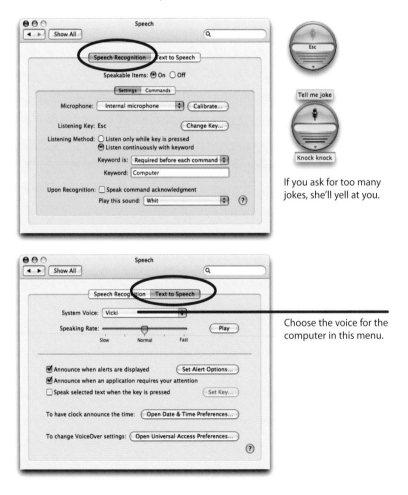

If you ask for too many jokes, she'll yell at you.

Choose the voice for the computer in this menu.

Keyboard & Mouse preferences: Adjust the response

For relatively minor adjustments, don't forget about the "Keyboard & Mouse" system preferences. The "Key Repeat Rate" determines how fast a key that is held down repeats itself across the page.

Keyboard & Mouse

If you're a heavy-handed typist and find extra letters and spaces in your documents, tell the keys to wait a little longer before repeating—use a longer "Delay Until Repeat," or turn off the repeat altogether.

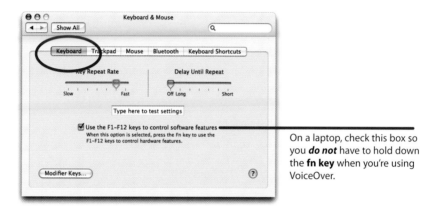

On a laptop, check this box so you **do not** have to hold down the **fn key** when you're using VoiceOver.

The "Tracking Speed" of the mouse refers to how far you have to move the mouse to make the cursor move across the screen. The slower the tracking, the farther you have to move your mouse and your hand. But also, the slower the tracking, the easier it is to click directly on tiny little things.

If you find you can't double-click fast enough, slow down the "Double-Click Speed." The other options you see in this pane are for a two-button mouse.

Keyboard & Mouse preferences: Control the keyboard shortcuts

If some of the keyboard shortcuts you use regularly are a little difficult, use this "Keyboard Shortcuts" pane to change them. You can even click the **+** sign and add your own keyboard shortcuts for commands you use often.

The option for "Full keyboard access" lets you use the Tab key to select *all* controls in a dialog box, not just the text boxes and lists. That is, if there are radio buttons (the round ones) or checkboxes (the square ones) in a dialog box, every time you hit the Tab key it will select the next active button; use the arrow keys to select the inactive ones.

For instance, in the dialog box below, the Tab key will highlight the active button, "Keyboard Shortcuts." If you want to choose any of the other buttons to its left, use the Left Arrow key.

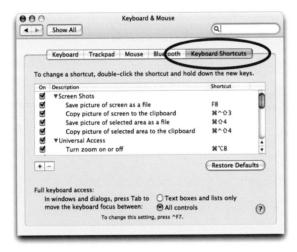

And there's more!

To enlarge everything on your screen and still see the whole screen (as opposed to enlarging a portion of it with the Zoom feature, as shown on pages 397–399), use the "Displays" preferences and choose a lower resolution: the lower the numbers, the lower the resolution and the larger the items on your screen.

To change the sound level, play sound effects for actions on your Mac, choose a microphone or speakers, and more, use the "Sound" preferences.

What You've Learned

▼ The very basics of how to use VoiceOver, and where to go for more help.

▼ How to customize VoiceOver to suit your needs.

▼ How to enlarge the icons and text labels.

▼ How to adjust the contrast of the monitor or change to black and white.

▼ How to zoom in on an area of the screen.

▼ How to make the screen flash when you can't hear the audio alert.

▼ How to use Sticky Keys to type a keyboard shortcut in sequence.

▼ How to slow down the Mac's response to the keyboard.

▼ How to control the cursor using the numeric keypad.

▼ How to enlarge the size of the pointer.

▼ How to tell your Mac what to do with speech recognition.

▼ How to change the computer's voice.

▼ How to adjust your keyboard and mouse to suit your own movements.

▼ How to change keyboard shortcuts and to make your own.

▼ How to change the resolution of your screen so everything looks bigger (or smaller).

▼ How to change the sound level.

Keyboard Shortcuts

Command F5	Turn VoiceOver on or off
Control Option	All VoiceOver commands start with these keys
Control	Pause or resume VoiceOver speaking

The End **Matters**

Glossary

Most words are defined as I use them. Please see the index!

active window

The *active window* is the one that is in front of everything else and is selected. You can tell if a window is active because the three little buttons in the top-left corner are in color, and the title bar icon is not shaded. It's important to become aware at all times of which window is active because that is the window that will accept any command. For instance, if you press Command Shift N to create a new folder, that new folder will appear in the active window (or on the Desktop, if the Desktop is active). If you press Command W in just about any application or in the Finder, it will close the active window. **To make any window active** (or the Desktop), single-click on it.

alias

An *alias* is a "go-fer"—it goes for things and gets them for you. It's nothing all by itself; it's merely a representative icon (only 2 or 3 k in file size) that is *linked* to the original. You double-click the alias and it goes and gets the real thing and opens the real thing for you. The advantage of this is that you can put aliases in multiple places for easy access (you can have as many aliases of an item as you want). Some applications cannot open properly if you move them out of their folders, but if you make an alias of that application, you can put it anywhere.

An alias icon has a tiny arrow in the bottom-left corner of the icon so you know it's a go-fer.

You can throw away an alias and it does not affect the original at all. You can move an original or rename the original or the alias and everything still works fine.

Methinks I scent the morning air

To make an alias, select a file; press Command L.

colored labels

To *color-code* a file, Control-click on it and choose a "Color Label" from the menu that pops up. Once a file is color-coded, you can search for it by its label, organize your files, etc. To change the names of the labels, use the Finder preferences: Go to the Finder menu and choose "Preferences…." Click the "Labels" menu and change the names.

extension

An *extension* usually refers to the short code at the end of a file name. It might be from two to six letters. This extension tells the Mac what to do with that file.

ApplePro Tip of the Week.webloc — *This extension, .webloc, tells the Mac this is a web page location.*

You might not see the extensions. If you like to have them visible all the time, go to the Finder preferences (from the Finder menu, choose "Preferences"). Click on the "Advanced" tab. Put a check in the box to "Show all file extensions."

To show the extensions temporarily or to check to see what the extension is for a particular file, use the Get Info window (explained below). You'll see an option for "Name & Extension" that will tell you what it is and let you hide or show it for that selected file.

Do not add or change the extensions yourself! The Mac has become very fussy about these extensions and you run the risk that the file will not open if you change its extension without knowing what you are doing.

Get Info window

The *Get Info* window has a secret "Inspector" mode. If you select a file and press Command I, the Get Info window appears for that one particular file. But if you select a file and press Command Option I, you get the *Inspector* window, which looks exactly like the Get Info window *except* the Inspector window will change depending on what you click. That is, if you display the info for one file, then select another file, the content of the Inspector changes to display the next file. Try it.

You can also get the Inspector with a contextual menu: Control-click on a file, then hold the Option key down and you'll see "Get Info" change to "Show Inspector."

screenshots

To make *screenshots* (pictures of the screen), use these shortcuts:

Full screen: Command Shift 3

Selection: Command Shift 4, use the target cursor to select the area.

The above screenshots land on your Desktop labeled "Picture 1," "Picture 2," etc. They are in the PNG file format.

Selection you can paste: Command Shift 4, the target cursor appears. Hold down the Control key and drag to select the area. Now you can paste the screenshot somewhere.

string

A *string* is simply a line of characters that you type. If someone tells you to "enter a search string," all it means is to enter the words you want to search for.

Symbols

Each key has a **symbol** by which it is known. These are the keyboard symbols you will see in menus and charts:

⇧	**Shift**	↻	**Escape (esc)**
⌘	**Command**	⇞ ⇟	**Page Up or Page Down**
⌥	**Option**	⌫	**Delete**
⌃	**Control**	↑↓←→	**Arrow keys**
↩	**Return**	⌤	**Enter**
⏏	**Eject**		

A

colophon!

I wrote and indexed this book directly in **Adobe InDesign** on a Mac G4. The fonts used are Minion Pro for body copy and Myriad Pro for the heads. I wish I could have been allowed to use something really sassy here and there. Some fun face from **Veer.com,** like Gizmo, above.

The tigers on the divider pages are in the Albuquerque Zoo. John Tollett shot the photos and designed the pages.

All of the photos on every chapter opener are from **iStockPhoto.com,** a really great and very affordable stock photo site (you won't believe how affordable). They're amazing.   ;-)